MW00998028

# Accounts Payable

SUBSCRIPTION NOTICE

This Wiley product is updated on a periodic basis with supplements to reflect important changes in the subject matter. If you purchased this product directly from John Wiley & Sons, Inc., we have already recorded your subscription for this update service.

If, however, you purchased this product from a bookstore and wish to receive (1) the current update at no additional charge, and (2) future updates and revised or related volumes billed separately with a 30-day examination review, please send your name, company name (if applicable), address, and the title of the product to:

Supplement Department
John Wiley & Sons, Inc.
One Wiley Drive
Somerset, NJ 08875
1-800-225-5945

For customers outside the United States, please contact the Wiley office nearest you:

Professional & Reference Division
John Wiley & Sons Canada, Ltd.
22 Worcester Road
Rexdale, Ontario M9W 1L1
CANADA
(416) 675-3580
1-800-567-4797
FAX (416) 675-6599

John Wiley & Sons, Ltd.
Baffins Lane
Chichester
West Sussex, PO19 1UD
UNITED KINGDOM
(44) (243) 779777

Jacaranda Wiley Ltd.
PRT Division
P.O. Box 174
North Ryde, NSW 2113
AUSTRALIA
(02) 805-1100
FAX (02) 805-1597

John Wiley & Sons (SEA)
Pte. Ltd.
37 Jalan Pemimpin
Block B # 05-04
Union Industrial Building
SINGAPORE 2057
(65) 258-1157

# Accounts Payable

## A Guide to Running an Efficient Department

*Mary S. Ludwig*
Editor of IOMA's Report on Managing Accounts Payable

John Wiley & Sons, Inc.
New York • Chichester • Weinheim • Brisbane • Singapore • Toronto

This book is printed on acid-free paper. ♾



Published simultaneously in Canada.



***Library of Congress Cataloging-in-Publication Data:***
Ludwig, Mary S.
Accounts payable : a guide to running an efficient department / Mary S. Ludwig.
p. cm.
Includes bibliographical references and index.
ISBN 0-471-29857-3 (cloth : alk. paper)
1. Accounts payable. I. Title.
HF5681.A27L83 1999
658.8'8—DC21 98-28232
CIP

Printed in the United States of America.

10 9 8 7 6 5 4 3 2 1

*for Lara and Ben, my two special joys*
*and*
*Celeste Schacht, Nancy Lewko, Ron Schacht,*
*and*
*Hal Schaeffer*

# Contents

## Contents

Contents

## Contents

Contents

# Preface

Throughout this book, especially where benchmarking data is provided, reference will be made to the Institute of Management and Administration (IOMA), a newsletter publisher. It publishes the newsletter, *IOMA's Report on Managing Accounts Payable*, on which some of this book is based. When John Marqusee, the former chairman of the company, came up with the idea for the newsletter, it did not seem like the wonderful idea that it turned out to be. The market, it appears, is anxious for much information about accounts payable. And, to the surprise of many, this function is much more than one of a few clerks merely paying bills.

Those who doubt this theory should realize that *The Wall Street Journal* featured accounts payable in a page one story just a few years ago. The people who populate these departments and those responsible for the function tend to be well educated, innovative people who realize that what they do and how they do it can make a very real difference in their company's bottom line. It is a function that requires individuals who can do more than just process bills for payments. Knowledge of matters such as electronic data interchange, fraud and check fraud protection techniques, corporate procurement cards, payment timing, benchmarking, 1099s, and travel and entertainment reimbursements are just a few of the areas that a good accounts payable professional needs to know about.

This book addresses the above mentioned topics after investigating the best ways to handle some of the more traditional functions. These include invoice handling, check printing and signing, avoiding duplicate payments, improving accuracy, and working to reduce the number of rush or emergency checks. The book also looks at the professionalism that has crept into most accounts payable departments and offers the accounts payable professional career advice that is relevant to the field.

Running an effective department requires good management skills. The book provides some guidance on those special people issues that are relevant to accounts payable. It provides advice on staff motivation and dealing with morale issues that can be a problem when accounts payable departments are overworked.

Many people do not realize the full range of management issues that can affect accounts payable. These issues are occasionally resolved by the accounts payable manager. However, in most companies it is necessary for the accounts payable professionals to take guidance from others in setting policies in these areas. Yet, it is often up to the accounts payable professional to bring these issues to the table so that company policy may be set. Such matters as taking discounts, cleaning up vendor files, and payment timing are often beyond the control of the accounts payable manager. This person often needs to bring the issue to management's attention so that company policy can be set. Often, if the accounts payable person does not raise the issue, the matter will be ignored—often to the detriment of the company's bottom line. These issues are identified and discussed in detail.

Travel and entertainment reimbursement fall under the accounts payable umbrella in most organizations—a fact that many accounts payable managers wish were not so. This tedious and time consuming process brings many accounts payable managers more than their fair share of headaches and problems. The topic is examined in depth and techniques that work and best practices are discussed. Additionally, the VAT refund process is discussed for those companies whose employees travel overseas.

One of the biggest innovations in accounts payable today is the introduction of technology. It has made possible major improvements. Electronic data interchange, imaging, the internet, e-mail and new software applications are discussed in detail in ways that will help the accounts payable professional do a better job.

Technology is not the only issue to make a big impact on accounts payable. Several other topics are making their mark as well. The one change in the last few years that will ultimately make the biggest difference to the way accounts payable is done in many companies is the introduction of corporate procurement cards. Similar to charge cards, these are used to make payments on small dollar goods. The definition of small dollar varies from company to company. The use of these cards cuts down the number of invoices flowing through accounts payable tremendously. To work well, corporate procurement card programs must be set up correctly, management and end users must be convinced that the cards are right for the company and the procedures for using them must be integrated into the day-to-day workflow. The book takes an in-depth look at these issues.

Accounts payable post audit firms and benchmarking are two more topics that were not heard of until the last few years. Now, most leading edge accounts payable departments use one or both. The audit firms review payments after the fact and recover any duplicate or erroneous payments. While many claim never to make a duplicate payment, the rapid growth of these companies would seem to indicate otherwise. The book discusses the issues accounts payable needs to address when selecting and using post audit firms. Similarly, benchmarking has become a big issue and the book also provides some benchmarking statistics.

The book has an entire section devoted to fraud. While this may seem like overkill at first glance, consider the fact that check fraud is believed to be a $10 billion industry in the United States. And that is just one type of fraud that accounts payable professionals need to concern themselves about. While fraud stories make interesting reading, there are many things accounts payable professionals need to know about fraud and fraud protection in order to protect themselves and their companies. The book investigates the topic thoroughly from the perspective of the accounts payable professional. The book closes with several case studies—in-depth stories about real life accounts payable professionals who have accomplished extraordinary things by taking the extra step.

Reading this book will give the professional a thorough understanding of the issues accounts payable managers face every day of their working lives.

# Acknowledgments

For the last four years, I have had the privilege of working at a New York City–based newsletter publishing company, known as IOMA. The congenial working atmosphere along with the unique management support make working a pleasure. For this I am very grateful. Special thanks must go to John Marqusee, Perry Patterson, and David Foster for providing this environment.

This book would not have been possible if I had not spent the last three years conversing with, in writing, in person, and via e-mail, a very large group of innovative accounts payable professionals and the vendors who provide all sorts of services to this group. The conversations, suggestions, and recommendations from both parties all have found their way into the editorial content.

Finally, John Wiley & Sons, Inc., and the editor, Sheck Cho, have been ideal partners for this endeavor. They have made the project manageable and kept the stress level low—for which I am grateful.

# Part One

# Traditional Functions

On those rare occasions when most people give accounts payable a thought, they focus on some of the topics covered in this section. Few realize the amount of work needed to get a simple check prepared to pay an invoice. Even fewer realize that their own careless actions cause accounts payable much unnecessary work while simultaneously putting the company at risk for a duplicate payment and possibly even fraud.

So, what's the big deal most think, the company receiving the extra payment will return it, right? WRONG—most won't and they don't even inform the payor of the mistake. What's worse is that companies that make one duplicate payment are apt to have poor controls and thus make many more errors. The chapters in this section will look at some of the traditional accounts payable processes and suggest ways to improve productivity while simultaneously tightening controls and reducing the number of mistakes.

# 1

# Invoice Handling

The primary function of any accounts payable department is to pay the company's bills. This deceptively simple concept can, and usually does, get quite complicated. Bills for businesses come in the form of invoices and will be referred to as such for the remainder of this book. When the invoice is presented for payment, most companies match it against a purchase order and a receiving document and *if* all three match, the invoice is paid on or after its due date. This is what is referred to as the "three-way match"—a term accounts payable professionals know as well as they know their own names.

Now some might say that this is where the problems start, but in actuality, the problems can and often do start long before this match takes place. Incomplete purchase orders, purchase orders never completed, purchase orders never sent to accounts payable, inaccurate purchase orders, lost invoices, late invoices, early invoices, inaccurate invoices, incorrect receiving documents, receiving documents not checked, and invoices sent in for payment two or more times are just some of the problems that can occur—before the match takes place. You will note that all of these problems are caused outside the accounts payable department, but all will have to be rectified by someone in accounts payable. And, as you read this book you will see, this is just the beginning of the issues faced by the professionals who work in the department. With accounts payable there is definitely more than meets the eye.

## 1.1 THE INVOICE

Invoices are usually sent by the supplier as soon as the shipment is made. However, a few crafty vendors predate them. The reason for this is simple. The invoice does not have to be paid until a set number of days after the invoice date—although some in the field say the set number of days is after the receipt of the invoice. Regardless of which approach is used by your company, it is in the best interests of your supplier to get that invoice in your hands as quickly as possible to get the clock ticking.

Where the invoice is sent is also an issue. Some companies have them sent straight to the accounts payable department for processing. This makes a good deal of sense if purchase orders are filled out entirely and correctly. In fact, if there are good controls on the purchase order then, in theory, there would be no reason for the invoice ever to go any place other than accounts payable. However, in many organizations, there are problems with the purchase order and the invoice goes to the purchaser for approval before payment.

Even in those organizations where an approval is needed in order to make payment, invoices are sometimes sent first to accounts payable. Why? So they can be logged in and accounts payable can follow up to make sure they are returned on a timely basis. It seems that in many organizations invoices have a way of disappearing into thin air with no one ever admitting having received them. Then when the supplier calls looking for payment and the invoice cannot be located, the supplier is asked to provide a copy, which it gladly does.

While at first glance this may not seem to be a big deal, it is. First, much time is wasted looking for the missing invoice. When it cannot be found and a second is sent, the possibility of a duplicate payment has just been geometrically increased. For those who think a mountain is being made out of a molehill, reserve judgement until Chapter 4, Errors and Duplicate Payments, is read. Delays of this sort also mean that any discount that might have been available is lost. But perhaps the biggest problem occurs when the missing invoice suddenly appears. In many cases both the original and the copy end up in accounts payable approved for payment. Depending on the controls in place, the second payment may or may not be caught! The phenomenal growth of payment recovery firms (see Chapter 23, Post Audit Firms) gives testimony to the fact that this is a serious issue in corporate America today.

## 1.2 PURCHASE ORDERS

In the best of all worlds, the purchasing department fills out a document known as the purchase order (PO) when ordering goods. This document should contain every tiny detail regarding the order, including the price, quantity, payment terms, and all other pertinent details. A copy of this should be sent to accounts payable where it will wait to be matched with an invoice and receiving document. Problems with purchase orders can include: They are not sent to accounts payable, they are not filled out correctly, and so on.

The other issue regarding POs is that there are many goods ordered in an organization for which no purchase order is completed. Magazine subscriptions, conferences, interest expense, and rent are just a few examples. The list is endless. In these instances, a check request may be completed or the invoice may simply be approved for payment and forwarded to accounts payable. These non–PO purchases represent a major headache in many organizations.

## 1.3 RECEIVING DOCUMENTS

The third part of the proverbial match, the receiving documents, are, most often, the weakest link in the whole process. The reason for this is that the receiving departments in many organizations do not accurately check the goods that come through the department. Whatever is marked on the packing slip is often marked off as having arrived with no one in the receiving department actually counting.

## 1.4 PROPER INVOICE HANDLING

Those wishing to reduce the time spent with these pesky documents need to determine what changes can be made in the way their invoices are handled. The following suggestions offer accounts payable managers strategies to become more efficient in dealing with their company's invoices:

**Insist that all items sent for payment are coded.** Many accounts payable clerks end up taking on the responsibility for coding—something that is supposed to be done either by an accountant or a purchasing agent or the person submitting the bill for payment. Insist that all invoices sent for payment include a valid general ledger (G/L) code.

**Enter invoices one at a time.** Batch entry can cause problems. Entering invoices grouped by vendor as one invoice can cause problems. When there is a question about an individual invoice, it will be difficult to answer under such circumstances. It will also be difficult for the vendor to determine which invoices have been paid, and which ones have had deductions taken.

**Assign complete responsibility for accounts alphabetically.** This approach clearly delineates who is responsible for what and makes it easy to forward vendor inquiry calls as well as invoices for payment.

**Use adjustment letters to describe discrepancies to vendors.** Many of the calls received by accounts payable from vendors stem from differences between the amount of money they believe they are owed and the actual amount they receive. Formulate adjustment letters to vendors and subcontractors to explain any deductions taken. This will greatly reduce the number of phone calls asking for explanations and will make it easier for the accounts payable clerk when such calls do come in. The clerk will be able to easily determine why the deduction was taken in the first place. There is another side benefit to these letters. Statements from these vendors no longer contain open items that the company has no intention of paying.

**Work more closely with suppliers**. By letting suppliers know what accounts payable requirements are for invoice processing, you will be able to streamline the voucher processing. This effective move can also lead to better relations with those suppliers.

**Make better use of computer systems.** Paper-based systems are time consuming and often inefficient. Teach people to look up invoices on the system and not to need to see the paper. The result of this is that time spent both processing and searching for invoices in the files will decrease.

**Enter data directly from invoices.** Much time is gobbled up in some organizations entering data into a data entry form. The information is then taken from these forms and entered into the computer system. This often unnecessary step is just one more example of an unneeded process that can introduce errors into a system.

**Have all invoices sent directly to the accounts payable department.** Have this done rather than having the invoice sent to the department that actually initiated the purchase. This one simple step can save an enormous amount of wasted time.

## 1.5 ENTRY BY MONTH-END

Month-end cutoffs can cause real problems for the accounts payable department. Items that are not entered may not be paid on a timely basis resulting in lost discounts or, even worse, late fees. Those who deal with this issue on a regular basis know this is often the result of an invoice sitting on someone's desk either until the last minute or until the vendor calls looking for payment. In addition, many executives let the bills pile up, then send a big batch down to accounts payable at the last minute. When this coincides with a month-end cutoff, it is almost guaranteed to cause problems. And, if this should happen at quarter- or year-end cutoff, tensions are bound to increase—especially if the vendor needs to show the payment on its quarter- or year-end reports.

There are ways to avert this type of crisis. They include:

Ask other departments that might have a lull at deadline time if some of the data entry work can be shifted there.

Hire temporary workers to help with the overflow.

Ask key supplier to send the invoices a little earlier.

## 1.6 TIMELY APPROVALS

How often have you lost a discount because, although the invoice was received on a timely basis, you didn't have the necessary approval to pay it equally promptly? Once the invoice is received in accounts payable, it has to be sent to the appropriate party for approval.

E-mail can be used to facilitate this issue. Some report success with using a transmittal sheet for control purposes. However, the best way to draw attention to this is setting up a special general ledger account for late fees. This draws attention to this largely hidden matter. Since the late fees will be aggregated in one place, it is relatively easy to show the financial impact. Of course, it only shows part of the affect. The amount of lost discounts will not be similarly quantified. Still, it gives accounts payable professionals a starting point for quantifying the results of sloppy practices.

## 1.7 UNIDENTIFIED INVOICES SENT TO ACCOUNTS PAYABLE

A real time waster for accounts payable professionals is the invoice that shows up bearing no clue as to who ordered the goods and whether or not the items were ever received. These are generally for items ordered without a purchase order. This puts accounts payable managers on the spot—if they allow it. A number of professionals indicated they do not pay such invoices nor do they spin their wheels trying to determine who placed the order. When vendors call looking for such payment, they are simply told to contact the party who ordered the goods.

This solution may not be acceptable in all organizations, but it makes life a little easier in those accounts payable departments where it is used. It should be noted that the lack of the desired information on the invoice may not be the fault of the company employee. It may simply be due to carelessness on the part of vendors who are often not fastidious in preparing invoices. Why should your staff be responsible for another company's slipshod practices?

Whether or not the severe approach is used, the following steps can alleviate headaches caused by unidentified invoices.

Send a memo or an e-mail to everyone in the company asking that all invoices include the name of the party ordering goods. This enables the accounts payable department to obtain necessary approvals and track down other needed information.

If managers agree, inform the appropriate staff that invoices received without this information will not be processed for payment.

Make sure that your policy is explained to all new hires.

Accounts payable professionals who are successful in getting their invoice handling under control will have taken one step on the path to a smoother-running department.

## 1.8 USE BEST OF TERMS

Pay according to the terms recorded on the purchase order and the quantity received. Some suppliers put terms on their invoices that, if not checked, would have resulted in payments earlier than the purchasing department had agreed to. Others include terms that are more stringent than those agreed to with purchasing. This is just one reason why getting a completely filled out purchase order is so important. Always pay according to the purchase order unless the terms on the invoice are better. Then use the terms on the invoice and inform purchasing so they can use this information the next time they order. Using this approach will result in the best of both worlds for the company.

## 1.9 GOODS IMPROPERLY ORDERED OUTSIDE PURCHASING

One of the areas ripe for overpayments (and duplicate payments as well) are those goods ordered outside the purchasing umbrella. While it is sometimes appropriate for departments to order goods, many professionals recommend that a purchase requisition be filled out at the time of order to notify the accounts payable department of the upcoming bill. Purchasing may then create a purchase order and mark it as bill only—no receiver forthcoming. Unfortunately, most people wait until the invoice arrives and then do an after-the-fact purchase order. This is a waste of time and only serves to paper the file to make the auditors think there are controls in place.

### (a) Why Should a Company Care?

For starters, there is a big pricing issue. Most companies negotiate contracts with lower per-item prices to take advantage of the volume of goods purchased. When an employee buys something outside of this contract, they usually end up paying more for the item than they would have had purchasing arranged the transactions. Sure, it may only be a few dollars each time, but those few dollars have a way off adding up real fast.

This type of ordering can also circumvent company pricing guidelines. If everything goes through purchasing, information can be accumulated so as to negotiate better vendor pricing.

### (b) How Can a Company Stop This Activity?

Communication and management backing is the key to eliminating this type of behavior. In order to make sure that everyone abides by the ground rules, there needs to be consequences for those who go outside the proper channels. This, of course, is very difficult in the corporate environment but perhaps a charge against the personal bottom line of the executive who is ultimately responsible. If a bonus is tied to bottom-line profitability, this might be an effective route. Getting such a policy implemented will be virtually impossible for an accounts payable manager—unless there is strong upper management backing. What the accounts payable professional can do is to spell out for management the actual effect of the purchases made outside the channel.

## 1.10 NON-PURCHASE ORDER BUYING

There are times, however, when it is appropriate for a party other than the purchasing department to acquire goods or services for the company. The overriding principle in such instances is that there be someone who is ultimately responsible for authorizing and monitoring such expenditures. Check requests are the way most companies handle this issue. They should be kept to a minimum. However, if complete coding information is required on the check request, accounting will have the necessary information to include for complete vendor analysis.

## 1.11 GETTING OTHERS TO FOLLOW ACCOUNTS PAYABLE'S GUIDELINES

Many accounts payable departments have trouble getting the rest of the company to follow their payment procedures. Draft an easy reference guide for all standard procedures in an attempt to make them not only more user-friendly, but easier to locate. Such a guide can help reduce the enormous amount of time educating other professionals in the organization in the proper procedures for disbursements.

## 1.12 INVOICES WITHOUT INVOICE NUMBERS

Missing an invoice number often leads to duplicate payments. Many accounts payable professionals, when paying an invoice with no invoice number, simply make one up. While dummying in an invoice number might make the system work, it does have its pitfalls—especially for those who routinely use the date as their invoice number. A better way is to make up a dummy number that includes some unique identifier to the vendor, for example, a combination of digits from the vendor's phone number and the date. And, whenever paying an invoice with no invoice number, check to make sure it hasn't already been paid. This is the type of thing that often leads to duplicate payments.

## 1.13 INVOICE AMNESTY DAY

One of the dirty little secrets in most accounts payable departments is that invoices with problems tend to disappear. Rather than pretending that this doesn't happen, successful department heads are introducing "invoice amnesty day"—with no finger-pointing and no recriminations. Once a year, hold an invoice amnesty day. Each staffer is asked to clean out his or her desk and may submit invoices that have been sidelined for various reasons—no questions asked. You will be surprised at the number of invoices that crawl out from under rocks. Such a move may also improve morale as the hidden invoices often weigh heavily on the staffers minds.

## 1.14 REDUCING THE NUMBER OF INVOICES

As anyone even remotely involved with the accounts payable function can tell you, payable departments are being inundated with an increasing amount of work. Companies acquire other companies or simply expand and the workload grows. Yet the accounts payable department is expected to handle additional responsibilities with no extra staff. In fact, at some companies they are expected to handle the increased workload with a smaller staff.

In the doing-more-with-less environment permeating most of corporate America today, accounts payable professionals are adopting a variety of techniques to reduce the number of invoices coming into their departments.

In most organizations these initiatives are long-term projects and require approval from upper management. So review your options: decide which will not only work in your organization but are most likely to fly and begin a campaign to "educate and implement."

### (a) Summary Statements

Most accounts payable managers are loathe to pay off a statement. They want an invoice that can be used for the three-way match. In fact, some wish they could get rid of statements since they occasionally are used, in error, in place of an invoice resulting in a duplicate payment. However, there are instances where paying off a statement makes a lot of sense.

If you do a good deal of business with a given supplier and most of the transactions are small dollar amounts, you might consider ignoring invoices with that particular vendor. A number of accounts payable managers report that instead of paying many small invoices from the same vendor each month, they pay once a month from the end-of-month summary statement. This can greatly reduce the number of small, bothersome invoices in the department. It also helps reduce errors as small invoices are the ones that tend to get paid twice—and are never uncovered.

It also makes things easier for the supplier. Instead of getting many small checks from you during the month, one larger one is received. If you are remitting to a lockbox, the supplier will save banking fees. You might raise this when trying to negotiate such a deal. In addition, if your supplier knows when to expect that single check, it will be better able to predict its cash flow. By pointing out the benefits, you may even be able to get your terms stretched a little!

### (b) Corporate Procurement Cards

Perhaps even more bothersome than many small payments to a few large vendors, are many small payments to a wide variety of vendors. Most companies find that over 90% of invoices paid represent less than 10% of funds disbursed. In growing numbers these companies are turning to corporate procurement cards. Once again, use of these cards will drastically reduce the number of invoices sent to accounts payable for processing.

This application will work with some of the large vendors discussed above in the summary billing section. If you can get them to accept credit cards, your life will be made quite a bit easier. Only one payment will need to be made to cover payments to a variety of vendors. And, best of all, these payments are typically made at the end of the billing period.

Most accounts payable professionals using these cards report that once the original reluctance to their use is overcome, the cards are embraced wholeheartedly. When management realizes that the strict controls that can be imposed limit their exposure, they are more likely to go along. It is also a positive experience for employees who are empowered to use the cards. As card issuers continue to refine their cards and solutions are found to some of the accounting issues that cloud this usage in some corporations, we expect use of the cards will skyrocket. See Chapter 22, Purchasing Cards, for more details on this subject.

### (c) Evaluated Receipt Settlement (ERS)

Also called invoiceless processing, this is a concept that a few companies swear by and the rest avoid like the plague. It requires partnering with your supplier and cooperation from both the purchasing department and the receiving department. The concept is quite simple. Normally, accounts payable waits for an invoice and then matches it to the purchase order and receiving document and then processes the invoice for payment should everything be in order. With ERS, the accounts payable department simply mails the payment to the vendor at the agreed upon time if the purchase order and receiving document match. The invoice is never mailed or included in the process.

Obviously, this can only be done with vendors who agree to implement this process. It also requires accuracy on the purchase order and in the receiving department. Goods arriving from a vendor must be checked carefully before receiving signs off as the receiving document will be the only one received from the vendor. Also, purchasing cannot be sloppy about filling out its purchase orders. The POs must also include the payment terms spelled out in detail. If you don't have your own house in order, don't consider this technique. See Chapter 14, Alternatives to the Three-Way Match, for more details on this technique.

### (d) Revamping the Purchasing Process

This is a very sensitive area. In most organizations, the purchasing department will not take it well if the accounts payable department suggests it revamp its operations to make accounts payable's life a little easier. But, the reality is that accounts payable pays for sloppy practices in purchasing. Not only do careless practices result in extra work for payables, but in lost discounts as well. While it is often difficult to quantify the cost of such procedures, those lost discounts are fairly easy to add up.

The following practices in purchasing will reduce the amount of time spent in the accounts payable department fixing purchasing's mistakes:

- Automating POs.
- Consistent purchasing practices throughout the organization.
- Integration of the purchasing, receiving and A/P functions.

Certain organizations purchase the same item, or types of items, from a number of different suppliers. If this number could be reduced, so, too, could the number of invoices. Finding a diplomatic way to make such a recommendation is not easy. Ideally, if you go high enough in the organization, it would come from the person responsible for both departments.

A few accounts payable managers have had success taking a more devious route. When the number of suppliers is reduced, those who remain get more business. In these situations, many competent purchasing professionals are able to negotiate pricing breaks for their companies based on the increased volume. By pointing this out to the right purchasing person, and then letting them take credit for the savings, some accounts payable professionals have been able to influence purchasing without being offensive.

### (e) Integration of Purchasing and Accounts Payable

As shown in the sections above, the workflow of the purchasing and the accounts payable departments are closely aligned. The actions of one can directly impact the results of the other. A number of organizations have moved the two under one umbrella having both report to the same department head. Taking this approach a step further, a few organizations have integrated the accounts payable department into purchasing. This trend has become such a hot topic, several conference organizers have planned conferences focusing on this very issue while others are including it in their more general A/P conferences.

### (f) Automating Purchasing through Electronic Data Interchange (EDI)

One of the best ways—not only to reduce the amount of paper flowing into the A/P department, but to improve the accuracy of the information—is to use EDI in all phases of the procurement process. This starts with the PO which is sent electronically to the supplier. In some organizations this is as far as the use of EDI goes.

Others go one step further and receive invoices (and advance shipping notices) via EDI.

This is where EDI stops in many organizations because of the "float issue." Many companies don't pay electronically because they don't want to give up the savings associated with float. However, this is missing the big picture unless the amounts of money involved in each payment are very large. Why? Because the cost of issuing a check far exceeds the small float savings. But try to convince most financial managers of this relatively simple fact and you'll find yourself beating your head against the wall.

Several innovative managers have moved to financial EDI (FEDI) while simultaneously holding on to part of the beloved float. They've done this by renegotiating terms with the supplier. Since the supplier benefits by having a better handle on its cash flow, some are agreeable to this negotiation. Others are not. While FEDI is desirable, accounts payable managers will benefit from embracing EDI even if they can't talk the company into the final part.

### (g) Imaging and Workflow

With the price of technology dropping rapidly, companies that just a few short years ago found imaging too expensive are now reevaluating it. This doesn't mean this technology is cheap but rather that it is now more affordable for certain organizations.

Those most successful with imaging can scan an invoice into their system the minute it enters their door. The original paper document is never touched by human hands again. The imaging systems index the information. This allows easy document retrieval at a later date.

The necessary information is taken from the invoice electronically. This drastically reduces rekeying errors. The document can then be passed around the organization as needed: it can be accessed by different individuals and departments. Copying costs are eliminated and storage costs greatly reduced.

The conversion to an imaging system can be time consuming.

Many take this opportunity to review their current workflow processes and eliminate unnecessary steps. Employees will need to be retrained to use the new machines. Some may be resistant to the changes. But once the system is up and running, most are pleased with the results.

The accounts payable world is, as is the rest of the business community, changing quickly. It is no longer cost effective to do things the way they have been done since time immemorial. Anything that reduces the ever-growing volume of paper crossing accounts payable managers' desks is welcome. The techniques just discussed are a few of the ones sweeping accounts payable departments.

## 1.15 HANDLING BILLS WITH REMITTANCE ADVICES

Bills for services such as telephone and utilities often require that a stub be sent along with the check so the receiving company can apply the payment correctly. This is something that most of us do as a matter of course when paying our own personal bills. However, it can be a major time waster when paying such bills for a company. Many companies have found solutions to this annoying problem, some of which may work in your organization. They include:

Eliminating the process of sending payment stubs with our utility and telephone bills. Reference the account number as the invoice number with the invoice date.

Contacting the utility company and asking for a consolidated statement of all accounts. Cut one check for all accounts and return the stubs to the utility. This does not completely eliminate the problem but does limit the extent of the damages.

Use a subscription service. This technique works well for those organizations that have many subscriptions. Some companies offering this service are:

EBSCO who charges 15% for each subscription. EBSCO's number is (800) 367-6247. Its address is P.O. Box 1943, Birmingham, AL 35201-1943.

Turner Subscription Services. Its address is 116 E. 16th St., New York, NY 10003. (800) 847-4201.

# 2

# Check Preparation Printing and Filing

Most people who don't work in accounts payable do not realize how much time it actually takes to get a check out the door. Some companies have their checks printed, signed, and put in an envelope for mailing entirely by machine with little or no human intervention. These companies are a distinct minority. Even those that do use the above mentioned technique, still must have some human handling on certain checks. For starters, certain payments, such as utility bills, require that the payor include a remittance advice with the payment. Others will sometimes include a copy of the invoice being paid. At this time, no computer exists that will take whatever attachments are desired and include them with the check.

## 2.1 A MORE COMMON APPROACH

Typically, corporate America prints its checks in one of three ways:

1. Checks are outsourced and printed by a third party.
2. Checks are printed on a laser printer.
3. Checks are printed on a line printer in continuous form and have to be burst.

In both the second and third approach checks can be either signed by the computer or hand signed.

## 2.2 MANUAL SIGNATURES

Where they are hand signed massive human intervention is required not only to sign the checks but to get them to the appropriate parties for signature. What typically happens is the checks are burst apart and reattached to all the backup documentation and then taken in batch mode to an authorized signer who reviews the backup and signs the check. This is where the problems multiply. Finding an available authorized signer can sometimes be a problem. It is not uncommon for checks to sit for days unsigned until someone has the time to review and sign the checks. Then the clerk who is responsible for the checks is called to retrieve them.

In some organizations, two signatures are required. The process of finding a second authorized signer then begins with the same issues as with the first signer. The longer it takes to get signatures on the checks, the more likely it is that vendors will call looking for their payments. When one of these vendors gets irate or threatens not to make future shipments, a search must be made to find their check. If a company has more than one check run a week, it is quite possible that there will be several batches making the rounds for signature. Which batch is the check in? In a two-signature environment, the clerk must then identify which signer has the checks. It is not unknown for a manual check to be drawn in these circumstances—leading to not only the possibility of a duplicate payment, but the likelihood of such an event.

This treatise is not meant to discourage companies from using manual signatures. They have their place—especially for high-dollar payments and in those environments where the controls over payments before reaching accounts payable are weak or nonexistent.

Once the checks are signed and returned to accounts payable, someone in the department must:

Separate the checks from all the backup.

Prepare an envelope and stuff the check in it.

File the backup.

Mail the checks and/or call internal personnel who need to pick up certain checks.

## 2.3 LIMITING TIME SPENT GETTING CHECKS SIGNED

Finding the signer is only half the battle. Getting that person to focus and actually lift a pen to sign the check is the other half. Accounts payable departments often find their schedules ruined by the bottleneck of harried executives required to sign the company's checks. It's often a low-priority task as far as these individuals are concerned—low priority, that is, until a major supplier refuses to make further shipments.

Most accounts payable departments would be more productive if the wasted time spent stalking authorized signers could be eliminated—or at least reduced. Many professionals simply throw up their hands in disgust, thinking that this is a situation that can't be changed. But that is not necessarily so. Accounts payable managers at a variety of organizations report success in diminishing this problem through the following techniques: raising limits for dual signatures; raising limits for electronic check signers; using electronic check signers for recurring payments; appointing backup signers; using electronic check signers for approved POs; and scheduling check signing meetings.

### (a) Raising Limits for Dual Signatures

By simply raising the level at which two signatures are required on a check, the number of checks requiring two chases will be reduced—and in most cases, reduced drastically. This is due to the fact that, as most accounts payable professionals are well aware, small checks represent a high proportion of all checks written. Simply raising the limit from $5,000 to $10,000 can make a huge difference.

Companies requiring two signatures on all checks might consider moving to one for small checks. Once a level of comfort is reached with one signature, the issue of raising the limit can be broached. The banks on which the check is drawn should be contacted to make sure that the instructions they have on file regarding signatures on your checks are up-to-date.

With a smaller number of checks requiring two signatures, the accounts payable associate responsible for obtaining those precious "John Hancocks" will have an easier time. Persuading that second signer to stop what he or she is doing when there are only five checks to sign is much easier than it is to stop and sign 25, or even more.

### (b) Raising Limits for Electronic Check Signers

Use of an electronic check signer completely eliminates the problem—well, almost completely. Most companies using these machines have controls in place that require two people to be involved in the signing operation. Since the people involved in running these machines are generally part of the staff, a regular schedule can be developed, and will be adhered to in most cases. This is generally a much easier situation.

Some computers will sign the checks as part of the print cycle. The use of such computers will resolve the check signing issues in much the same way as the separate machines currently available do.

### (c) Electronic Signers for Recurring Payments

Rent, mortgage payments, lease payments, interest payments on fixed-rate loans, and a variety of other payments are made on a regular basis by many companies. Since these payments are recurring, never change, and are always for the same amount, there is really no reason why they have to go through the manual check-signing process.

These items are perfect candidates for the electronic signer. Should you be successful in convincing management to go this route, it is possible to take it one step further. After some ease is gained with the process, search out other payments that the company has a contractual obligation to pay. The easiest examples are utility bills and interest on floating rate loans. Once the invoice has been approved, it could go through the electronic signer with no further management review.

### (d) Electronic Signers for Approved POs

Along the same lines, invoices that are matched with approved POs should not really require a manual signature. Once the three-way match has been made, signifying that the goods were ordered and received, a manual signature adds nothing to the process. What this does is force the controls back to the first line of defense—the approval of the invoice. If that is done correctly, why involve highly compensated management in signing the check? This will be a hard sell at many companies—especially where large invoices are involved.

### (e) Backup Signers

One of the problems often encountered in trying to get checks signed is that the authorized signer simply can't be found. The signer may be out to lunch, traveling, or in a meeting. Eventually, the checks get left in the office of the signer—requiring a few reminders to get the checks signed. This situation can be remedied by simply designating pinch-hitter signers to be used whenever the first level cannot be found. If several such individuals are appointed, the problem may rectify itself.

This is true because some of the authorized signers, despite vocal complaints to the contrary, love to sign checks. Whether it be because of the perceived power, or the need to be wanted, or the attention, is not clear. But what is apparent is that when alternatives can be found, the formerly recalcitrant signers often reform their check signing behavior. Several accounts payable managers report that this solution works wonders with signers who like to play hard to get.

### (f) Check Signing Meetings

Some truly busy signers don't realize the inconvenience they are causing the accounts payable staff. A few managers have reported success by merely scheduling a meeting with the offending individual and explaining how this behavior affects accounts payable. This has to be done tactfully. Finger-pointing rarely helps any situation.

The problem can sometimes be rectified by scheduling regular meetings with the check signer several times a week to get the checks signed. By sitting with the individual as the checks are signed, the accounts payable manager guarantees the checks will be processed. These meetings generally last no more than 15 minutes. At first glance, it may appear that time is being wasted, but this is not true.

For starters, the morale of the staff improves when the associates see that the manager is willing to take on the disagreeable task of getting the signatures. Often times, the signers are a little short on people skills and few accounts payable clerks like trying to get them to stop what they are doing and focus on the checks.

This time can also be used to improve the visibility of the accounts payable department. These meetings provide the opportunity to point out the department's accomplishments. This can gradually increase the signers' appreciation for the job the accounts payable department does. This can pay off at year end when it was time to get raises for the staff approved.

While all of these techniques will not work at all companies, at least one or two should work at most. The resourceful accounts payable manager will review the techniques discussed and find ways to reduce the awful amount of time wasted as frustrated staff associates try to get signatures.

## 2.4 MAILING VERSUS PICKING UP CHECKS

Having checks picked up is an annoyance for the accounts payable personnel. They either have to call the appropriate parties or e-mail them. People tend to drift down to accounts payable whenever it is convenient for them—and usually when it is most inconvenient for the accounts payable personnel. Some companies have gotten around this issue by establishing a preset time each day when checks are available for pickup. This only half solves the problem because just like there are emergency checks there will always be someone who can't make at the preordained time and insists on coming at a time convenient for them.

However, there is a more basic issue. Allowing checks to be hand picked up makes it easier for an internal employee looking to commit fraud to do so. How? It's simple. They can get their hands on the check and divert it. In a more devious scheme, a few employees have been known to submit phony invoices and then pick the checks up and deposit them into their own bank accounts. This topic will be discussed in detail in Chapters 28 and 29, Check Fraud and Employee Fraud, respectively.

Most experts recommend that all checks be mailed—even employee travel and expense report reimbursements. The value of the time saved far outweighs the small postage savings accrued by not mailing the checks.

It should be noted that all the functions surrounding the check printing and signing are sometimes handled in the treasury or accounting departments. This typically happens in organizations that have a smallish accounts payable department. The reason for this is the segregation of duties concern. Many try and segregate these responsibilities as much as possible. Thus, if there are only one or two people in accounts payable, the responsibility may be moved elsewhere. Some larger organizations concerned about segregation of duties move these functions to other departments, as well. However, typically the checks go back to accounts payable for mailing and the filing of backup documentation.

## 2.5 CHECK FILING

The filing of the backup documentation can take a monumental amount of time. Traditionally this paperwork was filed alphabetically by vendor. This took an incredible amount of time that did not necessarily add anything to the process. However, whenever anyone needed to check if an invoice had been paid it was easy enough to go to the file and pull the copy of the invoice. This assumes that the company only has set up one file for each vendor. But, as anyone who has ever worked in accounts payable will tell you, multiple vendor files have been known to creep into existence. Thus, a company that buys from IBM might have a file called IBM and another called International Business Machines. Now, when the accounts payable staffer goes to check the file to determine if a particular invoice has been paid, he or she will only get the right information if they happen to hit the file that has that particular paid invoice in it.

Additionally, many companies have discovered that the time spent filing alphabetically bore little benefit to the company. As technology wends its way into the accounts payable department, more companies are finding solutions to this filing problem that ultimately save them much time and boring miserable work. The ultimate solution is imaging but this is not practical for companies of all sizes. Companies that image all their paperwork have no need for paper files and typically send all paper to cold storage—or even destroy it immediately. However, these systems are often rather expensive at present and are not a realistic solution for mid-size and smaller firms.

Nevertheless, many of these companies have come up with a workable solution. If the company's computer system is sophisticated enough to allow someone to peek through the files and determine when a check was issued and what batch it was included in, most of the problems disappear. Why? Because all the backup can be filed by batch with little time spent on filing. The documentation within each batch can be alphabetized or filed by vendor or check number. Thus, for each check run, one big file can be created instead of having someone go through the huge paper files and put each little chit in the right place.

## 2.6 TIMESAVING TECHNIQUES IN THE CHECK PRODUCTION CYCLE

One of the facts of life for accounts payable managers is that the handling of checks can take a large amount of time. Anything that can be done to reduce this time is money in the bank. Five areas that can be "reengineered" to save time are:

1. Multipart checks.
2. Filing systems.
3. Check runs.
4. Travel and expense checks.
5. Purchase cards.

### (a) Multi-Part Checks

At many companies, standard procedures require a carbon copy of a check be attached to all invoices and check request forms. This simple task can take many hours each week without adding much value to the process. Many accounts payable systems provide complete information on checks issued. Attaching the copy does nothing for the company. Eliminate this laborious task. When the company's check stock runs out, it may be able to save a few more dollars by ordering checks without that carbon copy.

### (b) Filing Systems

Some companies have saved time and money simply by changing the way they handle filing invoices and related materials. This can be done in several ways. Many companies match invoices with checks and then file the two documents together. This is time consuming. Simply file the invoices separately from checks. From this simple change, companies save many hours each week. Others have had success by moving from filing by voucher number to a two-part check/alpha filing system.

### (c) Check Runs

The other area of frequent debate in accounts payable departments is check runs. They are time consuming. However, if they are not done often enough, the demand for exception or rush checks increases and can really eat into the department's time. The right number of check runs depends on many factors. Most of those able to increase productivity by focusing on their check runs reduce them.

Reducing check runs from nightly to once a week can save time and money. One of the biggest concerns with reducing the number of check runs is that discounts will be lost. However, this does not have to be the case. Employees know when the check run is and are more timely about getting their expenses reports and any other special check requests in before the weekly run.

### (d) Travel and Expenses Checks

Another time stealer for the accounts payable department are Travel and Expenses (T&E) checks—not only printing but distributing them as well. Here's how some companies get away from this problem completely: The accounts payable system sends a file to the payroll system and employees are reimbursed in their paycheck. This has significantly reduced the processing time and employees know exactly when to expect their reimbursements.

If the time spent on distributing T&E checks is excessive, some companies have had success simply mailing these checks to the homes of their employees.

Those contemplating either of the above suggestions should be aware of another problem that is sometimes encountered. Occasionally, an employee will hide T&E reimbursements from a spouse. Beginning such a plan will bring an outburst of complaints from such employees—although it is unlikely that they will reveal the real reason for their objections.

### (e) P-cards

One of the biggest time savers for the accounts payable departments worldwide was the introduction of purchasing cards (P-cards), also referred to as corporate procurement cards. These credit cards effectively eliminate many small-dollar invoices from the check production cycle, effectively saving time and money for the company using them. As their popularity grows and the services offered by the card issuers improve, the cards are expected to make a major impact on the accounts payable world.

Some companies have given such cards to their accounts payable managers with instructions to use these cards to pay any invoice where the card can be used if the invoice is under a certain preagreed on limit. Subscriptions, seminars and conferences are perfect applications for this timesaver. For more information see Chapter 22, Purchasing Cards.

By this time, those reading this will be able to see that although the check signing and filing process can be time consuming, there are techniques that innovative companies can use to decrease the amount of time spent on the process.

# 3

# Exception and Rush Processing

A "rush check" is any request that does not go through normal channels and disrupts the normal work flow of the payables department. Those who do not work in the department often think that the accounts payable manager is making a mountain out of a molehill when a big deal is made of a request for an exception or rush check request. What these individuals do not realize is that it takes anywhere from 15 to 30 minutes to handle such a request. This is time taken away from the normal work process and it can happen to the accounts payable manager many times in a given day—if it is permitted. Now, everyone understands that there are true emergencies. However, if a close look is taken at the situation in those companies where there are a large number of rush check requests, it is usually revealed that the large number of requests are due to inefficiencies outside the accounts payable department. Even worse, from the accounts payable department's staff's point of view, the large number are often due to carelessness and mistakes made by others.

There is another danger associated with rush checks. Even those who are not interested in whether they are creating additional work for the accounts payable staff, should be concerned about the possible negative impact rush checks can have on the company's financial position. Rush checks tend to be manual checks, that is, they are rarely produced by the computer system. Thus, the information needs to be entered at a later time to ensure that the company's books are correct. There is often a lag in completing this and at times it does not get done. This opens the door to duplicate payments and in some cases fraud. Issuing a large number of manual checks will be a matter that most outside auditors will bring up in the management letter. In a well-run company, it simply should not happen. Not only does permitting rush checks on a regular basis add work to the accounts payable department, it can put the company at financial risk—something that should concern all executives. The reality, though, is that it is unlikely they will ever be eliminated.

## 3.1 DEALING WITH THE ISSUE

Given the seriousness of the matter, most accounts payable managers look for ways to alleviate the problem and decrease the number of these interruptions. A few techniques that work and can be implemented rather easily include:

Ask a few questions.

Education.

Just say NO.

Change procedures.

### (a) Ask a Few Questions

Begin by closely questioning the person making the rush request. Often it can be determined that the check can be handled through normal channels and still meet deadlines. If after questioning, it appears that a rush check is needed, try one other simple thing. Look over the request and the documentation. Often, the person requesting the check hasn't looked closely at the bill or has provided, unintentionally, wrong information. The bill may not be due when they think it is. Or they may have added a few days to the time frame just to be on the safe side. Most accounts payable professionals will be able to convince these individuals to put the request through normal channels.

### (b) Education

The next strategy is a long-range approach. It involves educating everyone in the company on the way the payables department works and the time requirements to get checks through the process. Some companies can turn checks around in a few hours, and some, especially those requiring multiple approvals or signatures, can take several days or longer. The longer the cycle, the more likely you are to have rush requests.

Start by writing a memo detailing the work flow, including realistic time frames. If checks need two manual signatures (yes, there are companies that still do that) and one of the signers is apt to take two days, factor that into your timing. If the process is complicated, try flow-charting it. From this, draw up a simple memo to all who request checks. The document should give them guidelines on the appropriate time frame for submitting check requests. Be realistic. Including very optimistic times is just buying trouble down the road when accounts payable can't deliver. Of course, it is prudent to check with the supervisor before releasing this memo.

Keep copies of the memo around and when someone requests a rush check that could have been handled under normal circumstances, give them another copy along with their check. Try to do it without being annoying—something that is easier said than done in many cases. Over the long haul, education is probably the best way to reduce this problem.

### (c) Just Say NO

In truth, many of these so-called emergencies are the result of someone else's carelessness. If it happens only once in a while, that's one thing. But in many instances, it is the same few people making most of the unnecessary requests. Sometimes people have to be hit on the head with the proverbial two-by-four before they learn. In this case, the two-by-four is refusing their request. Before doing this, be sure there is full support of the department head. One thing is certain with this approach: There will be a ruckus over this. But sometimes, you just have to take a stand. Be forewarned that not everyone will be willing to do this. So, there's a good chance there will be an argument with the department head about this as well.

In all probability, there will be some financial impact to the company, either a late charge or a higher cost. So when a stand is taken, don't do it on a huge invoice. And be prepared for a fight—which may ultimately be lost. But word will get around, and others will begin to get their requests in on time.

Some companies don't have check runs every day. This only increases the number of rush check requests. Consider adding a check run if your volume has increased or there seems to be a good number of checks that must be rushed through.

Finally, realize that in most organizations this problem will probably never disappear. No one in their right mind will tell the president or some other high-level officer that they can't have their rush check because it could have gone through normal channels if it had been handled correctly.

### (d) Change Procedures

Sometimes, despite good intentions, it's the accounts payable department that needs changing. This is most likely to be true in a growing dynamic company where procedures have not changed to keep up with the expanded requirement.

## 3.2 HARD-LINE APPROACH

When all else fails, and the requests for exception processing continue, it's time to take off the kid gloves. When that happens, it's "no more Mr. Nice Guy." Here are some ways to reduce the number of such requests in those circumstances:

Prepare a form for special checks to include who is requesting the check, an approval signature and the date the check is needed. Next, require that the controller or CFO or other high- level executive approve all these requests.

Make it difficult. Ask a lot of questions. Those encountering this process once find they have no great desire to repeat the experience and the number of requests usually drops precipitously.

Document the costs associated with preparing a rush check. When upper management is presented with the results of such a study, they gave full support to A/P's initiatives in reducing these items.

Require multiple signatures. Add one line to the check request form as well as requiring three instead of two signatures in order to get it. On that line the requestor had to explain why the check was needed on a rush basis instead of through normal channels.

## 3.3 IDENTIFYING THE RUSH CHECK TROUBLEMAKERS

Try keeping a log of all these checks issued. Make sure to identify not only the culprit, but the reason that the check is needed. After a month or two a pattern may emerge. If it can be identified, then the chance of eliminating it increases. Once you have identified the pattern, see what you can do to eradicate the cause of the problem and you will have reduced the number of rush checks handled in the department.

### (a) A Picture's Worth a Thousand Words

In an attempt to make management see the value of enforcing compliance with a no-manual-check policy, track the amount of time spent on the handling of manual checks. Begin by having the staff keep a log of all requests. Each time someone had to stop working to handle such an item, the time spent handling the item was monitored and entered in the log as well. The log should also contain information regarding who is requesting the special item and the reason it is needed on a rush basis and can't wait until the scheduled check run. At the end of the month, calculate how much time was spent on normal check runs and how many checks were produced. From this information calculate how much time was spent handling a check that came through normal channels. From the log data, calculate the time spent per check on the rush items. Take the average salary of the staff and calculate a per check handling charge. Present all this information in a report with bar graphs. These graphs will bring home the point that manual checks are much more costly than checks handled through the normal process.

### (b) Identify the Laggards

From the log information, identify the worst offenders and the reasons for their requests. In most organizations, a few names will show up on the report with much greater frequency than others. Present this information to management along with a request that a new hard line be taken on special requests. This will help get the top-level support needed when instituting a hard-line approach to rush checks. The graphs in the reports bring home the points and can make the difference between getting management support and not.

## 3.4 NEWSLETTER

Sometimes it seems like everyone in the company makes the same mistakes repeatedly when submitting invoices for payment or check requests. This often leaves accounts payable managers frustrated by their inability to communicate simple information to a large audience. A growing number of innovative professionals have found a unique way to deal with this issue. They communicate on a regular basis with the entire company by means of a companywide two- to four-page accounts payable newsletter on a quarterly or even monthly basis.

While this might not be needed in all cases, nor will all A/P managers have the time available, the following guidelines will help those looking to begin such a publishing venture.

Remember, the goal is to update and educate the rest of the company and to get them to handle everything relating to accounts payable in a way that will make it easier for the accounts payable staff to do their jobs. But, the true goal can not be obvious in the newsletter. Show the readers what's in it for them. Self-interest motivates most people and showing them how they will benefit will increase the odds of getting their help. Just don't put them to sleep in the process.

Give it a snappy title. The Leland James Service Corporation calls theirs the "Accounts Pay-Zette." The company also has a smaller publication used primarily within the accounts payable department that they call, "Practically Paid." Others, such as Talisman Energy Co., devise titles that creatively take advantage of the company's name. In this case, the monthly newsletter is called, "Tali Ho." A very large computer company calls their newsletter, "The Armadillo Express." Guess what state the accounts payable department is located in? Other titles that are being used include "Accounts Payable Newz" and "Accounts Payable Focus."

Devise a masthead and use it with every issue. This will give your periodical brand recognition. It doesn't have to be anything fancy either. With the graphics and variety of fonts available in today's word-processing programs, it is not difficult to come up with an attractive design.

Use the same color paper to reprint the newsletter each time. This will also help with recognition.

Keep it short. The best in-house productions are either two or four pages. Remember the goal is to get the audience to read what is written and if it's too long, it will simply get tossed in the circular file.

Try to make it entertaining as well as educational. One organization includes a quiz. Another gives all the articles titles from movies. Anyone who could find all the movie titles in the newsletter was invited to send in their name to be included in a drawing for a special prize. The real purpose, of course, was to entice the reader to go through the entire issue. Theme issues also work sometimes. Be careful though—if it is too cute, the readers may become engrossed in the witticisms and miss the educational points.

Get everyone involved if possible—but have someone who is a good writer edit the final version. Let them be ruthless. If the newsletter is not short, concise, and entertaining, it won't get read and the whole purpose will be negated.

Keep it upbeat and don't forget the reader's thinking, "What's in it for me?" Find a way to convey your messages without preaching or lecturing.

Produce it on a regular basis so the readers will know when to expect the next words of wisdom. The most successful are either monthly or quarterly.

Use the newsletter to introduce new employees and announce promotions. This provides the perfect opportunity to remind everyone of the person's responsibilities in a very blunt manner. It's not at all inappropriate to end an announcement with something like, "Call John with all your questions about ABC."

Changes in procedures can also be reported in the newsletter. If many people are doing the same thing incorrectly, try announcing a new procedure for that process. In reality, this will simply be reiterating the old procedures, but this won't offend all the dimwits who insist on doing things their own way.

Use the newsletter to periodically review who is responsible for what areas in A/P.

Include as many phone numbers (and e-mail addresses) as possible. If the manager does not want to receive any calls, however, don't include that phone number.

Toot your own horn with short updates about accounts payable department successes.

Before starting such a publication, most accounts payable managers will need approval from their superiors. Some have found that a separate newsletter isn't necessary if there is already a company newsletter. In these instances, many have had success simply writing a column for that publication.

Some who use A/P newsletters report good results from a question-and-answer column. Readers are invited to submit questions. Bribe friends into submitting questions that need to be answered.

Also consider accepting submissions from other related departments, such as travel, payroll or purchasing that are relevant to accounts payable matters.

## 3.5 CONCLUSION

Rush checks will never go away completely. Those who find ways to reduce the number will find more time to handle more productive matters. If all else fails, try the approach of more than one accounts payable manager. Post a sign saying something to the effect that "a mistake on your part does not constitute an emergency on mine."

# 4

# Errors and Duplicate Payments

Despite their best efforts, accounts payable managers continue to be plagued by erroneous payments. The ever-increasing number of accounts payable audit firms gives testament to the fact that this remains a serious and financially troubling issue. Some experts estimate that the number of such firms has grown from 20 to 30 in just the last few years—and they all seem to be making money. One of the largest, Howard Schultz & Associates International, reported it had found $560 million on behalf of its clients in 1997 alone.

## 4.1 STATISTICS

Figures taken from the *Managing Accounts Payable* benchmarking survey prepared by IOMA help put the seriousness of this matter in perspective. It is fair to assume that these figures understate the problem for the following two reasons:

1. Not everyone is willing to admit the full extent of their payment errors. Like weight and age, people tend to underestimate when talking about their own mistakes.
2. The numbers reflect only the errors managers know about. Obviously, they can't report the overpayments and duplicate payments they are not aware of.

Although recipients of this survey were asked for the percentage of errors made on vendor payments, a full 20% wrote in less than 1%. This tends to give credence to the theory that some companies do not know the exact extent of the problem. The remaining 80% reported an average error rate of 1.91%. Of those, 70% of the payments were reissued.

The same question was asked of T&Es. In this case, 25% indicated less than 1% and the other 75% averaged 1.32%. In this case, half the payments were reissued. These are serious numbers.

## 4.2 TYPES OF ERRONEOUS PAYMENTS

One of the first steps to be taken in eliminating payment errors is to identify the types that can occur. The most common include:

Duplicate payments.

Invoices paid for an incorrect amount, that is, $1,000 instead of $100.

Paying for items, such as freight or insurance, that should not be paid for.

Discounts not taken.

Fraudulent payments.

Aside from the obvious reason, fraud is included in a discussion of erroneous payments, as the same lack of controls that permit erroneous and/or duplicate payments also allow fraudulent ones to slip by.

## 4.3 LOW-TECH SOLUTIONS

While it is probably next to impossible to completely eliminate erroneous payments, many actions will reduce the number of these mistakes. Accounts payable professionals have reported some success in this area by:

- Cleaning up master vendor files (for a detailed look at this issue, see Chapter 10, Master Vendor Files).
- Instituting controls on adding and deleting information from the vendor files.
- Paying only from original invoices.
- Setting up strict rules for handling invoices with invoice numbers.
- Insisting that POs be completely filled out before being sent.
- Canceling all invoices once they are paid.
- As part of the annual review, having an external auditor review controls.

It may not be possible to enforce all of these rules. Insisting that you will pay only from an original invoice sounds nice, but there are times when the bill is legitimately lost in the mail. However, setting strict controls when an invoice is not an original will reduce the number of such payments. For a detailed look at this issue, see Chapter 5, Paying When the Original Invoice is Not Available.

Similarly, many employees are successful in convincing their auditors to exclude certain recommendations from the management report. (No one likes to be criticized to upper management—it is generally not seen as a good career move.) However, if you persuade the auditors to remove something from the management letter, don't immediately forget about it. Consider whether the criticism was legitimate and what you can do to correct the condition.

## 4.4 HIGH-TECH SOLUTIONS

The items discussed above were of the simpler variety. Other actions that can be taken generally require management backing. They include:

Receiving as many invoices as possible electronically.

Doing the three-way match electronically.

Hiring a third-party firm specializing in reviewing bills and contracts to recover funds (see Chapter 23, Post Audit Firms, for more details.)

Asking the audit firm to point out weaknesses in your procedures.

Tightening controls as recommended.

## 4.5 OTHER LONG-TERM SOLUTIONS

The best approach that the accounts payable professional can take in solving the erroneous and duplicate payment issue will also help in other aspects of the job. By keeping up to date on the latest techniques and approaches, a professional will be in the best position to do the most effective job both for themselves and the company. As many accounts payable professionals are well aware, there are not a lot of resources available for those looking for accounts payable help, but they do exist. They include:

Reading all relevant information in trade publications.

Joining professional organizations, such as the International Accounts Payable Professionals and the Treasury Management Association.

Participating in local chapter meetings of professional organizations.

Getting on the Web and joining in accounts payable discussion groups (for an example, see IOMA's home page (www.ioma.com).

Asking an expert, also on the Web, for advice (www.recap-inc.com).

## 4.6 MOST IMPORTANT RESOURCE

Most companies overlook their most valuable asset when it comes to plugging the leaks—their own employees. The people involved in the day-to-day activities of the business usually know where and how the problems can occur. Unfortunately, they are rarely consulted and even less frequently listened to. So, start by asking the people involved in the daily processing of payments where they perceive the holes to be. You might be surprised to hear what they have to say.

## 4.7 TOLERANCE LEVELS

One of the most popular recommendations made to accounts payable professionals is to set tolerance levels for which discrepancies will be ignored and vendor invoices can be paid. Some companies set these as a discrete dollar level, say $5.00, and others as a percentage of the face value of the invoice up to a certain amount, say $50. This approach is not without critics.

### (a) Small Amounts Add Up

It is all too easy to overpay an invoice when the extra amounts involved are small. However, if a company receives many small invoices from the same vendor, the amounts can quickly add up. Another way these amounts accumulate is when the vendor passes along charges that it is supposed to pay. This often happens with freight and insurance charges. But, the same financial impact can be achieved with 100 charges of $3 as with one $300 charge. Skeptics may wonder whether or not this was an honest mistake on the part of the vendor.

### (b) Check the Invoice

When it comes to checking invoices, here's what a few innovative billers do. The invoice indicates the correct terms. It may also indicate in tiny print that there can be a 1.5% late payment service charge. There is a statement on the invoice reflecting the amount due if paid before the discount date. It is correct. Now, here comes the kicker. In the "pay this amount" box, the figure shown reflects a late fee for one month. If the accounts payable clerk paying the bill does not stop to foot the amounts on the invoice, the amount paid will include the late payment service charge. Nowhere on the invoice does the correct figure appear—not even in tiny print.

## 4.8 HANDLING DISCREPANCIES

For the reasons discussed earlier, many experts recommend resolving all variances—no matter how small. There are a few unscrupulous vendors who will use information about your tolerance levels to their advantage. Accounts payable professionals who know exactly which charges their companies are responsible for paying and which they are not are in a position to save their companies huge amounts of money—even if it is 35 cents at a time. Those who refoot all invoices will discover the few dollars spent to buy calculators is money well spent.

Not everyone will agree with this point of view. It may be less relevant in some industries than others. However, if it is not a real issue, why are accounts payable audit firms doing so well? And why do accounts receivable managers want to run for the hills when they hear such a firm is auditing one of their client's books. Those wishing to take a middle-of-the-road approach might try investigating all discrepancies, regardless of size, for a month or two. The results of that investigation should provide the necessary guidance to determine what is appropriate at each company.

## 4.9 ACCURACY AND TIMELINESS

Many duplicate payments occur because the original invoice was not paid on a timely basis or the accuracy of the payment leaves much to be desired. When a payment is made for an incorrect amount, the likelihood of the receiving party being able to apply the cash diminishes greatly. If the cash isn't applied, the recipient will think the payment has not been received and will call looking for its money. More than occasionally a second payment is made. By focusing on these two key areas, the number of duplicate and erroneous payments will be greatly reduced. The greatest success tends to come when focus is placed on three different areas:

1. Procedures.
2. Purchase orders.
3. Invoices.

### (a) Procedures

The most obvious place to start, when concerned about accuracy and timeliness, is with the procedures being used. And that is just what many successful A/P professionals do. Savvy professionals continue to search for solutions by modifying their procedures. The A/P manager at a mid-size insurance company says his dilemma is that "As the disbursement unit of a group of insurance companies, we are often in a situation where we must answer to other departments as to 'Where did that check get sent?' and 'So and so didn't get their check!' When dealing with one of our companies specifically, we found it very difficult because the majority of the time, their feedback occurred after the fact, when it was out of our control to resolve the situation." Many reading this would tell him that this predicament is not peculiar to insurance companies, in fact the majority of accounts payable managers have to deal with it. Here's how several companies have addressed this issue:

> Review existing procedures and clarify those that are not crystal clear. These might include things as simple as writing the receiving party's name on our source documents during the backup/source matching process.

Never assume anything and clarify via phone call all questionable items.

Rotate duties within the department to prevent boredom. A side benefit to this is that the staff is cross trained and this enables the company to have more than adequate backup in case of abscences.

Requests for payment often come in to accounts payable with too few details and no audit trail documentation. Take requests for payment with insufficient information (which can include missing account numbers or documentation), and send them back to the originating department until the proper information is collected. This common sense solution will work in most organizations—when it has management backing. So, make sure you have it before implementing such a hard line approach.

Try the KISS (keep it simple, stupid) solution for those who code incorrectly. Develop a one-page reference chart of accounts for each office. It should include only those account numbers used in that office. This should eliminate most, if not all, of their coding errors.

### (b) Purchase Orders

In most companies, the primary piece of documentation regarding a purchase is the Purchase Order (PO). For many it is their Bible. While the PO is usually under the purveyance of the purchasing department in manufacturing companies, that is not the case at those institutions where no such department exists. In those cases, the modus operandi will be slightly different. Here are some of the problems encountered by accounts payable professionals and how these messes were solved:

Consider the case of a Wisconsin college. "Our biggest problem," says the A/P supervisor, "is that we do not have a purchasing agent so this falls to the accounts payable area to control. We have redefined our Purchase Order system and have a closer working relationship with departments and use e-mail and computer systems a lot more."

The A/P manager at a retirement community has the opposite problem. "With eight departments, each doing their own purchasing, sometimes using the same vendor," grumbles this professional, "I would receive an invoice and have to search the company to see what department had ordered the product." But this innovative manager came up with an easy-to-implement solution to this messy problem. "Now we use the department number as part of our PO number," she explains. "It has really helped identify the purchaser."

### (c) Invoices

Invoices also play an important part in the life of an accounts payable professional. While many consider the PO the Bible for a transaction, most are willing to forget it should a better price or terms appear on an invoice. In many organizations, invoices must be approved for payment before a check can be cut. Getting approved invoices back is the bane of existence for many accounts payable professionals. When this problem is not controlled, duplicate payments multiply.

**(i) Timeliness.** Here's how some handle the problem of getting them back on a timely basis:

Explaining how he deals with the issue of getting invoices approved in a timely manner, one A/P professional says, "We make copies of invoices sent to departments for approval and if not returned within a couple of days, we call them." Like others in the same situation, he spends more time than he'd like on the phone trying to track down approvals.

Others choose to keep on top of the matter on a regular basis. The accounting supervisor of a freight transfer company reports having implemented a recurring e-mail message to all department heads stating the importance that all invoices and expense reports be received in accounting prior to the month's end. That's just the beginning of the process for this persistent supervisor. "Failure to comply with our e-mail," she says, "will result in accounts payable copying late arrivals of invoices and discussion with department heads in our monthly review." This hardline approach usually works but often makes an enemy out of the offending employee.

**(ii) Large Numbers of Small Invoices.** The other problem with invoices that drives accounts payable managers crazy is the large amount of small invoices. These are difficult to track and often get paid more than once. Since the individual amounts involved are not huge, no one gets overly upset if they are overpaid. But small amounts add up. This not uncommon situation is dealt with in several ways, including:

Consolidating many items on each invoice.

Using corporate procurement cards for low-dollar purchases.

Paying once a month from a statement rather than individual invoices.

## 4.10 TIMING ISSUES

Many companies look for ways to stretch their payments to vendors. This is especially true for large invoices. However, those that do this are increasing the chances of a duplicate payment. Unfortunately, few realize this. When a payment is delayed, most vendors will send a second invoice. Some do not mark it as a copy or duplicate invoice. When the invoice shows up, it looks like a new invoice and is often processed for payment.

Processing a second invoice for payment does not present a problem for those companies that have good controls for duplicate payments. However, many do not. Thus when this second invoice gets processed through the system, it gets paid. After all, it's not a copy and if it is not so marked, the accounts payable staff will have no way of realizing that it has already been paid. This issue is compounded by the fact that many vendors do not tell their customers about duplicate payments and even the most scrupulous will take some time in reporting the overpayment. After all, the receiving company must identify the second payment; applying unidentified cash is not a top priority in most organizations.

## 4.11 CONCLUSION

Now many reading this are probably thinking that this is not a big issue, but it is. Some companies, including more than one well-known company, have been known to send duplicate invoices that are not so marked. Making the matter even worse, there are reports that some of these duplicates contain different invoice numbers. This is extremely important as many of the procedures companies use to determine if an invoice has already been paid focus on the invoice number. If a different invoice number is supplied, the invoice looks new.

This discussion is not meant to scare the reader but to put the issue into proper focus. Perhaps the biggest indication of the size of the problem of duplicate payments is the continuing emergence of accounts payable audit firms. (See Chapter 23, Payment Recovery Firms, for more information about them). If duplicate payments were not such a big issue, these firms would have no work—and they are thriving with new companies popping up on a regular basis. Duplicate payments are a problem in most companies—and not doing something about them has a direct and very negative impact on the company's bottom line.

# 5

# Paying When the Original Invoice Is Not Available

Those not intimately involved with accounts payable are probably wondering why a chapter is being devoted to paying when an original invoice is not available. The reason is quite simple. Payments made against copies of invoices account for a good portion of all duplicate and fraudulent payments. Virtually every accounts payable professional would like to institute a policy of never paying from anything but an original invoice. Yet, realistically speaking, this is not possible. Invoices do get lost or mutilated.

In the *1997 Managing Accounts Payable Benchmarking Survey*, respondents were asked whether payments at their company were made without the original invoice or receipt. The responses were divided almost right down the middle, with a slight majority (51.5%) indicating they made payments from copies.

## 5.1 WHO PAYS FROM COPIES

With some variations, the larger the company, the more likely it was to allow payments from copies. The two statistical bumps in this pattern are firms with between 250 and 499 employees and those with between 1,000 and 4,999 employees. The former group was slightly more likely to pay from a copy and the latter slightly less likely to do so than a straight-line analysis would suggest.

The breakdown of data by industry was all over the lot. Not-for-profits take the booby prize in this area, with fully 60% of them making payments from copies. Companies in both the health-care industry and the nebulous category known as other have the strictest policies in this regard, with only 40% making payments from copies. For a complete breakdown of figures by company size and industry, see Exhibit 5.1.

*Exhibit 5.1* **Who Pays From Copies**

| | *Yes* | *No* |
|---|---|---|
| *Total* | *51.5%* | *48.5%* |
| **By number of employees** | | |
| Up to 99 | 37.5 | 62.5 |
| 100 to 249 | 43.0 | 57.0 |
| 250 to 499 | 55.0 | 45.0 |
| 500 to 999 | 52.7 | 47.3 |
| 1,000 to 4,999 | 49.0 | 51.0 |
| Over 5,000 | 64.6 | 35.4 |
| **By industry** | | |
| Manufacturing | 56.4 | 43.6 |
| Finance | 50.9 | 49.1 |
| Utilities, transportation | 49.0 | 51.0 |
| Private practice | 49.0 | 51.0 |
| Nonprofit | 60.0 | 40.0 |
| Wholesale/resale distribution | 55.0 | 45.0 |
| Health care | 40.4 | 59.6 |
| Education | 42.3 | 57.7 |
| Communications | 53.3 | 46.7 |
| Construction | 45.0 | 55.0 |
| Other | 40.0 | 60.0 |

(Source: IOMA)

## 5.2 CONTROLS WHEN USING COPIES

There is good reason for the controversy surrounding the making of payments without an original invoice or receipt. If payments were only made against originals, there would be no duplicate payments (or very few). Thus, companies that do make payments from copies should have strong controls in place to ensure that the payment has not already been made. These firms also need to ensure that if the original does surface, a payment will not be made against it when one has already been made against a copy. Many stamp the copy either duplicate or copy and then file it away. That's great except when the original finally finds its way down to accounts payable, it often gets paid—after all it's an original invoice. Unless the files are checked for each and every payment, there are good controls in place, or someone remembers making the first payment, a duplicate payment will be made.

There is also the concern that the payment has already been made and that's why the original invoice cannot be found. If the vendor applied the cash incorrectly on its own books, it will look to them as though a payment had not been made—even though one has. Additionally, if the payment was mailed to a lockbox, the vendor may have received it but not updated its records. And there are a few unscrupulous vendors who claim they have not been paid when they actually have. Thus, whenever a payment is being made from a copy, there are concerns that the payment will be made a second time, it has already been made or perhaps, the request is fraudulent. It's easy to see why this topic generates so much concern.

## 5.3 COMMON TECHNIQUES TO ENSURE A SECOND PAYMENT WILL NOT BE MADE

Many companies used similar processes to eliminate duplicate payments. The following list provides a number of solutions that work at various companies. Not all will work in all companies. What is applicable to each organization will depend in large part on the other controls and processes in place. The solutions most commonly used include variations on the following:

- A search routine by vendor for the dollar amount and/or the invoice number.
- The approval from one or more senior-level managers for payments made without an original.
- The payment of only those invoices that are long overdue. Each company has its own definition of what long overdue is.

## 5.4 CONTROLS WHEN PAYING FROM COPIES

There are a wide variety of procedures companies can use in order to ensure the payment being made from the copy is legitimate and that another won't be made at some future date. As you review the following list, you will note that many of them seem to make life a little more difficult for the person trying to get a payment made from a copy. That impression is correct and there is a very good reason for this. Payments made from copies are time consuming and put the company at risk as discussed above. Such payments should only be made when all other avenues have been exhausted.

It is easy for the requestor to simply have the vendor fax over another copy of the invoice and then have the accounts payable department pay it. Unfortunately in many instances, the original invoice is lying on this very person's desk and when it does eventually surface, it is forwarded for payment because the person has long forgotten it has been paid. This is rarely done out of malice, usually just plain laziness. By making it difficult, the requestors may decide that it is easier to submit invoices for payment when received or search their desk for the missing document. In either event, you are changing bad behavior patterns for the future.

## 5.4 Controls when Paying from Copies

Listed below are procedures that have worked in a number of organizations:

Require a signature approval from one or more high-level executive before issuing a check.

Research the company's records thoroughly to detect a prior payment.

Double-check to ensure that the original invoice was not paid.

Print out a payment history for the supplier in question and check on the invoice number and the dollar amount.

Check the master vendor file to ensure that no previous payment was made. Review all possible vendor files. In many instances, there is more than one vendor file per supplier.

If purchasing makes the request for the payment, insist that a valid PO and an unmatched receivable transaction exist.

If non-PO, search the payment history for possible duplicates.

Review the purpose and reason for the request.

Get a sign-off from purchasing for all requests without original invoices.

After research has been done to determine that the payment has not been made, the copy is marked with a stamp reflecting this fact.

Run the information through a search routine based on the invoice number and dollar amount involved.

Stamp the copy "Copy of Original" and pay only after the system is checked for duplication.

Require an explanation for the lack of an original invoice with the payment request.

Only pay on a copy if the invoice is severely past due and a thorough review of the files has been completed.

### Paying When the Original Invoice Is Not Available

Review requests for payment without the original invoice on a case-by-case basis to determine if it is advisable to pay.

Copies used for payment purposes are marked "Certified Copy" so that the staffer processing the item can double-check the system to detect duplicate payments.

Get a copy of the Purchase Order and receiving document.

Require a memo requesting the payment from a copy and have it signed by two senior-level managers.

Have a form signed by both the requestor and the Chief Financial Officer.

Pay only those invoices that are more than 90 days past due.

Only those invoices under $250 may be paid without the original.

Require that the check-request form be co-signed by an officer of the company.

Allow payments from faxes but never from statements.

Place all requests for payments from copies in a tickler file for later follow-up and research.

Have the request for payment signed by the individual who has the primary relationship with the vendor.

Use Evaluated Receipt Settlement (invoiceless processing), thus eliminating the need to receive an invoice. For more information about ERS see Chapter 14, Alternatives to the "Three-Way Match."

Issue payments only on those items that are more than 45 days past due.

Research the possibility of a duplicate payment manually.

Pay from copies only if the invoice number is completely legible on the copy so that it can be checked for possible previous payment.

### 5.4 Controls when Paying from Copies

Those who have been paying from copies should reevaluate that process and decide whether or not they are comfortable with the policy. If they decide to go forward with such a policy, then they will need to make sure they have the appropriate controls and procedures in place to make sure that they are not paying twice or paying something they should not.

# Part Two

# The People

The most valuable asset any company has is its employees, and this is especially true in accounts payable where the staff is responsible for the outflow of firm's cash. Until recently few recognized how vital these professionals are to the organization and how treating them with dignity and respect can make a big difference both in the department's productivity and the corporation's bottom line.

One of the best kept secrets in many companies is the fact that the people who toil in their accounts payable departments are bright, innovative, hard working, and resourceful. Given just the tiniest bit of encouragement, these individuals work wonders with limited resources. They know the current procedures and for the most part they know where the weaknesses in the processes are. Ask for their ideas, encourage and offer positive reinforcement for their successes—and then watch out—the sky's the limit.

# 6

# Making Your Accounts Payable Department First Rate

Today's accounts payable departments are a far cry from the preconceived notions held by most people. If, and this is a big if, they even give accounts payable a second thought, most will envision one or more low-level clerks writing checks while surrounded by mounds of paper. Nowhere in this vision is there a computer, a fax machine, or anything else high tech. Creative, educated, innovative employees are also not part of this picture. Nothing could be further from the truth. While accounts payable departments often have to fight with the powers that be to get the necessary equipment, most accounts payable departments are staffed with intelligent enterprising people. These individuals are responsible for one of their company's most valuable assets—its money—and for the most part, they take very good care of it.

## 6.1 TYPICAL ACCOUNTS PAYABLE DEPARTMENT

Of course, there is no such thing as a typical department. However, we have a few statistics, from an IOMA benchmarking survey of over 700 companies, that give a rough idea of what an average accounts payable department looks like. The size of the department, obviously, depends on what work is handled in the department. Certain functions, such as 1099s, petty cash, T&E, and payroll may or may not be handled within accounts payable. Similarly, coding, check printing, check signing, general ledger work, wire transfer activity, and other functions may also be done outside the department—or not. In fact, in a survey at its accounts payable conference, RECAP Inc. discovered that the only function handled by 100% of the accounts payable departments of the attendees was the paying of invoices. The IOMA statistics show:

> One-third of all companies have an accounts payable staff of two or fewer employees.
>
> Another 30% have between three and five.
>
> Only 89% have more than 20.
>
> 10% have between 11 and 20.
>
> Just under 20% have between six and ten.

The large number of companies with small accounts payable staff sizes also implies that many of the functions discussed in this book are performed in other departments—most commonly the controllers or accounting and in some cases treasury or finance.

## 6.2 WHO RUNS THE DEPARTMENT?

Much of the work is repetitive, yet if it is not done properly, there is a direct and immediate impact on the bottom line. The accounts payable manager has to be able to keep the staff motivated and errors minimized while simultaneously looking for ways to improve the productivity of the department. Additionally, they often have the ability to save the company money or even, in a few instances, make it a few dollars. So, who does corporate America entrust with these responsibilities? Here are some statistics, again from the IOMA survey, about these managers.

Approximately two-thirds of all departments are run by women.

The average age of the manager is 39 for women and 40 for men.

Female managers average 16.9 years experience with 7.2 of those years being spent in accounts payable while their male counterparts have 17.4 years total experience with just .2 of a year less time spent in accounts payable.

## 6.3 HOW TO ASSEMBLE YOUR OWN ACCOUNTS PAYABLE DREAM TEAM

Finding and maintaining the perfect mix of employees in any accounts payable department takes an incredible amount of hard work on the part of the accounts payable manager—with a dash of luck thrown in for good measure. Just when the ideal composition has been achieved, invariably a monkey wrench in the form of a promotion to another department, or a job at another company for a key employee, wreaks havoc with the hard-won departmental harmony. Finding the right people for the positions is critical to the success of the department.

This is made all the worse by the downsizing and reengineering facing many professionals today. Many who know their company is reengineering, or may be having mandatory staff reductions in the near future, are reluctant to hire new people, especially those who already have a job. It also makes outside candidates leery of accepting a position that may be eliminated in only a few months. Yet, accounts payable professionals still have to get the work done. Here are some ways you can assemble the best staff possible.

### (a) Know the Numbers

First, A/P professionals must know the number of invoices handled in their department, where they come from, what the terms are, how many come from each vendor group, and so on. Those who do not have a good grasp of what they are currently dealing with are in a very poor position to recommend change.

### (b) Maintain a Minimal or No Backlog

In order to move ahead, all processing backlogs must be eliminated. Otherwise, the entire focus of the department will be grinding out the work rather than spending time evaluating new and more efficient ways to do things. Backlogs tend to create additional work as staff members search through piles of unprocessed invoices for the one that must be paid now. This fire fighting time could be better spent on more meaningful work.

### (c) Set Up a Vendor/Customer Relations Group

Rather than have every employee distracted by vendor inquiries, assign this responsibility to one or more employees who do nothing but answer vendors' inquiries. This will free the remainder of the staff to work without constant interruptions. Others have had success by setting aside a specific time of the day when vendor inquiries will be handled. Such an approach should be instituted with great care as it may offend certain of your larger customers on whose business your company's livelihood depends.

### (d) Don't Accept Shoddy Behaviors

Most of A/P staff's time wasters are due to mistakes made by others. If the behavior of those individuals could be changed, then perhaps the number of discrepancies—and time—would decrease. Partially tie the purchasing manager's compensation to purchase order accuracy. In some organizations this is a big issue and offers the opportunity for big improvements, if possible. Obviously this is a management initiative but it can bring big productivity gains to the accounts payable department.

Pay on a PO only once. Thus, a supplier sending a partial shipment would get paid for that first shipment. Payment for the remainder of the shipment theoretically could not be made. It will not take long for suppliers to learn not to send partial orders.

By identifying the things done by others that cause A/P additional work, the accounts payable manager will be able to go about trying to change that behavior to better meet the department's needs.

### (e) Involve Employees

When looking to improve operations, many managers overlook their best resource: the staffers currently doing the job. Ask those employees for their suggestions. They will have many good ones.

### (f) Track Productivity

Track individual employee productivity but be cautious about taking the results at face value. People will figure out how you are tracking them and then go out of their way to make the numbers look good. For example, if you track the number of invoices handled by each employee, some may go out of their way to get the easy invoices.

### (g) Always Be Creative

Use technology wherever possible to improve productivity, being as creative as possible when looking for productivity gains. Don't add staff until it is clearly absolutely necessary since no one likes to be in the position of having to let someone go. Use temporaries until a full evaluation determines that there really is a need for an additional person.

### (h) Take Full Advantage of Technology

Use the technology you have to its fullest capabilities. When purchasing new technology make sure that it will make the group more effective. Don't purchase it because everyone else is using it. Many professionals have found ways to use simple programs like word processing and spreadsheet analysis to make forms, prepare reports, and even prepare employees' T&Es.

### (i) Make the Best Use of Existing Personnel

Have management and existing personnel pick up some of the slack. This works well in those instances when the manager can show the staff that mandatory cutbacks have been avoided due to this action. It also doesn't hurt if the employees picking up the extra work are paid overtime.

Use temporary workers for long-term assignments when either downsizing or reengineering would otherwise require job cuts.

Use temporary workers to handle overload periods.

Cross train personnel so they can pitch in when there are work crunches in other parts of the department. This also makes staff members more promotable and more marketable should the unthinkable happen.

Rewrite job descriptions to upgrade accounts payable positions so that staff members can be paid market salaries. This will help keep those key employees who might be lured away by one of your competitors offering a more attractive compensation package.

Retrain employees whose tasks have been automated. This will improve employee morale throughout the department, while making them more marketable.

Put those few employees whose work has deteriorated on notice. By giving warning and offering help to overcome deficiencies, many marginal employees will become productive and make meaningful contributions. Should they not come up to speed, there will have been sufficient notice. Also, an employee who is put on notice and does not have the inclination to improve may go out and find another position, relieving the accounts payable manager of the unpleasantness associated with fixing the distasteful situation.

Add additional personnel to handle increased workloads and to provide existing personnel more time to improve current procedures.

Make the accounts payable department staff realize they are part of a larger team and not a separate, discrete function. This will increase their esteem and confidence.

Where appropriate, convert long-term, temporary personnel into permanent employees. In these instances you will have a good idea of the person's work ethic and ability and will save yourself a lot of time and effort training a new employee. Many times temps turn out to be the best candidates for jobs. They've had a chance to try you out and know exactly what they are getting into.

Nip troublemakers in the bud.

## 6.4 PROCEDURES MANUAL

Since many accounts payable departments have grown gradually or evolved as part of the accounting department, few have a written game plan. Procedures are developed in kind of a hodgepodge with much of the knowledge about how things work and where information is located often residing with one or more individual. Should that person get sick or worse, get another job, the company is left in a lurch. Every accounts payable department should have a procedures manual. This not only serves as a guide in cases of emergency, it will give the manager the necessary documentation to prove to management just how professional the staff is and how much work they are handling. Until the list is completed, few understand the scope of information that is needed in order to run a successful department.

The guide can also be used to determine if there are any efforts that are not needed. We are not going to claim that this will be the most interesting book ever written, but it is essential that every department have one. As an added benefit, it will make the auditors happy. The following guidelines will help you prepare a usable manual:

Make this a group project in which the entire department can participate. Some have even found that an activity such as this is great for getting individuals to work as a team.

Make a detailed outline of all topics that need to be included in the manual. Think of it as a detailed table of contents. With a little organization, it probably can be used for that purpose.

Assign overall responsibility for the project to someone who gets things done on a timely basis. The person should also be someone who gets along with most of the staff.

Divide the topics and have each member of the staff write one or more sections. Having the sections written by those intimately involved with the work will ensure that the information is accurate.

Have each section reviewed by another member of the department. Try to not have two people review each other's work. Many people tend to be sensitive about their writing and changes must be handled with tact.

Make sure all who participated in the project get credit for their work—possibly include a page in the front listing all the authors.

Once it's done, don't forget about it. It's not difficult to update something like this once a year. But let it sit on the shelf for several years and you'll find yourself back at ground zero when the manual needs to be updated.

Accounts payable departments without such a manual leave themselves open to criticism when duplicate payments or fraud are uncovered.

## 6.5 TECHNOLOGY MAKES SERIOUS INROADS INTO ACCOUNTS PAYABLE DEPARTMENTS

It's hard to believe that just ten years ago computers in the accounts payable department were an exception rather than a norm.

Now they are commonplace and accounts payable managers are finding innovative ways to use them to improve departmental productivity while simultaneously tightening controls and reducing costs. In the following sections, we explore how some are putting theirs to use in six A/P areas.

### (a) Check Printing & Signing

The biggest change is the shift away from mainframe printed checks to those that can be printed from personal computers on the department's laser printers. In some cases, companies using this technology have been able to completely eliminate handwritten rush checks. The ripple effect from this is there are then fewer duplicate payments. Why? Because many duplicate payments arise when a rush manual check is written but not entered into the accounting system. When a second request for payment is made, the invoice does not appear to have been paid.

Check printing on laser printers also allows companies to eliminate large supplies of checks. No longer is it necessary to have preprinted check stock. The computer includes the necessary bank information and company logo at the time the check is printed. This is especially useful to companies that have many different bank accounts for different purposes. Laser printers have many control features built in and, if set up correctly, actually offer more fraud protection than multipart checks traditionally used by companies.

Most of these printers have the capability to have checks automatically signed, although not every company goes that route and some do so only for smaller checks. (Each has their own definition of what a small check is.)

The final savings comes from the fact that companies no longer need to purchase and house the check bursting machines needed to handle those three-part computer checks.

### (b) Online Wire Transfers

As anyone who uses wire transfers will attest, they can be time consuming and expensive if done by phone. However, since they are typically done for large dollar payments or in cases where it is imperative that the funds arrive by or at a precise time, many companies pay the price. However, by initiating your transfers online through a computer, it is possible to cut these exorbitant fees. With proper controls, the initiation of wire transfers online with the bank not only lowers fee but saves a great deal of time. The emphasis must be on proper controls.

Some also use this online technology to issue and amend letters of credit.

As banks become more cost conscious, they focus on the true cost of taking a wire transfer by phone. It is time consuming for the bank and consequently, very expensive. Increasingly, banks are trying to move their customers to online wire transmissions by increasing the cost for wires called in. Some banks charge $50 for a wire in such a case. If your bank has not started to increase these charges, don't be surprised to see them do so in the future.

### (c) Online Three-Way Matching

There are now a number of software programs on the market that allow the accounts payable department to automate the traditional three-way match (print order with invoice and receiving document). These programs only spit out the exception items where the documents don't match. As you might imagine, this is not only a big timesaver, but also helps reduce errors—the less human intervention, the fewer errors.

### (d) E-mail

Intercompany e-mail is a big help to the accounts payable manager. When accounts payable professionals need to notify people to come pick up their checks, they can simply send an e-mail message. If appropriate, it can be broadcast to the entire company just by clicking on a few extra buttons. This technology can be used at companies of all sizes. Many companies successfully use e-mail for intercompany communications. Other applications include:

- Streamline and shorten the time span for T&E reports to be reimbursed.
- Better communications between departments.
- Quicker responses to A/P problems or queries.
- Notification of T&E electronic payments.
- Nudge executives that are a bit slow in getting invoice approvals back to A/P.

### (e) Delegate Data Entry to Users

Traditionally, much of the invoice data entry has been done in the accounts payable department. With computers on most employees' desks, this is no longer a necessity. Some organizations have pushed this responsibility back to the department approving the purchase. Expect to meet some resistance from those departments who are overworked and/or are not eager to take on additional tasks.

### (f) Use of Networks to Reduce Paper Flow

The amount of paper generated in an accounts payable department and sent to other departments can be enormous. However, networks can alleviate this problem.

## 6.6 OUTSOURCING

Business consultants are all touting the benefits of outsourcing. From the company's perspective, at least initially, outsourcing can seem to make sense. The outsourcer takes a task, outside of the target company's core competency, and performs it at a lower cost. The target company can then focus on the tasks it does best.

In theory this seems to make sense. In the most horrific cases, the target company lays off the employees who are then rehired by the outsourcer, usually at a lower salary and with fewer, if any benefits, to handle the same work. Now, right off the bat, how committed do you think these employees will be working for less money, with no security, doing the same tasks? Off the record, the very consultants who vigorously recommend outsourcing will concede that yes this does happen—but so what? It's easy to see that it is not their jobs at stake. If it were, they might have a different perspective.

But, putting the human concerns aside and looking at the issue from the business point of view, does it make sense? The answer will vary from organization to organization, of course. In general, it might make sense only in certain very limited technical tasks. The best example that springs to mind is the case of VAT refunds. Most companies will not have enough employees with significant international travel to make it worthwhile to have one or more staff members become expert enough to handle this nightmare of paperwork.

### (a) State of Outsourcing in Accounts Payable Today

The only place, aside from some of the extremely specialized applications, where outsourcing appears to be making any inroads is in check printing where a few, mostly large, companies are allowing their banks to handle their check printing.

Most companies are extremely reluctant to have their accounts payable information leave the company. Additionally, they like to have control over the payment timing—especially at those times of the year when cashflow might be tight. The state of outsourcing and accounts payable today was summarized best by a speaker at a recent conference who said, "Everybody is talking about it but no one is doing it."

### (b) Outsourcing Case Study

Several years ago, when a large well-known technology company decided to outsource its accounts payable function, one of the options not considered was keeping the function in-house. As part of a companywide head count reduction, management had decided to send the function outside. When the team responsible for evaluating the issue interviewed potential candidates to handle the work, they discovered what many other accounts payable professionals have found at both big and smaller companies alike: They could do the work better and cheaper in-house if they reengineered.

Making this discovery was just the beginning. The accounts payable team then had to win over managers focused on reducing staff. They were lucky in that management was open-minded enough to allow them to make an internal proposal along with the outsourcing organizations. The accounts payable manager for this company explained how the team succeeded in getting the bid and lowering costs dramatically enough to keep the account.

### (c) The Investigation

Once the order was received to outsource the accounts payable function, a methodical approach was taken. The requirements for all five accounts payable locations (including one that was already outsourced) were summarized, and a request for proposal (RFP) was sent to seven companies. Four companies responded to the RFP and two seemed to meet the company's needs, including price requirements. Company representatives traveled to these two organizations and viewed their operations.

At this point, the idea was beginning to emerge. Could the accounts payable department do it better and more cost effectively? The team thought so and approached management about the possibility of the company making its own bid. Management agreed to look at an in-house proposal along with the proposals from outside vendors and decided to give the existing department a chance to continue doing the job.

### (d) The Reengineering

When the process began, per item handling costs were $10.05. Nine months later, this had been reduced to $6.37. These cost reductions resulted from several innovations:

Consolidating several field locations.

Doing accruals quarterly rather than monthly.

Implementing use of an approval stamp.

Making the audit process more sophisticated.

Discontinuing the process of manually decrementing purchase orders.

Reorganizing vendor files alphabetically.

Converting check stock to a one-part form.

Acknowledging decrease in volume due to companywide layoffs.

Generally moving to more efficient systems.

But, reengineering is an ongoing effort and the company didn't stop here. A year later, the company had further reduced its per-item costs to $4.95, despite a 35% to 40% increase in volume. This was done by:

Using electronic approvals.

Streamlining the accounts receivable refund process, thus eliminating paper.

Converting all agency and contractors to an EDI system.

Arranging contractual payments.

Eliminating hard copies of purchase orders.

Streamlining AMEX processing.

Negotiating an AMEX partnership pricing agreement to allow the company to pay a portion of an employee's American Express bill directly to AMEX instead of to the employee, resulting in a decrease in the number of client held-days and a discount.

Initiating use of auto accruals.

Introducing a companywide newsletter about accounts payable. It was created in an attempt to reduce the number of phone calls received in the department and the other inconveniences caused when employees outside the accounts payable area handle accounts payable matters incorrectly. The newsletter offers other departments tips for the proper handling of accounts payable-related matters. This innovative effort was taken on by one of the accounts payable staff members.

## 6.7 MOVING FORWARD

The company has further reduced its costs to $3.65 per item by continually reviewing its operations and implementing new technologies and procedures. For example, the company has just begun using procurement cards—a change that makes the company optimistic about still more cost reductions.

The company saw enough advantages to handling the accounts payable work in-house to offset the few disadvantage:

The accounts payable department did not reduce its head count.

The work is not part of the company's core competency.

The company is less flexible than an outside agency would be should it suddenly have to respond to a dramatic increase in volume.

The company also still had the administrative support costs associated with keeping the function in-house.

However, the lower per-item costs, the lack of implementation fees, and the staff's demonstrated ability to manage both costs and head count far outweighed these and other minor disadvantages. And, of course, the existing staff knew the company's ways much better than an outside party. It is noteworthy that, unlike most organizations, this company knows and measures its costs on a very regular basis. Not only are the costs measured, they are reported to management. In conclusion, the company's accounts payable manager points out that the staff would not have been competitive if they had not pushed hard to reengineer their processes.

# 7

# Managing the Staff

Working in accounts payable in many organizations is often a thankless job. In many organizations, the people in the department are given little or no respect, compensation is poor and the thought that some of the employees might actually want a career path is alien to most in management. These attitudes are reflected back, making it difficult for the accounts payable manager to manage the staff in a manner to produce the most error-free work as possible. This is a shame because the way the accounts payable functions are performed can have a direct impact—either positive or negative—on the company's bottom line. This is starting to change in a growing number of organizations as management focuses on the functions and begins to realize the profit potential of the department along with the fact that there are many innovative people toiling away in those jobs.

What's more, if these people are asked for suggestions, many have useful ideas that ultimately save the company money, improve productivity, and reduce the number of duplicate and erroneous payments made. However, if the staff is treated poorly, the members are less likely to offer suggestions or look for ways to improve departmental productivity. In Chapter 8, Staff Motivation and Morale, there is an expanded discussion on ways to motivate the staff.

## 7.1 TRAINING

Up until a few years ago, very few companies ever offered any extra training to their accounts payable professionals. For starters, very little was available. Now a number of organizations have accounts payable conferences that run anywhere from one to five days. The level of information varies in these sessions. There is a list of these conferences in Chapter 31. In addition to accounts payable training, professionals need to learn about a variety of other topics, including accounting, technology matters, people management, dealing with difficult vendors, and so on. This training can also be informal by reading either on ones own or of material provided by the company.

### (a) Who Needs Training?

There are several reasons to emphasize training. No one would expect an accounts payable clerk to do a three-way match if the clerk has never been shown how to do it. Most accounts payable managers make some attempt to train newcomers. Unfortunately, some only do this if the person is new to the field.

If a professional from another company is hired, often only minimal time is spent giving that employee on-the-job training. This is often a mistake, as different companies have different procedures and guidelines. What is standard operating procedure in one organization may very well cause trouble at the next. Rush checks often cause trouble: Some companies are quite flexible about issuing rush checks while others are not. A person coming from a company that grills someone asking for a rush check may be committing political suicide by trying that in the new organization. The accounts payable manager who makes sure that new employees are given adequate training usually finds it to be time well spent.

Beyond the issue of learning the basics, there are other reasons why training leads to a more productive team. Encouraging the accounts payable staff to obtain new skills will not only enable them to do a better job, but will put them in the position of being able to make suggestions that will improve the way the department is run.

### (b) Effective Training

In order to get the most out of your training periods, it is necessary to give a little thought to the entire process. Begin by preparing the information to be taught. This might be as simple as making an outline to use to make sure that all the pertinent points are covered. It might also include making copies of appropriate handouts for each of those attending your training session. These handouts could include worksheets, outlines, and even additional related articles for your staff to read at a later time. If the same material is used periodically, make sure and review it before each session. Certain topics may have changed, some of the material may become outdated, or perhaps supplementary material may need to be added.

Once the material is together and the presentation is ready, decide how and where the training will be done. If a large group is involved (e.g., training the entire staff on a new system or procedure) a conference room may need to be reserved. This also lets the staff know that they are special and the topic to be covered is important. For some, it will be the first time they are in the conference room.

If the instruction is to be one-on-one, an office might work well. Depending on the situation, it might also be appropriate to train at the staff member's desk. This is especially true if a computer system is involved, especially if it is only at the employee's desk and not in the office.

Make sure to encourage staff members to ask questions. Remind them that there is no such thing as a stupid question and then reinforce that concept whenever a question is asked—no matter how basic it might seem. Comments like, "That's a good question," or "I'm sure others are wondering the same thing," will make staffers less reluctant to ask questions.

Go over each step in detail. Just because something appears simple to a manager doesn't mean it will be as readily apparent to the staff or to someone hired from the outside. They may not have the years of experience dealing with the intricacies of the company's financial systems or its executives.

Do not feel that the manager must do all the training. If there is someone on staff who is particularly good at one facet of the operation, let that person do that part of the training. Not only will the manager have saved some time by delegating, but it will increase the staffer's morale.

### (c) Follow-Up

Once the training is completed, half the job is done. Don't assume that since questions were answered and everyone looked like they knew what was being discussed that the task is over. Check up frequently on the work based on this new training in the beginning. If a new form was introduced for rush checks, check all the forms for the first week. If there are errors in the way the form is being used, talk to the individuals involved. If a number of people seem to be making the same mistake, consider that the problem may have been with the instruction, and schedule a follow-up meeting. Review the mistakes and then ask for more questions. If the problems are minor, it may be possible to get by with a memo addressing the problem point in detail, rather than tying up everyone with a meeting.

Some accounts payable managers report that they like to schedule follow-up meetings even if there are no major fiascos with the new procedures. Their reasoning is that they can discuss with their staff how the new procedures are working and what, if any, additional problems are being caused. It is not always possible to anticipate the full extent of a problem until you are up to your knees in it. Look what happened to America Online when they offered unlimited Internet access for a flat fee. Quite often there are unanticipated consequences to even the simplest changes.

Training can take what seems like an inordinate amount of time—time that could be spent doing a million other things. However, the extra time invested in training your accounts payable staff will earn many dividends as your people make fewer mistakes and are able to handle a larger, more complex work flow with less supervision.

## 7.2 FINDING CHALLENGING WORK FOR THE STAFF

Trying to motivate people beyond the eight-to-five mentality and trying to make the routine seem less boring is a common problem facing managers today. Others find themselves trying to stimulate a staff that has no interest in making changes or taking on additional responsibilities. Some ways to challenge the accounts payable staff include:

Involve the staff in an improvement plan by making them owners of the project of procedures and policies that are being changed. When people have a say in how things work, they suddenly find them more interesting.

Make several changes simultaneously. While no one feature alone is responsible for lightening the load, each contributes to making the work more meaningful.

With a decentralized staff, use a custom training manual and arrange for special staff instruction. Have an accounts payable staff member from the home office visit each region for two weeks, giving comprehensive training sessions to those in the field. This results in a more productive staff—and less complaining.

## 7.3 LISTENING SKILLS

Accounts payable managers often complain that their bosses don't listen to their ideas, but how many are aware that their own staffers—and an occasional vendor—might have the same complaints about them? Good listening skills don't come automatically. Of the four basic communication skills—reading, writing, speaking, and listening—the first two are taught to almost everyone, the third to some, and the fourth to very few.

This is doubly unfortunate, because we do more listening than anything else: One study found that people typically spend 9% of their time writing, 16% reading, 30% talking, and 45% listening.

### (a) How to Improve Your Listening Skills

The manager who listens will be a much better manager. While everyone thinks they listen, many are actually thinking about their response rather than truly listening. The accounts payable professional who wants to manage better will need to listen better. A few tips to help managers listen better are:

**First, resolve to improve.** Wanting to improve listening skills is the first step in the right direction. Admitting there might be a problem in this area is the beginning. Once the issue is recognized, resolving to do something about it will become much easier.

**De-emotionalize listening.** Psychologist Carl Rogers pointed out that each person brings a unique point of view to communication. On hearing certain words, a set of emotions is activated. It's a good idea to sit down and list the words and ideas you feel most strongly about, whether positively or negatively. Tell yourself: "Next time I hear the term 'EDI,' instead of turning off, I'll deal with it in a positive way, which I'm now going to predetermine." De-emotionalizing dialogue is one of the hardest things for anyone to do, however. If a staff member (or boss) comes to your office happy, upset, or crying, it's difficult to respond in a noninvolved way. We tend to pick up on emotions. If we do, we're probably not listening, however. In contrast, the manager who remains calm can control the dialogue, bringing it from the realm of the emotional to the rational.

**Positioning.** Don't violate other people's "body space." Getting too close to staff members physically can make them feel threatened. Although the proper distance varies from person to person, two feet or so is a good rule of thumb. If the person you're speaking to seems uncomfortable that close, step back a few inches. If you're having trouble getting the person's attention, however, you might try moving closer and then stepping back. Chances are, you'll be able to start communicating.

**Feed forward.** Show interest in those speaking and in what they have to say. For example, look them in the eye. And ask questions that show an understanding of what they're talking about.

**Use your eyes.** We communicate with our actions in addition to our words. Some 80% of the emotion in a speaker's message is conveyed by body language.

**Feed back what you understand the speaker's message to be.** Repeat back what you think has been said in your own words. The speaker will either correct you or confirm that you understand what has been said. This is especially important when a vendor is complaining. There is plenty of time to think while the other person is talking. The average speaker talks at 125 words a minute, but can think at 500 words a minute. That should allow plenty of time to listen to what's being said while composing an answer.

**Question the speaker.** If you don't understand, ask the person to clarify, justify, or expand. Of course, if you're in what could be perceived as an inferior position (say the speaker is the hostile head of purchasing or an important, but belligerent, vendor), it's only natural to hesitate. Most people don't mind questions—they're flattered by them, because they show you're interested.

**To internalize, repeat the speaker's key points to yourself several times.** Dale Carnegie suggests that if you repeat people's names silently three times in the first two minutes after hearing them, you will remember them. This tactic also holds true for the points they are making.

**Learn the power of silence.** This may be the most productive of all listening techniques. Remaining silent is a way of honoring another. When doing so, look at the other person, and he or she will probably speak up. This strategy is extremely useful if you've asked a difficult question of someone and the person doesn't answer right away. There is a natural tendency to speak to fill the void, but avoid it.

## 7.4 HIRING STAFF

There are many excellent books on the market regarding hiring and interviewing practices. It is beyond the scope of this book to discuss the subject in any sort of a comprehensive manner. However, there is one point that we would like to address regarding filling a position. Many people overlook the obvious when there is a staff opening. Some accounts payable managers forget to look right under their noses when a key position becomes vacant. Others get hung up on the fact that they would like the new hire to have a particular type of experience. When they get caught up in this type of reasoning, they miss all the advantages of hiring someone already on board. These include:

An existing employee knows how the company works—its corporate culture and unwritten rules, and the many quirks of the company's executives and key managers.

Promoting from within generates goodwill and improves morale within the department, possibly opening up a vacancy for another promotion.

The internal candidate is a known quantity, and with an outsider, no matter how much checking and interviewing you do, you never really know what you are getting.

The existing productive employee who was passed over may become disgusted and either turn into an unproductive employee or leave the company completely.

Many who work in accounts payable are not used to speaking up for themselves and asking for promotions or the opportunity to fill existing openings. Others may not even consider the option because they are certain they will be denied. The next time you have an opening, take advantage of the opportunity to improve morale and hire what just might be the best candidate for the job—the internal one.

## 7.5 OVERTIME: A SERIOUS ISSUE

In some companies, the work flow is uneven, resulting in required overtime for the accounts payable staff—whether those people want to work it or not. Mandating overtime can lead to serious morale and productivity issues. Many companies get around this concern by simply hiring temporary workers. They also do this to fill in for regular staffers who are on vacation. This approach will work best when a little thought and planning goes into the process. To make the most of temporary workers:

Give the staffing service as much notice as possible.

Inform the service if you have any flexibility as to hours and skills.

Be firm about your requirements when there's no room for compromise.

Get quotes from several different outfits to make sure you are paying a market rate.

Give the temporary workers adequate training to do the tasks you need them to do.

Handled correctly, temporary workers can provide a real boost to an accounts payable department's productivity. Handled poorly, they can create more work than they complete.

# 8

# Staff Motivation and Morale

There are many fine books on building morale and motivating staff. This chapter takes a quick look at a few techniques that work particularly well in accounts payable. However, those professionals who wish to become world class managers are urged to study in detail some of the books that thoroughly address these issues on the market today. Management skills are extremely important in improving departmental productivity. The manager with the right skills can inspire the staff to produce more work than one who has poor managerial skills. Yet, these attributes are often overlooked when promoting someone to the position of accounts payable manager.

If accounts payable managers could take a pill that would make them first-class motivators, most would do precisely that. However, as those who have ever faced the task of inspiring a group of discouraged staffers know only too well, it's not that easy. Adding to this hurdle is the fact that even with high corporate profitability, some companies still insist on cutting staff and/or giving meager raises.

## 8.1 MOTIVATION TECHNIQUES

Given this challenge, accounts payable managers are still succeeding in motivating their staffs. For the most part, success comes not with one or two big steps, but with a series of smaller moves. It's an ongoing process: You can't give the staff a pep talk and expect everyone to remember it for the next three months. In fact, such a move might backfire and do more harm than good. Successful motivation comes from making it a part of your daily management skills. Some of the techniques being used today include:

**Actions speak louder than words.** The staff will pick up on the manager's mood and tempo. If you say one thing and act in a contrary manner, they'll mimic your behavior rather than your words. Good work habits are contagious—and so are poor ones.

**Have high, but realistic, expectations.** If you set your standards high, your staff will have to hustle to meet them. When they do, they will feel like they have accomplished something. Make sure to let them know you appreciate their hard work. Otherwise, your staff may feel as though you are never satisfied.

**Use praise abundantly** and in public, criticism sparsely and always in private. The old adage about being able to catch more flies with honey than vinegar applies in spades when it comes to motivating a staff. Let them know when their work is good and make sure others, like the boss, hear about their outstanding accomplishments. Everyone likes to receive compliments. Along the same lines, no one likes to be criticized, yet occasionally it must be done. Be as gentle as possible. Let the person know it is the task, not the individual, being criticized. Most important, never ever do it when others are around. Such an action can seriously affect the motivation of the individual involved.

**Share credit for a successful project.** Many managers forget to credit their staff for an assignment successfully completed. This is critical when the exposure for the task extends outside the department and others might not realize that more than the manager was involved. While forgetting to share credit might have a minimal immediate impact, don't look for much staff support the next time a big project comes your way.

**Set up each person to succeed.** Nothing succeeds like success itself. Carefully evaluating each person's capabilities and assigning work so everyone can complete it successfully will motivate the staff. This tactic will also gently move them on the path to trying a more difficult portion of the job the next time around. However, if a staffer is assigned a task that is completely beyond his reach, he won't even try.

**Include everyone wherever possible.** It's easy to rely on a few superstars within the department and ignore the rest. By giving the special or choice assignments to only a few individuals, the rest begin to feel that it doesn't matter what they do, and their productivity plummets.

There are a few lucky souls to whom this stuff comes naturally. For most people, however, staff motivation is not second nature. Most accounts payable managers need to work at improving these on an ongoing basis. Try including a few of the previously mentioned ideas on a day-to-day basis. The results may be surprising.

## 8.2 EVALUATING YOUR OWN MOTIVATING SKILLS

Looking at yourself objectively is difficult, no matter what your profession. This task of self-evaluation becomes all the more challenging when you are forced to assess your own managerial skills. Most accounts payable managers like to think they are good motivators, but on close inspection this often turns out not to be the case. With accounts payable departments continually being pushed to do more work with smaller staffs, there's an almost inevitable danger of both morale and motivation suffering.

Accounts payable managers who are able to motivate their

staffs will find that, almost miraculously, the morale problem evaporates. They will be able to kill two proverbial birds with one stone.

To discover whether you are a good motivator, or only think you are, take the following quiz. Then, if you have the courage, have the staff take the quiz on a confidential basis. By comparing the staff's responses with your own, problem areas will be readily identifiable. The results will also reveal whether you and the staff are on the same wavelength.

**Is success rewarded in your accounts payable department?** Much of the day-to-day work in accounts payable is routine. It requires continual attention to detail. The only time many in the accounts payable department are noticed is when something goes wrong. This is unfortunate, since many staffers do an excellent job, which is simply taken for granted. Motivate the staff by giving them praise and recognition for their first-rate work and doing it frequently.

**Is hard work rewarded?** When someone is out sick or on vacation, and the rest of the staff picks up the extra workload, do you give them special recognition? Or is it simply expected? By rewarding your hardest workers, heavy workloads become an opportunity to win recognition and respect. It is also a way to motivate the staff to help out when the chips are down. If you have heavy workloads at month's end, like many accounts payable departments, but find many of your staffers asking for vacation at that time of the month, you could have a serious morale problem—with no one taking any ownership for the departmental work.

**Are standards high?** When you see the department's error rates beginning to drift upward, do you just shrug your shoulders or do you try and figure out what the problem is? Accepting pedestrian results motivates no one and guarantees mediocrity. Let the staff know that you expect the very best from them—and they'll give it.

**Does information flow upward?** The very best ideas and suggestions for work flow improvement often come from the people who actually do the work. How many members of the accounts payable staff feel comfortable enough with your management style to offer their thoughts? Staff motivation is highest in those departments where information and insight flow up. If the staff does not volunteer this type of input, ask them for their thoughts on problem solving and improving procedures. If you have a problem getting checks turned around quickly enough, ask the staffers who actually handle the checks to identify the problems. They will be able to tell you which signers hold on to checks and which executives routinely submit incomplete check-request forms. They will also tell you who the worst offenders are when it comes to rush checks.

**Are office politics discouraged?** Organizations where politics flourish usually have lower productivity and higher morale problems than those where people are rewarded for the work they do rather than the games they play. Read the riot act to staffers caught developing alliances at the cost of performance. The accounts payable clerk that rushes checks through for a few friends or political allies undermines the hard work done by the rest of the department to eliminate such checks. Similarly, cliques can undermine morale and should not be tolerated.

**Do you use the power of persuasion rather than simply ordering staffers to do what needs to be done?** Ownership of a decision can mean the difference between a highly productive staff and a poorly motivated one. Explaining the reasoning behind a decision can make a big difference. This is especially important when implementing changes that require more work with no corresponding increase in productivity. In the last few years, as companies become more aware of the impact of check fraud, many accounts payable departments are being forced to implement checks and balances regarding check storage. On the face of it, these changes mean more work. If staff members understand the full implications of a stolen check, they are more apt to cooperate with the new lengthy procedures. They may even offer a few additional suggestions of their own.

**Does the department work as a team?** People work better when they feel that everyone is striving for the same goal rather than proceeding separately. If the whole department tries to reduce the number of duplicate payments made, each person is apt to do what he or she can to make sure mistakes are minimized.

**Is office authoritarianism avoided?** Leaders, rather than commanders, are what make an organization run smoothly, whether it be the military or an accounts payable department. A commanding managerial style can have a de-motivating effect on the staff. The reason for this is simple: It prevents staff members from coming forward with both problems and solutions. It also chokes creativity.

**Does the work connect with the whole?** Can the accounts payable staffers see where they fit into the big picture? Staff who are led effectively to see how their individual assignments fit into the whole are more apt to be productive. The staffer who understands the necessity of processing a certain number of checks per hour is more likely to try and meet that goal than one who feels as though whatever he or she does doesn't matter and makes no difference in the overall well-being of the company.

**Are top performers adequately rewarded?** Nothing can be more disheartening to good workers than to feel that hard work is not rewarded. Money is the worst reason to lose good staff. Yet it happens more frequently than most accounts payable managers might want to acknowledge. Although you may not be able to do a lot about the pay levels for some of your staff, try to keep the salaries and benefits in line with what others in your area are paying.

Some accounts payable professionals will not need to ask their staff to complete this quiz. As they read through the questions, they will be able to identify their own weaknesses when it comes to motivation. It doesn't hurt to periodically brush up on people skills as this is an area that is often given short shrift when it comes to training—yet it can be vital.

## 8.3 MOTIVATING THE SEEMINGLY UNMOTIVATABLE

Everyone has run into the truly unmotivated employee—the one who could care less about his or her work, mistakes made, money lost, or even the effect of his or her actions have on others within the department. For some unexplainable reason, this type of employee often gets dumped into the accounts payable department whenever the company does not wish or can not terminate the person. Yet, while this situation might seem hopeless at first, several innovative accounts payable managers have found ways to get this type of employee moving.

**Case 1:** The Underachievers. Try finding an interesting project to assign totally to the unmotivated person. Tell them what is expected but not how to get there. Let them know that they are totally in control of accomplishing the task by the means they feel are the best (within reason, of course) and ask them to keep the manager posted.

It seems to give them a sense of motivation and pride to be entrusted with something entirely and realizing that the end result will be a reflection of their capabilities alone. They will try to do the best job they can and might even look forward to more challenges.

**Case 2:** The Dictator. The lead person is running the department like Hitler. Quickly change the responsibilities of this person so that she works alone without supervising others. With this simple change, morale in the whole department should pick up and unmotivated employees are no longer an issue.

**Case 3:** The Loners. When everyone has a "mine vs. theirs" attitude, it gets in the way of getting the work out. Convince the group to work as a team and that projects are the group's responsibility and attitudes will change.

**Case 4:** The Followers. Everyone has them. The group that takes on the posture of the moment. Hire several new motivated staff members whose mood and attitude are contagious. The followers will begin to take their cue from the new employees. Team building motivational techniques recommended in several management books will also help. And if there is a ringleader who tends to "lead" in the wrong direction, look to move that employee into a less prominent position, or possibly out of the department.

## 8.4 TAKING ADVANTAGE OF THE STAFF'S KNOWLEDGE

Accounts payable professionals often overlook one of the best resources available when it comes to solving problems: their own staff. Gather together the staffers who worked on the issue for a pizza luncheon and present the problem. The knowledgeable solutions that can emanate from such a meeting are often mind-boggling and all for the price of a simple luncheon. The same can be done over coffee and donuts in the morning. The beauty of these inexpensive meals is that not only do staffers come up with great solutions to everyday problems, the little extra attention motivates the staff—especially if done in an organization where the accounts payable staff has been given very little.

Don't be surprised if the first time such a meeting is held, few suggestions are offered. Many of the staffers will be so surprised that someone actually wants to hear what they have to say that they will be hesitant to offer suggestions. However, once a few of the recommendations are implemented and the person on the staff acknowledged for their contribution, expect to be inundated with suggestions—most of them worthy of further investigation.

Of course, a few of the suggestions will be really bad. Never ridicule the person making the point, simply indicate that you will take it under consideration or think about it and thank the individual for their input.

## 8.5 DEALING WITH ATTITUDE PROBLEMS

Despite their best efforts, a good number of accounts payable managers occasionally find themselves saddled with staffers who have serious "attitude problems." In general friction in accounts payable is due to one of three causes:

1. The accounts payable staff is exposed to *all* the major work-related stress elements: high volume, demand for 100% accuracy, constant interruptions, demanding customers, and relatively little positive feedback.
2. The "doing-more-with-less" perspective of certain management teams who think employees should be happy just to have the job—regardless of the number of hours they must work.
3. Personality conflicts that normally arise from time to time.

Of course, in a few organizations, all three exist. These issues sometimes lead not only to the aforementioned attitude problems, but to low staff morale, as well. Solutions to this matter generally can be broken down into three main categories:

1. **Boosting Morale**
   a. Have an open door and an ear to listen and coach.
   b. Document and present staff requirements to upper-level management and obtain the additional staff needed.
   c. Get the staff exactly what they need—be it a simple calculator or an up-to-date computer.
   d. Whenever division closings, corporatewide downsizing or company acquisitions are announced, it is a pretty good bet that morale will decline significantly. Have regular meetings with the department and promote the positive aspects of the situation.

e. Identify the more mundane parts of the job that can be done with temporary help. This frees up the more experienced staff to be able to work on the more complex tasks. When the department members see that their work is valued spirits rise.

f. Periodically buy the staff lunch, coffee and donuts, or even an afternoon ice cream.

### 2. Effective Strategies

a. When dealing with a staffer who continually expresses her discontent with both the department and the supervisor, set a deadline by which time the malcontent is told to have all her work brought up to date. When the matter is laid out in black and white, the employee will get the message and hopefully get the work back on track.

b. Written notices and/or warnings to those who continually denigrate the company and managers but do not complete their work on time.

c. By being very clear about the importance of accuracy, timeliness, and internal controls right from the beginning, serious attitude problems within the department can be avoided.

### 3. Making the Work More Challenging

a. Review the work to eliminate the most tedious, repetitive, non–value added functions.

b. Assign the tedious work to temporary workers where possible.

c. Let all staffers work on "fun" projects from time to time—don't limit such assignments to one or two.

d. Ask for suggestions as to what assignments each would like to do. There may be a staffer who likes doing what others dislike.

e. Rotate the most disliked tasks so no one individual gets stuck with it constantly.

## 8.6 GETTING THE ACCOUNTS PAYABLE STAFF TO TAKE ON MORE WORK

Doing more with less is the mantra for the next century. With the constant push toward having each employee handle an ever-increasing workload, little thought or guidance is generally given concerning how this will be accomplished. Talk to most accounts payable managers and they report being asked to handle additional work without being given additional staff. Surprisingly, many are getting quite good at it. How are they doing this?

Making the best use of the technology available.

Education—by attending classes, accounts payable managers will learn how to get the most out of new software and hardware being thrust in their direction.

Not only is it imperative that the manager know how to use new technology effectively, so too must the staffers who will be using it every day.

The accounts payable departments in most of corporate America are filled with innovative, intelligent people who, given half a chance, will shine and have a very positive impact on the company's bottom line.

# 9

# Working with/for Purchasing and Other Departments

Although few realize it, a good accounts payable manager needs to have diplomatic skills that rival those of Henry Kissinger. By the very nature of the job, the accounts payable department will be at odds with virtually every other department within the company—especially purchasing, its historical enemy. This is due to the fact that in order for accounts payable to do its job well, everyone else in the company must do their job 100% correctly—and when does that happen? For this to happen:

Purchasing must completely and accurately fill out its purchase orders and forward them to accounts payable on a timely basis.

Everyone else must review and approve for payment all invoices as soon as they are received.

Employees must submit Travel & Entertainment expense reports for reimbursement on a very timely basis.

Receiving must check all receiving documents against goods actually received and not just blindly sign for goods.

In most organizations, this just does not happen. These natural causes of friction set the stage for the accounts payable department to be viewed as obstinate, uncooperative, and so on. When in actuality the cause of these problems is not accounts payable but some or all of the individuals discussed above. Accounts payable ends up fixing everyone else's mistakes and it rarely makes them happy.

## 9.1 WHY IS THIS IMPORTANT?

For starters, cooperation between departments tends to dramatically lessen frustration and stress. If that were the only reason, it would be enough. However, there are even more compelling reasons. By getting along with other departments, accounts payable is in a position to get the problems that are causing the tension fixed. This directly affects departmental productivity.

If this were not enough, there is another overwhelming reason for accounts payable to get along with purchasing. A small, but significant, number of companies are merging the accounts payable and purchasing departments. When this happens, purchasing generally ends up "ruling the roost." Trying to cooperate after such a merger has been announced, or is even rumored, is like locking the barn door after the horse has been stolen. The damage may be irreparable and the accounts payable professional who has antagonized purchasing may be skating on very thin career ice.

Better to try and bridge the gap between the departments long before a merger becomes a reality. Building interdepartmental cooperation should be a top priority for today's accounts payable professional be it with the purchasing department or any other department.

## 9.2 BASIC APPROACHES

Accounts payable managers often find themselves at odds with employees in other departments largely due to the nature of the tasks they perform. But the adversarial nature of these relationships can often be reduced through some commonsense approaches. Those who successfully strengthened their dealings with these other groups do it by focusing on communication and education.

### (a) Education

It's easy to get annoyed with others who make our lives difficult—especially when they seem to make the same mistakes over and over. However, sometimes they just don't know the proper procedures. Educating everyone in a company on the right way to handle their payables can be done in many ways. There are numerous innovative ways to accomplish this task. These include:

Compose an easy-to-use reference guide for all standard operating procedures to make it more user-friendly and procedures easier to locate. This should be distributed to all who are affected by the policies and who need to know the proper way to do things.

Hold intercompany seminars on accounts payable and the integration of its procedures with other departments.

Publish an accounts payable newsletter on a periodic basis. Address timely topics and repeat information on those procedures that people seem to forget.

If one department seems to make a good portion of the mistakes, develop a "cheat sheet" that applies strictly to that group. Include on it the proper procedures for that group as they relate to accounts payable.

Whenever a major new process is undertaken, retrain department heads. This is especially important when major new initiatives, such as ERS, are undertaken.

If a number of different departments seem to be having problems with the same area, go back and review that area. It is possible that it is accounts payable and not the rest of the company that needs some education. Is the process so convoluted or unworkable that it needs to be changed? Is there something that can be done to make it more user friendly?

### (b) Communication

Hand-in-hand with education goes communication in making things work better for the often unappreciated accounts payable department. Here's how some have had success by simply communicating better with their peers in other departments:

> "By taking the initiative to open up discussion on business needs, procedures, and system requirements," explains the general accounting manager at a midsize oil and gas production firm, "several process opportunities emerged. Better information was received from vendors, the expectations of all parties became known, and business knowledge of A/P staff was increased." This undertaking has paid off nicely. As the manager concludes, "Processing rates have shown a good increase and savings from adjusted invoices are up $600,000 per year, or 70% during the first nine months of the year." Of course, not everyone has results that are easily quantifiable, nor are the resulting savings this large at many companies.
>
> "We had to explain to other departments how important they were to ensuring the accuracy of our payables," explains the assistant controller of a Wisconsin company. "Once it was explained to the supervisors, they in turn discussed it with their employees." By telling her counterparts how important they were to her success, this intuitive individual was able to win them over. They were then receptive to listening to her requests and willing to go back and communicate her requests to their staffs.
>
> "A vendor support team was formed with people from A/P, purchasing, traffic, planning, and quality. Weekly meetings were held and different topics discussed," explains an accounts payable supervisor. Some of the topics

> included were: when a PO is not needed, receiving processes, freight bill payments, purchasing cards, invoice/PO discrepancies, and ERS. The results from this weekly meeting are worth noting. "The talking about these processes encourages people to think about why they do certain things and who it affects," continues the manager. "People are working smarter as a result," she concludes. This meeting also gives the accounts payable manager an arena in which to bring up topics that might not be otherwise addressed.
>
> "Quarterly accounts payable/purchasing/receiving meetings have opened up the lines of communication between the departments," relates a senior staff accountant. "Through these meetings we have worked through the frustrations of individuals and improved processes."

It is not always possible, however, to schedule such meetings. For a variety of reasons, some companies are reluctant to have them. But there are less formal options available to the accounts payable professional who wants to improve things. Several examples of how this has worked include:

> Often, it is only necessary to improve strained relations with one or two other departments. The accounts payable supervisor for a large lens manufacturer needed to shore up fences with the buying staff. She explains, "We have a meeting with the buying staff about three times per year. We discuss problems and how to solve them." This has resulted in all concerned working together and helping each other.
>
> Bottlenecks often occur when the accounts payable manager is directed to deal only with one or two individuals. The accounts payable coordinator at a hospital explains, "Most departments order through materials management and use wrong account numbers. I was instructed to deal with this

problem through materials management, and that they would deal with the department. This wasted time and the problem was not solved," laments this accounts payable professional. But a solution to the problem was found and implemented. "I requested that I be able to deal directly with departments and the employees responsible for the mistakes, instead of their supervisors or the initial contact." This obvious solution not only ultimately saved time but eliminated unneeded intervention in the loop.

Not all solutions need be that complicated, as the A/P bookkeeper for an education company explains: "I developed stronger relationships with other departments by letting them know that I'm always available to answer questions and deal directly with vendors/suppliers for them." This has probably won her much appreciation from those whose messes she cleans up.

The A/P manager at an audio/video equipment company has let her peers in other departments know that she wants things to work well in her department. She explains, "Now that they know I work with ideas aimed at making the A/P department a better division, things are running smoothly."

## 9.3 HANDLING THE BIG ISSUES

Getting cooperation from other departments can be a nightmare for accounts payable managers. In many instances, the other departments don't even realize that what they do causes huge headaches for accounts payable professionals. The issues that cause the biggest problems for accounts payable are: delays, missing information, getting appropriate information to accounts payable, and dealing with the purchasing department.

### (a) Missing Information

One of the biggest problem for many accounts payable professionals is that information provided is not complete. This wastes huge amounts of time as the accounts payable staff runs around and tries to obtain the missing data. Some techniques that will help solve that problem include:

Send out a weekly memo that lists the requisition number, PO number, vendor, and the date the invoice was received. The senior manager, if responsible for that area, was also sent a copy. This helps give the issue high visibility and also makes those responsible a little quicker in supplying the necessary missing documentation. No one really wants to see their name in this report, and no one wants to have to give lame excuses to their boss as to why the information hasn't been supplied. Including in the report the date the invoice arrived makes it apparent to everyone receiving the report that if a deduction is lost, the responsibility lies not with the accounts payable department but with the individual who failed to supply the information. In most firms, this solution can be readily implemented.

Purchase orders, or rather the lack thereof, can also cause nightmares for accounts payable professionals. An ongoing problem in many organizations is getting employees to write purchase orders at the time they make the purchase and have the PO referenced on the invoice. Insisting on this can save the accounts payable clerks hours of time they will waste tracking down who bought what. With the information on the invoice, much of the tracking is eliminated.

### (b) Getting the Information to Accounts Payable

Purchase orders aren't the only thing that can drive accounts payable professionals to distraction. Getting all data to flow to a central location, such as the finance department, is also a big problem in many organizations. The following solutions to this problem have been used in many organizations:

Have all vendors change their billing contacts to the accounts payable department. Most are happy to do this if they are informed that it means they will be paid quicker.

Inform the mailroom that anything relating to payments is to be sent to the accounts payable department.

In those instances where regional locations are paying invoices locally, cut them off at the pass. Prevent this by restricting G/Ls, giving no option but to come to accounts payable.

### (c) Handling Delays

Purchases made without a PO are not the only items that cause trouble. Often the delay in getting payment approvals from other departments can cause serious problems. Invoices received by other departments are not sent promptly to the accounts payable department. Packing slips are not forwarded to receiving, and that delays preparation of receiving reports. To avoid such hassles try:

Sending companywide memos to remind department heads of their responsibility for these documents. Additionally, for specific trouble spots, more frequent follow-ups are made. If a certain person or department always seems late in providing necessary information or documents, be proactive: anticipate the trouble and head it off before it occurs.

Meet with every department where problems are being experienced and work with them to implement procedures to make the process more routine. Again, by identifying the trouble spots and dealing with them on an individual basis, many communication problems can be resolved.

### (d) Dealing With the Purchasing Department

Somehow, it seems that the purchasing department and A/P are always at war. There has been some tension between accounts payable and purchasing in most organizations almost forever. A few tips for alleviating some of that tension are:

Set up monthly meetings with both departments to discuss any difficulties. By identifying these problems when they are small, big problems will not develop.

Have the staff from accounts payable and purchasing work in each other's departments. In this manner, staff see how what each department does affects the other. This gives both departments a better understanding of each other's needs—by walking in each other's shoes, each may come to realize that the other is not so bad after all—and they may also come to see what they are doing to make the other's life more difficult.

Occasionally special information may be needed and accuracy lacking. In one instance, it was necessary for accounts payable to know whether a product was taxable. Unfortunately, this information was never provided to accounts payable by purchasing. A lot of time was wasted tracking the information down. In this case the controller scheduled a training session for all purchasing personnel to explain the problem and to discuss how to handle out-of-state vendors in this regard.

## 9.4 SOME QUICK ANSWERS TO COMMON ANNOYING PROBLEMS

Accounts payable often is also at odds over very simple issues with other departments. Unfortunately, these problems cause much wasted time and effort. If these problems can be solved, the resulting savings can be in time or money or both. Some common problems along with the solutions that sometimes work are:

**Problem:** A/P is not perceived as being a quality organization that wants to process invoices in a timely fashion.

**Solution:** Begin tracking performance (both for A/P and employees in general); use an A/P newsletter and communicate with those affected.

## 9.4 Some Quick Answers to Common Annoying Problems

**Problem:** Other departments don't always provide the proper documentation when requesting a payment.

**Solution:** After threatening and warning, some have had success by taking the extreme route and denying payment without proper documentation.

**Problem:** Other departments don't cooperate in processing paperwork quickly and accurately.

**Solution:** Make the new employee orientation process educational, and stress the importance of paperwork. For existing employees with bad habits, provide a set of instructions.

**Problem:** Some departments forget to return paperwork and others return it filled out incorrectly. This results in A/P spending a great deal of time tracking down the appropriate approvals.

**Solution:** Keep track of the number of invoices sent back for approval and why. Then prepare a report for senior management detailing this information. Use this summary to initiate a discussion regarding how the matter can be resolved.

**Problem:** The purchasing department refuses to take ownership of the information provided to A/P. This results in many errors and causes additional work for A/P.

**Solution:** Set up a weekly meeting with purchasing to discuss the most recent discrepancies and point out what information is missing or was incorrect. Slowly but surely, the errors will decrease.

**Problem:** The advertising department was continually late in sending approved invoices for payment. Additionally, advertising often forgot to write up purchase orders and when it did, the project was rarely identified.

**Solution:** Give advertising their own purchase order system. This makes the tracking of invoices for that department easier to handle.

**Problem:** Communication and paper flow between purchasing and A/P is poor.

**Solution:** Open lines of communication and let purchasing know what your goals are. Take the time to understand its goals as well. When a vendor problem arises because adequate information was not received from purchasing, forward that call to the recalcitrant party in purchasing.

**Problem:** A/P lacks credibility within the company. This frequent problem can be the result of the action by others or due to poor management support.

**Solution:** Discuss the matter with your supervisor and get his or her backing for new projects.

**Problem:** New people don't understand accounts payable procedures and requirements.

**Solution:** Issue, or if appropriate, reissue, an administrative expense manual that contains all company policies as they pertain to A/P.

**Problem:** Poor relations often exist between the individuals who work in purchasing and those in A/P.

**Solution:** Work closely with the head of the purchasing department to try to defuse the issue. Set up monthly meetings and reports. This problem will not go away overnight but over time it can be ameliorated.

**Problem:** Other departments, not understanding A/P's requirements, sometimes feel that the A/P professionals are too critical and demanding. They are often unaware of all that must be done to avoid duplicate payments and to meet audit standards.

**Solution:** Work with these other departments and explain the need underlying each of your requirements. By educating them on the entire procurement/payables process, many of these issues fall to the wayside.

**Problem:** Adequate backup for payments is often not provided by the person requesting a payment. It then becomes necessary for A/P to check back with the person requesting the payment to get the necessary documentation. Time is wasted and discounts are often lost.

**Solution:** Show the offending parties exactly how much money is lost each time a delay causes the company to miss a discount.

**Problem:** The receiving department forgets to submit packing slips to A/P. Some who *do* remember, forget to mark the date the goods were received. This often results in past due payments and definitely results in early discounts being lost.

**Solution:** Set up a meeting with the receiving department and explain why these documents are needed and the financial impact of not having them.

**Problem:** Many discrepancies are uncovered when A/P does their three-way match. Some of these problems are caused by purchasing and/or receiving.

**Solution:** Set up a weekly meeting to discuss discrepancies. If these issues typically revolve around price and/or quantity, it may be time for purchasing to take a look at its own internal procedures. Accounts payable may be able to identify weaknesses in other departments. Of course, great care and tact should be used when relaying this information.

**Problem:** Other departments expect more from the A/P department than it can deliver. This often causes friction within the company and poor relations with other departments.

**Solution:** Put together an intensive realization program so that others have a clear picture of what A/P does and a list of what it does not do. This might even include sharing some volume numbers.

**Problem:** Other departments are consistently late sending work to A/P.

**Solution:** Create a log for each offending department and track their problems. Review the log weekly with the department head of each unit under scrutiny. Also, offer training to staff members from other departments. Let them see what you do with the information they provide. Also focus on the problems A/P encounters with late or incorrect information.

**Problem:** When things don't go smoothly (and when do they ever?), the A/P manager must often deal with angry employees in other departments.

**Solution:** Gather as much information as possible about the issue that has made the colleague so furious. Contact the appropriate party and sit down to discuss the matter. Listen to what they have to say. Apologize for any errors or miscommunications A/P caused. Stay calm throughout the discussion. Discuss with the other party ways that the problem may be resolved and avoided completely in the future. End each conversation, no matter how difficult, on a positive note.

**Problem:** The ability to communicate with the rest of the company can be difficult.

**Solution:** If you have companywide e-mail, use it. Also use it to communicate with those in remote locations.

**Problem:** A/P can spend a good deal of time tracking down the documentation required for employee travel and entertainment reports.

**Solution:** Use an online system. This allows for a quick and easy review. Refuse to process for reimbursement incomplete reports.

**Problem:** Many accounts payable departments waste much time trying to track down receivers to match up with their purchase orders and invoices.

**Solution**: Put the responsibility back on the shoulders of the purchasing department. Of course, getting purchasing to go along with this plan will take more than a little cajoling in most organizations. Still, it is worth a try.

# Part Three

# Management Issues

While it is true that accounts payable is fundamentally about paying bills, there are ways to handle it to maximize productivity and impact the financial bottom line positively. These issues should be addressed at the management level. Accounts payable staffers should not be put in the position of having to make decisions regarding payment timing, the taking of discounts, or using one of the alternatives to the three-way match. These issues should be discussed and decided at the management level and formal policy guidelines established.

Issues pertaining to the master vendor file and the outside auditor's management letter typically also need to be addressed at the management level. In some organizations the accounts payable manager will have adequate authority to handle these matter and in others, they will need to be pushed further up the corporate ladder. These chapters discuss the concerns relating to these timely issues.

# 10

# Master Vendor Files

Proper maintenance and control over a company's master vendor file will greatly decrease the chances for duplicate and erroneous payments and fraud. Yet, many companies do not give adequate thought or attention to this issue. Not only are the controls often weak, but the files are not purged nearly as often as they should be—in fact, some companies never purge them. Yet many companies do not pay adequate attention to one of the most basic techniques for controlling such payments: Proper handling of the master vendor file. As part of a recent benchmarking survey, IOMA asked some pointed questions about master vendor files.

## 10.1 THE DATA

The first factor investigated was the number of entries in the master vendor file. As might be expected, the larger the company, the higher the number of vendors in its file. On average, companies had just under 11,000 vendors in their file (see Exhibit 10.1 for a complete breakdown by company size). Note that 18 companies with over 100,000 vendors were not included in this calculation because it was felt they would bias the numbers for most organizations. Even smaller companies have an incredible number of vendors in their master file. Those with fewer

*Exhibit 10.1* **Size of Master Vendor File by Company Size**

| *Number of Employees* | *Averge Number of Vendors* |
|---|---|
| 0 to 99 | 2,338 |
| 100 to 249 | 3,553 |
| 250 to 499 | 5,781 |
| 500 to 999 | 7,017 |
| 1,000 to 4,999 | 14,520 |
| Over 5,000 | 28,199 |

(Source: IOMA)

than 100 employees have an average of 2,338 entries in their master vendor files.

Exhibit 10.2 shows a breakdown of the data by number of vendors. The greatest number of organizations, over 41%, have between 1,000 and 5,000 invoices, while another 31% have between 5,001 and 20,000. The chart also shows the breakdown of number of invoices by size of company. By comparing the number in your master vendor file with that of companies of like size, you will see how you compare.

## 10.2 CLEAN-UP POLICIES

One of the big surprises of this study is the purging policies that exist at many companies—or, rather, the nonexistence of such policies. Almost one-quarter of all companies report they never purge their master vendor file. (No wonder 18 companies have more than 100,000 entries in this file!) Another 12% of firms only review their file every three years. Exhibit 10.3 details this information by company size and industry. You will note how often companies clean up their master vendor file.

Looking at the number of vendors in the master vendor files, one has to question the clean-up policies at those firms with over 50,000 vendors. Even 20,000 seems excessive, except perhaps at really huge companies. While it's true that most companies set up employees who travel and request reimbursement as vendors, this

*Exhibit 10.2* **How Many Vendors Should Be in Your Vendor File?**

| *Number of Vendors* | *Percent of Companies* |
|---|---|
| Under 1,000 | 12.4% |
| 1,000 to 5,000 | 41.3 |
| 5,001 to 20,000 | 30.9 |
| 20,001 to 50,000 | 10.3 |
| 50,001 to 100,000 | 2.7 |
| Over 100,000 | 2.4 |

(Source: IOMA's 1997 Benchmarking Survey)

issue will only play a role in explaining away a small part of the distortion at the very largest firms. In all likelihood, those companies with inordinately large numbers of entities in their master vendor files have weak policies regarding clean-up.

## 10.3 MAINTENANCE POLICIES

It is astounding that almost one-quarter of the respondents report they never purge their master vendor files. This means that a vendor who was paid once, 10, 20, or more years ago, remains in the file. It also means that a company whose name was entered incorrectly remains in the file, as do duplicate entries for the same company. Thus, AT&T and American Telephone and Telegraph Co. could reside in the same file. Unfortunately, most computers would not realize that these two entities were the same company.

A full 12% of the companies surveyed report purging their file only once every three years. While this is better than never, it is nothing to brag about.

## 10.4 GOOD MASTER VENDOR POLICIES

Many professionals know their files should be purged more frequently, but say they just don't have the time. This is unfortunate,

*Exhibit 10.3* **Timing of Master Vendor File Clean-Up**

| | |
|---|---|
| Monthly | 4.7% |
| Quarterly | 3.3 |
| Yearly | 40.5 |
| Every two yrs. | 13.7 |
| Every three yrs. | 12.0 |
| Never | 24.3 |
| Other | 1.5 |

(Source: IOMA's 1997 Benchmarking Survey)

because lax policies ultimately cost companies money. When both IBM and International Business Machines are paid for the same invoice, your company loses out—even if the funds are eventually recovered. Even more troublesome is the fact that a clever, but dishonest, employee could present an invoice from a long inactive vendor and possibly get it paid.

It is probably adequate to purge vendor files on an annual basis. Less than half the respondents meet that goal. Not only are these companies wasting computer-storage space—though that is not an issue at every firm—they are geometrically increasing their chances of making a duplicate payment, or worse, processing a fraudulent invoice. While tighter control on the master vendor file won't eliminate these issues, it will decrease the likelihood of their not occurring.

## 10.5 TIPS ON SETTING UP THE MASTER VENDOR FILE

Setting up vendor files so they reflect all pertinent information and are tamperproof as well is not easy. Yet it is a task that is given little thought or attention at most companies which can lead to reduced worker productivity, duplicate payments, and in the worst case, fraud.

Make the file easy to use while incorporating as much information as possible. This increases the productivity of those using the files (they don't have to search elsewhere for information), while reducing the likelihood of duplicate payments. Much of the following advice is common sense—once it's been pointed out!

Use codes that incorporate the vendor's name.

Use the vendor's billing address (the "pay to" address). Putting the headquarter's address in the master file is not of much use since it is unlikely that there will be a need for that information.

Enter the vendor's 800 phone number not their toll number. If you're not sure what it is, find out. Not every company has an 800 number, but if they do let them pay for your calls.

Enter the vendor's discount terms.

Enter due dates to default on the invoice screen.

Enter minimum or maximum purchase and credit limits.

Enter the general ledger expense account number most frequently associated with the vendor. Let this be the default code if no information is entered in this category.

Where applicable, include a material or job cost number.

Designate independent contractors with their federal ID number.

Enter the sales tax distribution account.

Use the comment field for special coding or concerns.

Set up separate files for the same vendor where there are:

Significant differences in the types of purchases.

Discounts on some purchases and not on others.

Sales tax on only some of the purchases.

Give different vendor numbers if payments made to this entity are sometimes 1099 and sometimes for material. If you do this be very careful about duplicate payments.

## 10.6 WHAT INFORMATION SHOULD BE IN YOUR VENDOR FILES?

For starters, the file should contain the correct legal name. While this may sound quite obvious, it is often overlooked. If you think I'm wrong, check how many versions of IBM are in your vendor file. If you are like a good portion of corporate America, you'll have an IBM, an I B M, an I.B.M., an International Business Machines, and an International Business Machine Company. Get the drift?

Include the address, phone numbers, and primary contact. Some accounts payable professionals also like to include the company's 800 phone number if it has one. Then when it is necessary to call a vendor, the vendor pays for the call.

The file should also contain the standard payment terms for this vendor. Ideally, this should be written and signed.

Any other special features of the vendor's agreement, such as minimum order sizes, shopping policy, and so on should be included.

The file should also contain the federal tax identification number or the social security number of the party. All 1099 forms for independent contractors should be included.

And, finally, for a really complete master vendor file, include copies of all purchase orders.

Now some who are reading this are probably thinking this is an awful lot of stuff to include in the files but it will come in handy in the unfortunate event of a payment dispute with a vendor. It will also provide you with ammunition in the case of a terms dispute or a disagreement over what the vendor's policy is regarding minimum orders, terms, and so on. It's not possible to have too much information, but it *is* possible to have too little.

## 10.7 ADJUSTMENTS, CORRECTIONS, AND ADDITIONS

A properly controlled accounting system will limit access to the master vendor files. The ability to make changes to this file will be limited. Ideally, a report will be generated automatically by the system on a regular basis detailing all the changes and corrections made. This report will be reviewed in detail by a senior level executive.

One of the most common types of employee fraud relates to an employee with access to the master file. The employee goes into the system and changes the "pay to" address of one or more vendors to whom large checks have been issued. These checks are automatically mailed to the new address. Once the checks have been mailed to this phony address to which the employee has access, the system is updated again and the address is changed back to the original. Thus, limiting the number of people with the ability to update and change the master file is vital. This is not the only way the vendor file can be manipulated for fraudulent purposes, but it gives you an idea of some of the shenanigans that can go on when proper controls are not put in place.

## 10.8 MAINTAINING THE MASTER VENDOR FILE

In an environment where access to the master vendor file is limited, the procedures for updating it must be modified. The following steps will help:

- Have your data entry personnel keep a list handy for noting any adjustments that need to be made.
- Note the changes made to the file and include them in the vendor's permanent paper file.
- Never allow data entry personnel to make changes to the master file.
- Designate personnel responsible for semi-permanent changes to the master vendor file.
- Review master vendor lists on a regular basis.

Create more than one vendor file for the same vendor if there are consistent and differing types of purchases made by the same vendor.

Make sure that vendor price adjustments are kept current.

All necessary corrections and adjustments to the master file should be made at one time— by the individual authorized to do so.

# 11

# Terms and Taking Discounts

The taking of a discount when the payment is past terms is a sensitive topic on both sides of the fence. When IOMA asked almost 700 professionals about this touchy subject, almost 30% admitted taking all discounts offered, even if a payment was past the terms offered by the supplier. Keep in mind that the figure may actually be higher, since not all companies following such a policy are willing to admit doing so.

Roughly one-half reveal that they take all discounts within the terms offered, while a mere 7% refuse all discounts. Half said they always took it paying within the discount period, while the remainder did so sometimes, depending on their cost of funds. This could simply be because it has been so long since interest rates were high enough for most firms to justify not taking the discount. However, if and when rates shoot into the double-digit stratosphere again, this analysis will become more prevalent.

## 11.1 SHOULD THE DISCOUNT BE TAKEN?

"The only firing offense at our company," says one accounts payable manager, "is missing a discount." This may seem extreme, but those in the know realize the big effect discounts can have on the bottom line. That said, it's important to analyze the whole financial picture before taking all discounts offered by all vendors.

A recent survey of a large number of companies shows that just under half of them (49%) offer discounts to induce their customers to pay early. Of those, half offered a 2% discount and another 40% offered a 1% discount. At first glance, 1% or 2% may not seem like a big deal. But missing a discount can be a big deal at many companies.

### (a) Basic Calculations

Let's start with a hypothetical bill of \$100 with terms of 2/10 net 30, the most common discount terms extended. The bill can be paid in full in 30 days, but if it is paid in 10 days, a 2% discount can be taken; that is, only \$98 must be paid. Thus, the paying company will give up the use of its money 20 days earlier than was absolutely required. To determine whether this is financially advisable, take a look at these calculations:

$$\frac{\text{Amount of discount}}{\text{Discounted price}} \times \frac{\text{Number of days in the year}}{\text{Number of days paid early}}$$

The math in the example looks as follows:

$$\$2 \div \$98 \times 365 \div 20 = 37.24\%$$

A company in a net borrowing position would only take the discounts if its cost of funds were less than 37%. Now, with a result like this, the right action is pretty clear. But the results are not always this apparent.

The second most frequently offered discount in our survey was 1%. The reader who goes through the math will find the rate of return, or break-even rate, for that calculation to be 18.62% if the discount period is 10 days and the full payment is due after 30 days. In today's interest rate environment, just about every company would still pay early to get the discount in either of these examples.

### (b) Factoring in Real Life

But there's another possible scenario. Even when terms require full payment in 30 days, very few companies meet that deadline. If, in reality, full payments are not made in 30 days as requested, but in 45 days, the effective rate of the discount diminishes. In the case where payments are typically made in 45 days, the company is losing the use of its money 35 days earlier than otherwise required. In those instances the calculation should be as follows:

$$\$2 \div \$98 \times 365 \div 35 = 21\%$$

While this number is still awe inspiring, it's not quite as mind-boggling as before. And if compensation is typically given after 60 days the return drops to 15%—still impressive, but approaching the kind of returns financial executives are accustomed to seeing. If only a 1% discount were being offered, these returns would all be halved.

### (c) To Take the Deduction or Not

Each company has its own unique circumstances that must be considered when deciding whether to take the deduction. The accounts payable professional making this decision usually needs to do a three-part analysis, as follows:

1. Carry out the basic calculations as described above, using the figures and the terms as offered.
2. Then factor in reality as it exists at the company. If the company doesn't pay its bills until 15 days after the due date, include this in your second calculation. Sometimes companies will have different policies for different customers. A large vendor might insist on being paid right smack on the 30th day, while smaller customers may tolerate payments on the 45th or 60th day. In these situations, two or more sets of calculations will be needed.
3. The reality number, or numbers, must then be compared with the company's borrowing or investment rates.

Be sure to note that the cost-of-funds rate for this comparison is the company's rate on its short-term facilities, not its all-in rate. In this case, the analysis is a short-term one and it would be incorrect to incorporate longer-term rates into the analysis.

It is this final comparison that will determine whether to take the discount. The results might surprise you. There are a few instances where a company is better off financially if it doesn't take the discount. For example, a company that normally pays at 60 days would look carefully at a discount of 1%, since this turns into a return of 7.5%.

However, in today's conditions, if that company is in a borrowing position, it *might* be better off *not* taking the discount. While this is unlikely in the current lower-rate environment, it doesn't take much to change the balance in the equation—especially if longer terms are negotiated. The emphasis in the analysis is not only on the break-even calculations, but on the company's financial position as well.

### (d) Non-financial Considerations

There are three other factors that will influence a company's decision regarding the calculations on whether or not to take a discount. They include:

1. Cashflow. Sometimes a company that is stretched tight for cash will forgo all discounts as it simply does not have the cash to take advantage of discounts offered. This may be a sign that the company is having financial difficulty or it may simply be a function of the industry.
2. Company policy. As mentioned above, some companies take all discounts regardless of when the payment is made. The professionals at those companies will not have to worry about doing the necessary calculations to determine whether it is financially advisable to take the discount. It should be noted that such a policy should be approved by senior management and is not something that should be undertaken by the accounts payable clerk.

The reason for this is that certain suppliers are apt to become annoyed at such a practice and it could have other repercussions that far outweigh the financial benefit gained from the practice. Others do not seem to care.

3. Turnaround time. It is quite difficult to turn around a check in a short period of time, with all the approvals required in most companies. There are quite a few companies where this would be impossible, especially if the company only has one or two check runs each week. Those who can do it in 10 days should be commended.

## 11.2 AN ONGOING PROCESS

This analysis of discounts should not be a one-shot deal. It needs to be repeated periodically—at least once a year. Interest rates change, the terms offered to the company change, and the company may take on new suppliers or lose some of their existing ones. All of these events can trigger a change in the feasibility analysis. The decision made today, with today's numbers, may not be valid a year from now.

Many accounts payable managers do themselves a disservice in the area of discounts. They analyze the data, make intelligent decisions, and then forget about the matter. They underplay their importance to their companies. As a result, management doesn't appreciate the talent working in the trenches.

Professionals who want to make sure their departments get the recognition they deserve should take these calculations and present them in memo form to their superiors. Additionally, they should calculate the amount of money that the company saves each year attributable to the proper taking of these discounts.

Along the same lines, those who decide the company should not be taking the discount need to document their reasons and make sure management is aware of them and concurs. This is particularly important if the company practice had been to take all discounts at all times, a not uncommon procedure, since most people automatically assume that all discounts must be taken.

## 11.3 POSSIBLE PROBLEMS WHEN PAYING LATE

Many accounts payable professionals find themselves paying their company's bills later and later. Whether they do this under a management directive or of their own initiative, the result is the same. Every day that a company delays making a payment results in an improvement in the bottom line. This is because the money will remain in the bank earning interest or, if the firm is in a net borrowing position, it will not borrow the money, and thus pay interest, until the check clears the bank.

Given this obvious fact, there is ever-increasing pressure to hold off paying a bill until the last possible moment. What financial zealots often do not realize is that their aggressive payment policies may actually cost their companies money—and in a few cases, cost them dearly. Since few vendors complain if payments are a few days late, there is little pressure to pay on time. Herein lies the problem. Many vendors will not pressure the customer for the payment; they simply send a second invoice. Some, BUT NOT ALL, mark it Copy or Duplicate.

### (a) Real-Life Incident

A conscientious accounts payable professional related the following incident. His firm had paid an invoice from a generally well-respected Fortune 50 company twice. The amount was in excess of $150,000. The second invoice was NOT marked copy and was printed in a slightly different format. Needless to say, both invoices had been approved for payment.

This company was lucky: It discovered the duplicate payment itself. A phone call to the vendor revealed that it had already realized the payment was a duplicate and was planning on returning the money—in about three weeks, the estimated time needed to turn a check request around. All in all, the paying company would be out of pocket for a month, assuming there were no further complications.

The cost of this little mishap was $1,000, and it was invisible. This figure was derived by calculating the interest expense the paying company had to incur to borrow the extra $150,000 for one month ($150,000 × .08 ÷ 12).

This story had a happy ending: The purchaser realized it had made a duplicate payment and was able to ask for its money back. It was dealing with a reasonable vendor. It could have been much worse.

### (b) The Culprit

The real problem in this instance was the two invoices, neither of which was marked duplicate. While it's easy to blame the vendor, in all probability the paying company needs to take a closer look at itself. We can learn a great deal from Miguel de Cervantes, who wrote in *Don Quixote,* "Our greatest foes, and whom we must chiefly combat, are within." In this regard, there are several issues to be evaluated:

Why was the payment approved twice?

Why were there two invoices?

What kind of checking did the company do to ensure a duplicate payment wasn't being made?

The obvious answer in this situation is that the up-front controls were weak and the company just might have been guilty of paying late, giving the vendor the opportunity to send that second invoice, which caused all the trouble.

### (c) Solutions

Any company regularly making payments after the due date needs to have top-notch routines for detecting duplicate payments. Without such processes, the company will ultimately give away much more than it will save.

Many accounts payable professionals are convinced that their companies do not have a serious problem with duplicate payments. However, any time a vendor returns a payment and indicates that an invoice has been paid, it is a warning signal that you may have duplicate payment issues—it is highly unlikely that only one duplicate got through. Also, be aware that not all vendors will return duplicate payments. In many cases, these funds sit in an unapplied account, never to be reconciled, and are eventually dumped into miscellaneous income. After all, how many vendors are going to spend the time to uncover the problems of others, especially when it means they will have to return money? Unfortunately, as the increase in accounts payable audit firms indicates, this is not always the case.

## 11.4 ARE ALL POSSIBLE DISCOUNTS BEING TAKEN?

The answer to this question in most organizations is usually a resounding NO. Now many reading this are probably thinking that is not the case in their organizations. But there is a good chance that they are wrong. Finding ways to increase the number of discounts a company can take is something that the accounts payable professional can do that adds value to their firm. A few simple techniques that can be used are:

- Improve check turnaround procedures so it is possible to legitimately earn discounts.
- Make all involved in the process, especially tardy invoice approvers, aware of the financial benefits of earning such discounts.
- Insist on completely filled out Purchase Orders so accounts payable is aware of all discounts it is entitled to take.
- Use an accounts payable audit firm to determine if any discounts are being missed. If they were, change procedures to ensure all discounts are being taken in the future.
- Establish a good rapport with purchasing to make sure that accounts payable is kept in the loop when special deals are arranged. Occasionally the purchasing department will nego-

tiate an extremely attractive discount and then fail to tell accounts payable about it. This is especially true if it is a one shot transaction. If the discount is not taken, don't expect the vendor to give the excess money back.

Take all discounts offered by vendors even if the purchase order does not indicate one is available. Let the vendor come back and ask for the extra funds—few will as they prepare and provide the invoice.

## 11.5 SHOULD YOU TAKE . . .

A few professionals believe it is wrong to take discounts after the discount period has ended. Yet, all evidence indicates that a good portion of corporate America takes these discounts regardless of when the invoice is paid. A few things that are being done by those who wish to be fair without completely penalizing the company for close misses include:

Take a common sense approach.

A 15/15 formalized approach.

A five-day approach.

### (a) Take A Common Sense Approach

Take into account how close the company is to actually earning it. If it is only missing the discount rate by a day or two and the discount is not real deep, there is no harm. Also, does the vendor agree with how the time period is calculated; that is, from invoice date vs. invoice receipt date and check date vs. payment receipt date?

Evaluate the relationship with the vendor. If the vendor is doing its job, it will know you are taking unearned discounts and adjust the next purchase price accordingly. If that is the case, both the accounts payable manager and the sales rep for the vendor are playing with the same money. On the accounts payable side, the accounts payable professional can tell everyone about the great discount savings being taken, and at the same time, the sales rep can tell management about protecting the company's margin with a recent increase in the sales price. With competition the way it is, many sales reps are much more aware of margins (including the effects of proper cash management), not just sales price.

Consider whether there is the time to test the waters with certain vendors by taking an unearned discount and monitoring its effect on purchase price, delivery time, service provided, and so on. Most accounts payable professionals do not.

There is also the argument that even in business, sometimes a company just needs to do the right thing. Remember those Business Ethics classes!

But blatantly taking discounts after the due date has expired can lead to trouble. One accounts payable mananger relates the story that at his firm there was a high-level finance guy who suggested to upper management that all discounts be taken regardless of timing. While the finance guy has moved on to another company, accounts payable and purchasing managers are still trying to mend fences with vendors over the whole incident.

### (b) A 15/15 Formalized Approach

Once the decision to take the discounts under certain circumstances has been made, ground rules should be set. Here's how one company approaches the task:

The company uses a 15/15 rule. If it has not exceeded the discount date by 15 days and the discount amount is no more than $15.00, the accounts payable staff may take the discount. If either the day or dollar limit has been exceeded, the accounts payable manager must approve the invoice and discount issue.

### (c) A Five-Day Approach

The frequency of check runs can add a new dimension to this discussion. Those who have weekly check runs have added problems. One approach is to have a policy that trys to pay within five days on either side so it washes out. However, if an invoice did not process due to vendor errors, the company takes the discount based on dating from good receipt of the invoice. If a vendor fails to invoice with a discount and the company pays within the terms, it will charge it back. The company that does this, does so on an annual review basis. It reports that it has used this approach for over five years with virtually no complaints.

# 12

# Payment Timing

Once companies realize that payment timing can have a financial impact—either positive or negative—management begins to look at accounts payable with a different mindset. No longer is the department viewed as a clerical function, a necessary evil, but rather as a group handling a process that deserves focus, attention, and financial analysis. The harsh reality in corporate America as it heads into the twenty-first century is that any function that can be reengineered to make it more efficient will be. Since vendor payment timing has been completely ignored in many companies for so long, it is ripe for review. Payment timing is an easy and obvious hit for those that understand anything about cashflow. While, as discussed in the previous chapter, a few have ethical problems extending payment dates, it is becoming a financial reality at many companies as they search for ways to improve profitabilty any way they can.

## 12.1 CAN ANOTHER DAY BE SQUEEZED OUT OF PAYABLES?

The first step in such a process is to determine if payments are being made too fast. It would be foolish to delay a payment to a valid vendor that was already being paid late as compared to the rest of the industry. But, how can this be determined? Begin by comparing company data to some benchmark statistics. One such set of numbers is included in Exhibit 12.1

*Exhibit 12.1* **Payment Speed Data**
**Days Sales Outstanding by Industry**

| | *Qtr. 2 '97* | *Qtr. 1 '97* | *Qtr. 2 '96* | *Qtr. 1 '96* |
|---|---|---|---|---|
| **All Respondents** | | | | |
| Days sales outstanding | 43.2 | 43.7 | 45.3 | 45.9 |
| Percent current | 76.6% | 75.5 | 74.0 | 73.2 |
| Percent over 60 days | 6.5% | 6.8 | 7.2 | 8.0 |
| Percent over 90 days | 4.0% | 4.6 | 5.3 | 6.1 |
| Bad debt to sales ratio | 0.274 | 0.284 | 0.372 | 0.369 |
| **Manufacturing-Consumer Goods** | | | | |
| Days sales outstanding | 45.5 | 44.7 | 47.9 | 47.2 |
| Percent current | 80.0% | 80.0 | 77.7 | 77.6 |
| Percent over 60 days | 5.0% | 5.3 | 5.9 | 6.3 |
| Percent over 90 days | 4.0% | 3.8 | 4.5 | 4.8 |
| Bad debt to sales ratio | 0.294 | 0.208 | 0.478 | 0.374 |
| **Manufacturing-Industrial Goods** | | | | |
| Days sales outstanding | 43.1 | 44.3 | 45.0 | 47.0 |
| Percent current | 75.9% | 74.1 | 73.0 | 71.7 |
| Percent over 60 days | 6.6% | 6.9 | 7.8 | 8.4 |
| Percent over 90 days | 4.0% | 4.8 | 5.6 | 6.3 |
| Bad debt to sales ratio | 0.168 | 0.199 | 0.208 | 0.286 |
| **Agriculture/Mining** | | | | |
| Days sales outstanding | 39.8 | 37.6 | 40.1 | 40.8 |
| Percent current | 85.6% | 84.1 | 80.8 | 81.7 |
| Percent over 60 days | 6.1% | 7.4 | 7.1 | 8.4 |
| Percent over 90 days | 1.8% | 2.2 | 2.9 | 2.9 |
| Bad debt to sales ratio | 0.080 | 0.083 | 0.085 | 0.095 |
| **Transportation/Communications/Utilities** | | | | |
| Days sales outstanding | 34.4 | 37.0 | 37.9 | 38.2 |
| Percent current | 76.8% | 77.2 | 74.6 | 75.0 |
| Percent over 60 days | 6.8% | 6.3 | 6.7 | 7.7 |
| Percent over 90 days | 3.5% | 4.3 | 3.9 | 4.8 |
| Bad debt to sales ratio | 0.394 | 0.543 | 0.387 | 0.462 |
| **Services** | | | | |
| Days sales outstanding | 46.5 | 49.4 | 51.4 | 48.2 |
| Percent current | 66.3% | 67.6 | 64.2 | 62.3 |
| Percent over 60 days | 10.0% | 9.4 | 10.0 | 11.3 |
| Percent over 90 days | 6.5% | 7.8 | 11.0 | 12.6 |
| Bad debt to sales ratio | 0.500 | 0.614 | 0.774 | 0.780 |

*Exhibit 12.1* *(Continued)*

| **Wholesale/Retail** | | | | |
|---|---|---|---|---|
| Days sales oustanding | 42.8 | 42.7 | 43.7 | 45.2 |
| Percent current | 75.4% | 73.8 | 73.6 | 72.7 |
| Percent over 60 days | 5.9% | 6.6 | 6.2 | 6.8 |
| Percent over 90 days | 3.6% | 4.2 | 4.0 | 5.7 |
| Bad debt to sales ratio | 0.400 | 0.397 | 0.490 | 0.436 |
| **Other** | | | | |
| Days sales outstanding | 29.0 | 30.5 | 31.8 | 31.4 |
| Percent current | 80.0% | 67.5 | 72.5 | 67.5 |
| Percent over 60 days | 12.0% | 18.0 | 15.0 | 19.5 |
| Percent over 90 days | 2.0% | 4.0 | 2.0 | 2.0 |
| Bad debt to sales ratio | 0.010 | 0.055 | 0.055 | 0.010 |

(Source: IOMA)

### (a) The Data

Accounts receivable managers are often measured by the speed at which they can collect their company's receivables. This measure is called DSO (days sales outstanding), and it measures in days the time until an invoice is paid. The numbers in Exhibit 12.1 were tabulated in a publication for use by credit and collection managers. However, they can also be used by payables managers.

A company with net 30 days should, in theory, have a DSO of 30. A quick look at the table reveals that this is not the case. On average, for all companies responding to this survey, the DSO was just under 43 days. If you take off three days for mail time, it becomes apparent that most companies are mailing their payments on the 40th day—not the 27th, as might be expected. (For the purposes of this discussion, we are ignoring the impact of discounts.)

The data shows that for the quarter ending June 30, 1997, the average DSO for all companies was 43 days. However, this number varies greatly by industry. As the exhibit demonstrates, it ranged from 29 to almost 47 days. Information that shows the percent of payments reported as current is also included. While this figure is approximately 75% on average, it can range from just over 66% to more than 85%, depending on the industry. Similarly, data is given for percent of payments over 60 days and over 90 days.

### (b) Using the Information

Accounts payable managers trying to determine if their own late payment policy is appropriate can see what others in their industry are doing. Don't forget to include a few days for mail time and, if you have lengthy signature processes, an appropriate number of days for that. Once these adjustments have been made, see how the numbers stack up compared to others in the industry.

Several of the numbers in the exhibit may have to be used. Remember, these are calculated from the other side of the fence. To determine the correct benchmark, look at the industry of the company you are paying. A wholesaler might expect to be paid more quickly than a transportation company.

It is important at this point to remember that if not handled correctly, paying late can have consequences. Certain key suppliers may not tolerate it. Even more important is the fact that if good duplicate-payment prevention techniques are not in place, the company may end up paying twice. This, of course, completely negates any benefit the company may have accrued by paying a few days late. For more information on this topic see Chapter 4, Errors and Duplicate Payments.

### (c) Another Source of Payment Information

Check with the company's credit manager to see if the company is a member of the National Association of Credit Managers (NACM), Reimer Group, National Group Management Corp (NGMC), the Media Credit Association, or some other credit trade association. If it is, the company will have received DSO numbers compiled by these fine organizations. These numbers can also be used for this purpose. These organizations (which typically only release this information to members) can be reached as follows:

NACM: (800) 955-8815

NGMC: (215) 923-1765

Reimer: (216) 835-2477

Whatever comparison numbers are used, a review of them should be done every year or two as they do change. To get updated figures from IOMA for a modest charge call (212) 244-0360 and ask for the the most recent issue of *Managing Credit Receivables and Collections,* which contains DSO data. The company updates these statistics twice a year.

### (d) Payment Trends

While most accounts payable professionals like to think in terms of extending payments, overall, companies are collecting faster this year than last. There have been some significant changes as well. Those involved in the retail trade have made impressive improvements in their collection activity over the last year, improving their DSO figures by more than five days. That means if you are paying a retailer, you are likely to be pressured for an earlier payment.

The only place that there has been some success in stretching payments is the services industry, which shows only a slight decline (or improvement, depending on which side of the fence you are standing).

These figures are presented to provide a rough guideline as to what is actually happening in industry today. They can be used to provide guidelines to your activity, but do not assume the data is written in stone. If the company is way off in either direction, investigate the possibility of either accelerating or slowing down your invoice-paying speed.

### (e) Payment Timing in Difficult Times

Nothing disturbs the smooth operation of payables more than a directive from senior management to "stop paying the bills." Sometimes it happens because of tight cash flow or because owners want to cash out or look for banks or a prospective investor. Whatever the reason, there are some strategies that will help a manager get through this rough period without damaging a company's credit rating or reputation—and hopefully without going crazy. It should be noted that these strategies are generally approved by upper management before being implemented. Accounts payable managers are cautioned against undertaking any of these techniques without the expressed approval of their management.

### (f) Stretching Vendor Payments

The most frequently used, and potentially most damaging, strategy employed when companies are looking to preserve cash is simply delaying vendor payments. If the postponement is not too long, the strategy may work. However, companies that use this tactic run the serious risk of damaging their credit rating and their reputation with their suppliers. This is not a risk to be taken lightly.

Many vendors belong to industry credit groups where members get together for the express purpose of discussing the payment patterns of their customers. If it is discovered at one of these meetings that a given company is delaying payments all over town, these important suppliers may pull credit—seriously affecting the long-term viability of the firm in question. A company may be able to stretch payments by a few days occasionally, but it's not advised over the long haul.

### (g) Place Smaller Orders

A better tactic for conserving cash is, whenever possible, to simply place more modest orders. This may entail giving up certain volume discounts, but that is usually preferable to alienating a valued supplier. Obviously, the accounts payable manager cannot mandate such action, but it can be suggested during discussions about conserving cash and stretching payments.

### (h) Talk to Vendors

Many executives don't realize that honesty is the best policy when it comes to stretching terms. A number of companies have found, to their surprise, that this practice often works with preferred vendors. Those in seasonal businesses experience periods of cash tightness when products are being manufactured and then shipped to customers on open account. Inevitably, the situation is remedied as customers begin to pay for the goods ordered.

By discussing the matter honestly with valued vendors, many find the supplier is sympathetic to their plight and willing to show some leniency with regard to payment timing. If the company is a valued customer, the vendor will most likely try to be accommodating. Again, this is probably a matter that will be decided at the very top management level.

The important issue to grasp is that many companies experience temporary cash flow challenges. There are ways to deal with them so as not to damage relationships with valued suppliers. By analyzing the issues and devising workable solutions, a good working relationship with the vendors most important to the company may be preserved.

## 12.2 A FORMALIZED APPROACH

Rather than randomly holding on to checks for a few more days, companies are beginning to analyze their payment flows to determine where terms can be stretched, or optimized as those in the field like to say. The reason they say optimized is that in some cases, a shortening of terms may be called for. Now those reading this may be doing a double take—but yes, a shortening of terms may have a stronger financial impact. Why? The answer is quite simple. Sometimes by paying faster a company will qualify for a discount for the early payment. Thus, when undertaking a review of the timing, look at discounts that could be lost if terms are stretched. Also, talking to the vendors might uncover some hidden opportunities for discounts that are often overlooked or have not been offered to the company.

## 12.2 A Formalized Approach

### (a) How It Works

The payment timing model is based on an Excel (or other) spreadsheet specially designed to analyze the current payment patterns of the company and recommend new ones by interviewing the payables staff on an item-by-item basis. It begins with contractual terms on the invoice or those agreed to with the vendor. As most payables professionals will point out, however, these terms often have very little to do with the actual ones—especially if no discount is involved.

The review begins by selecting between 45 and 90 of a company's largest vendors for examination. Typically these will represent between 50% and 70% of the company's payables on a dollars-spent basis.

Look at each payment and determine what is the likely amount of time that it can be extended. Also search for missed discount opportunities, analyze check approval time, and record the terms of the most recent invoice. There is a wealth of information at the fingertips of the payables staff, which most organizations find invaluable. Some recommend that this information be presented to management for final approval. Once the program is in place, it must be monitored. Certain vendor payments may have to be adjusted if these valued suppliers complain. If there are no objections raised by other vendors, it might be appropriate to stretch their payments out farther.

### (b) Discounts

There is a second component to this analysis. It also searches for lost discount opportunities. In some cases, there are more savings for a company in identifying missed discounts than by extending their payments. Most companies will profess that they are taking all allowable discounts. According to experts, this is rarely the case.

Terms on bills will often change without the company realizing it. The newly improved terms don't get put into the payables system, or whoever is running the computer system doesn't fully understand it and some discounts are lost. Then there's everyone's favorite excuse: office politics. Whatever the cause, part of this analysis involves identifying missed discount opportunities.

### (c) Exception Items

Obviously, payroll and taxes cannot be extended. Factors and contractors are also not included in such an analysis. Others include equipment lease payments, utility bills, and sometimes rent.

### (d) Advantages of Hiring an Outsider

Not all companies have the time or expertise to complete such an analysis themselves. By hiring a consultant with specialized knowledge, you guarantee that the task will be completed in a relatively short period of time regardless of what else is going on in the company. The consultant also brings knowledge of how other companies are being paid. This information is not usually available.

It never hurts to have an unbiased third pair of eyes looking over your operations. Often, people are too close to a situation to be completely objective. The outside consultant doesn't have this problem. For a relatively small amount of money, you get a professional to take an objective look at your operations and tell you how they can be improved.

This is the type of service that your management team may not think of bringing into your department. Those professionals who know there is money to be saved if they could stretch their payables, might recommend to management that a payment timing analysis be employed in their company. One such company that offers such a service is Goldstein Golub and Kessler and Company, a New York accounting and consulting firm. Robert Jaffee, the company's director of treasury consulting, heads the program and can be reached at (212) 372-1324.

### (e) Savings

Without going into extensive detail, the savings for the stretched portion of a payment timing program can be calculated as follows:

Interest rate × payments × number of days extended ÷ 365.

To illustrate we give the example of a company with:

Borrowing rate: 9%
Annual Payments Extended: $20 million
Number of Days Extended: 10
Annual Savings:
$49,315 (.09 × $20,000,000 × 10 ÷ 365)

There are savings associated with finding missed discounts as well. For example, a 2/10 net 30 discount found will result in a $4,000 savings on a $200,000 invoice.

Payment timing is a delicate issue that, if handled properly, can make an impact on a company's bottom line. As corporate America continues to look for ways to squeeze more value out of its assets, look for an increased focus on this area.

# 13

# Audits and the Outside Accountant's Management Letter

The one place accounts payable managers don't want to see their names is in the management letter prepared by the company's outside auditors at the completion of the annual audit. In this document, the accountants communicate "reportable conditions and material weaknesses" in the company's policies and procedures to upper management. It should be the goal of all professionals to make sure that nothing derogatory about their work or the work of their department be included in this document.

Most auditors give the client a chance to respond to the charges. In those instances, the letter will contain both the points and the responses. Most auditors won't remove items from the management letter unless the issue has been resolved. Just promising to fix something won't get the accounts payable department off the hook. The matter has to be completely corrected.

## 13.1 BIGGEST PAYABLES ISSUES

The most likely situations to land accounts payable in the management letter are discussed in the following sections. While this list is by no means exhaustive, it does contain the most common reasons. These professionals also offered suggestions to avoid that distasteful experience.

### (a) Writing Checks Too Soon is a Big No-No

Now, before you skip to the next item because your company always pays at the last minute, realize that this is not the issue. Often, overzealous accounts payable clerks clean their desks every night. They do this by processing all vouchers the minute they hit their desks, although the checks aren't mailed until the appropriate time. This results in a large number of checks floating in limbo. This poor control practice just pushes the responsibility for these checks up the ladder and results in wasted time when clients call looking for payments.

Additionally, this looks terrible to the guy on the other side when the check is received a month or more after it is dated. On top of everything else, it appears as though the company is experiencing cash-flow difficulties. This is not the impression that most companies wish to give their suppliers.

### (b) Lack of Proper Controls on Check Stock and Signature Plates

Given the increased rise in fraud and recent regulatory changes making corporations more liable for check losses, lack of proper controls is guaranteed to bring a write-up in the management letter. One experienced auditor recounts the tale of finding a check machine with the signature plate in it while working late one night at a client's office. Check stock was apparently not well controlled either, as he was able to print (and sign) a check for $1 million. Being an honest man, he left it for the controller. This was definitely a situation where a picture was worth a thousand words and this controller got the message.

### (c) Lack of Adequate Segregation of Duties

Lack of the proper segregation of duties will get the accounts payable department into the management letter faster than almost anything else. In fact, that's what led to the downfall of the British firm Barings. While Nick Leesam wasn't the accounts payable manager, he was responsible for making the payments on his trading activity. At a minimum, the person approving a payment should be different from the one responsible for writing the check. Bank reconciliations should also be done outside the accounts payable department.

### (d) Vacation Requirements

People should be required to take vacation. In fact, many banks require employees to be away from the office for two consecutive weeks. The feeling is that in this time frame any internal fraud will be uncovered. While the employee is away, someone else should handle their daily work. This way, if any member of the staff has been able to perpetrate fraud, it will be uncovered during the person's absence. Make sure that someone else does the work. Otherwise the purpose of this requirement has been defeated. Those managers who give their staffers a hard time when they want to take vacation time should seriously reconsider that stance. An added benefit from this posture is the ability to cross train the staff and have coverage in case of emergencies.

### (e) Appropriate Approvals

All invoices should have the appropriate approvals. People sometimes get sloppy about this requirement, especially in organizations that are growing fast. Without clear approval levels and when multiple approvers for the same item exist, the chances for duplicate payments rises rapidly.

### (f) Appropriate Backup

The backup attached to any check request should be adequate and approved. Again, this is an area where fast growing companies often fall down. The flip side of the coin is that in certain organizations, everything under the sun is attached often making it difficult to find the needed information. So while it is important that the needed backup be attached, don't overdo it.

### (g) Use Careful Check Signers

All check signers should compare the data on the backup to the check. Otherwise, the check preparer may just as well sign the check. As silly as this may sound to the control conscious person reading this, many will sign whatever is placed in front of them trusting the person who prepared the check. Situations such as this increase the chance of check fraud. If the signer is just going to sign whatever is placed in front of him, the whole purpose of having manual signatures is defeated.

### (h) Controls on the Check Stock and Machines

The numerical sequence on checks (and check-signing machines) should be accounted for by someone other than the person preparing the check (or running the machine). Check stock should be stored in a secure, locked location. Access should not be given to those with responsibility for preparing the checks.

### (i) Invoice Controls

Yes, invoices need to be controlled. All invoices should be sent from mail opener to person responsible for making the payment. Why? This makes it less likely that the invoice will sit on someone's desk for days or weeks before it is submitted to accounts payable. It also helps lessen the chance of check fraud.

### (j) Paying from Copies

In an ideal world, no payments would be made from copies or duplicate invoices. However, corporate America is far from an ideal world when it comes to invoices. All duplicate invoices should be marked duplicate. This will minimize duplicate payments. For more information on how to minimize the risk when paying from copies, refer to Chapter 5, Paying When the Original Invoice is Not Available, which covers this topic in depth.

### (k) Cancel Supporting Documentation

All supporting documents should be canceled to avoid duplicate payment or fraud. This can be done by marking the material paid or by stamping it so. If this is not done, there is a chance that the document will be used as backup for another check request. This is a favorite technique for those few individuals intent on defrauding the companies for which they work. This marking should be done to all documentation—no matter how small the dollar amount.

### (l) Check Mailing Procedures

Checks should be mailed by a manager, not the person who prepared the check. Many auditors will insist that checks never be returned to the person requesting them but mailed directly to the intended recipient.

## 13.2 USING THIS INFORMATION

Many accounts payable managers have been successful in getting a sneak preview of the management letter before it is sent to the controller. Whether the draft is offered or obtained through some devious means, many take the opportunity when reviewing it to try to persuade the auditors to remove those points from the report that they feel are unreasonable.

More than a few payables professionals have been known to persuade their accountants that "this is not an issue." This is important for several reasons. For starters, getting the item off the list means it doesn't have to be addressed to the auditors' satisfaction, only your own. But there is another, more subtle, reason to avoid a debate with the auditors with top management acting as the referee.

In many instances, controllers and other members of upper management were hired from the very accounting firm that is now performing the audit. Should you get into a serious disagreement with the audit team, top management is apt to have a decided bias in favor of the auditors' point of view. Not only are they the experts, but in many cases a close relationship also exists and you are definitely the outsider.

The savvy accounts payable manager who handles these issues before the auditors arrive will sidestep many discussions with them about what does and does not belong in the management letter. After all, this is a list every accounts payable professional should want to avoid.

# 14

# Alternatives to the Three-Way Match

As companies look to streamline their operations and eliminate non–value added tasks, they turn their focus to the proverbial three-way match described in Chapter 1, Invoice Handling. The process can introduce errors in situations where there were no problems. It is costly and it is time consuming. Now, few would object to spending time and money to make sure a large bill is paid correctly, but spending $40 to make sure a $425 invoice is paid correctly just doesn't make good business sense.

So innovative professionals studying the situation devised alternative solutions to address this issue. The obvious answer is to eliminate small bills. This is not as ludicrous a solution as it might appear at first glance. Companies are switching to corporate procurement cards in droves as a means of eliminating small dollar invoices. The topic of corporate procurement cards has become a leading issue for accounts payable professionals and is examined in detail in Chapter 22, Purchasing Card.

Assuming the invoices remain, companies are using a technique called assumed receipt for small dollar invoices and evaluated receipt settlement for both large and small invoices. Both require procedural changes.

## 14.1 ASSUMED RECEIPT

When accounts payable receives an invoice, it assumes that the goods have been received, and rather than go through the tedious three-way matching process, the department processes the invoice for payment.

Some also call the approach "negative assurance" because copies of the invoices are sent to the appropriate party, and if that individual does not tell accounts payable not to pay, the payment goes out as scheduled. Some innovative companies are beginning to send the notification by e-mail rather than sending copies of the invoice. While this approach may seem new to many, some companies have used the process for several years. This technique is also sometimes referred to as "positive receiving."

### (a) How It's Being Used

As might be expected, million-dollar invoices are rarely paid without in-depth verification, even at companies using assumed receipt. Most companies set guidelines. For example, at one company, the policy applies to all invoices less than $5,000 that do not have an associated PO or any other preapproval mechanism in place. At Tandem, the policy applied to all non–PO based invoices less than $1,000.

As part of the assumed receipt process, a system-generated paper notice along with a copy of the relevant invoice is sent to the person who ordered the goods or services. The recipient then has 10 business days to respond to A/P to indicate that the invoice should not be paid or should be recoded. If there is no response, the system releases the invoice to pay against its payment terms. Some take this a step further. Don't send copies of invoices for amounts less than $500.

Another innovation some are using is moving to an intranet/e-mail delivery of the notice with ultimate availability of an image of the invoice via the intranet/e-mail platform. With this mechanism in place, no copies would need to be sent, but if the recipient had any questions about the item, he or she could view an image of it on the company's intranet.

The policy allows us to simplify and speed up the approval and payment process for small-dollar invoices. It permits the staff to spend a higher proportion of its time managing the payment of large dollar invoices, which represent the bulk of spending.

### (b) Disadvantages

The major concern for most companies considering such a program is the increased possibility of fraud. However, if good controls are in place and all participants regularly check the information accounts payable provides, the likelihood of this is minimal.

### (c) Getting Started

Obviously, the first step in getting an assumed receipt program up and running is education. Since this is a relatively new process, few in management will know what you are talking about. Thus, your first task will be to educate those who will ultimately make the decision to go forward. A clear and comprehensive communication across the company is key to a successful implementation. Developing a system-generated notice is also a critical step in the project implementation process.

Management is not the only group that will need to be educated. Once you've gotten the green light to implement the program, make sure that all the participants understand the program and know exactly what they are supposed to do. It won't hurt to point out how the program will benefit them, as well.

Gather information about other companies that have implemented this policy, regarding their experience and any associated risks. If the company is uncomfortable with this approach, use a smaller dollar limit to start the process and increase it later, as appropriate. Significant benefit could be derived from using even a $500 cutoff for the policy.

### (d) Results

How do these programs work? Is there an increase in duplicate and fraudulent payments? One company using assumed receipt estimates that no more than 100 payments (under $5,000) have been put on hold or removed from the system. There have been no instances of paying for merchandise that had not been received (departments would have seen the charge on their monthly accounting statements). How do they know this? They brought in an audit recovery firm in September 1996 to do up to a three-year study of its accounts payable system. They stopped after reviewing only four months' worth of invoices, stating that any further time spent would be wasted, since they found only one error, where the vendor had accidentally calculated an extra item into his handwritten invoice for $123. The accounts payable manager reports that based on the fact that check runs for these four months were in the tens of millions, and that this was obviously a human error, the company determined that its system was working very well. Few would disagree with her.

## 14.2 EVALUATED RECEIPT SETTLEMENT

Whether due to reengineering initiatives or at the behest of a large and powerful customer, more accounts payable managers are being directed to adopt Evaluated Receipt Settlement (ERS)—also known as paperless invoicing, invoiceless processing, and pay-on-receipt. "Although most reengineering concepts will reduce the cost of processing an invoice," argues Mark Becker, a senior consultant with Soltec, "they do nothing to eliminate the single largest inefficiency in accounts payable—the invoice itself."

To illustrate the uselessness of the invoice, Becker poses the question: "What value does an invoice add to the procurement and disbursement process?" In theory, this is true. It assumes, of course, that purchase orders (POs) are filled out completely and that terms of sale are included on the PO. For ERS to work, this is essential.

### (a) How ERS Works

The underlying principle behind ERS is quite simple. When a company receives something it ordered, it pays for it as agreed in advance with the seller. Becker explains the concept in a little more detail as follows:

"A company agrees to purchase goods and services using a PO with established prices and terms. When the goods are received (or the service is performed), the customer makes payment without the need for the supplier furnishing an invoice. The payment to the supplier provides the remittance information, including the supplier's shipping document number (i.e., packing slip number, bill of lading number), which replaces the invoice number for cash application purposes."

It is imperative that both the purchasing and receiving staff understand the importance of their functions should a company move to ERS. Packing slips must be verified and forwarded to accounts payable for matching against purchase orders, which must be completely and accurately filled out. Any discrepancies or returns must be clearly identified on the packing slips. Without these two important components, any ERS initiative will make more rather than less work for accounts payable.

### (b) Changes to The Process

Most companies that implement ERS have to make some changes to their work flow. As readers may have already guessed, ERS results in a two-way match instead of a three-way. This is a big timesaver that ultimately reduces the number of errors introduced into the process.

The lack of an invoice number can present a problem, though innovative managers have found workable ways to get around the issue. Many accounts payable departments that insist on an invoice number to pay have had success in using the packing slip number as the invoice number. On the other side of the fence, some sellers that must have an invoice number have been successful in using the invoice number as the packing slip number.

Pricing can be a key issue as well. "ERS requires the establishment of firm delivered pricing on POs," says Becker. "This means that miscellaneous charges such as pallets, set-up, and tooling must either be eliminated or factored into the item's unit price by the supplier." This is a big advantage to accounts payable. "Firm delivered pricing eliminates all of the work associated with tracking and payment on miscellaneous charges," explains Becker.

With the emphasis on completed POs and accurate data, many accounts payable managers using ERS report a reduction in the number of problems with suppliers.

ERS tends to be used more in certain industries than in others. The automotive industry and all those industries supplying it are big users of ERS. The implementation process is usually not as hectic or as complex as certain other process improvements. "Soltec clients are successfully launching ERS pilot programs in three to four months with as much as a 40% reduction in their invoice-transaction volume," says Becker. "Full launch for all suppliers is occurring two to three months after the pilot launch." Compare this with an SAP installation, which can take years and disrupt virtually the entire company.

### (c) Supplier Relationships

One of the first steps when beginning an ERS program is the evaluation of supplier relationships. This is typically done by purchasing with little input from accounts payable. However, when it comes to setting up guidelines for the operation of the ERS, accounts payable managers should do everything in their power to be included in those discussions. Why? Because they are the ones who are going to have to live with whatever decisions are made—and live with them every day.

In their zeal to get ERS going, upper management may cave in to unreasonable requests made by suppliers. In fact, they may not even realize the demands are unrealistic. If the operating procedures are not written with input from someone with in-depth knowledge of the way accounts payable functions, you may find yourself saddled with procedures that are difficult, if not impossible, to use.

If ERS is done properly, it can be a real boon to accounts

payable. You will soon have fewer suppliers and so will be able to develop a closer working relationship with the chosen few. This will be a real benefit when it comes to reconciling payment discrepancies.

### (d) Operations Accounting

Once the program is operational, the ongoing requirements often fall on accounts payable's shoulders. Preparation of the remittance advice changes as the information, such as an invoice number, that is normally included is no longer available. Most companies faced with the dilemma of what identifier to put on the remittance advice go with the supplier's packing slip number. This allows the supplier who receives the payment to correctly identify and apply the money.

Some suppliers, especially those that rely heavily on invoice numbers, will make the packing slip number and the invoice number the same. Other information that may be present on the remittance advice includes: the shipping date; the discount dollar amount as per the packing slip; the gross dollar amount as per the packing slip; the net dollar amount as per the packing slip; and the type.

Additionally, the remittance advice may include the following optional data: quantity received; unit of measure; unit price; item number; purchase order/release number; extended price for each item received; receiving location reference; and sales tax.

This identifier should be selected when the program is being established. It should be information easily accessible to the accounts payable department. This is the type of detail that is often overlooked when accounts payable is not involved in setting up the program.

### (e) Corporate and Local Purchasing

When using ERS, correct and complete information on the purchase order is imperative. Unfortunately for accounts payable professionals, although they must rely on this document, they have virtually no control over it. It is therefore crucial that the importance of filling out the purchase order completely and correctly be impressed upon the purchasing top brass.

Accounts payable professionals will need to complete a thorough review of the purchase orders to make sure they contain all necessary information, including freight charges and one-time, lump-sum payments. They must also contain firm prices and timely price updates. Volume-sensitive pricing, prices quoted at market, and retroactive increases or decreases all must be indicated on the purchase order.

Working with purchasing on this matter consistently will put the accounts payable professionals in the best position to make ERS work in their company.

### (f) Supply and Material Control

In many organizations, receiving documents receive scant attention. There is not the thorough checking of the contents of a shipment against the packing slips that one would hope for. When discrepancies arise because of this, it is the accounts payable professional who is stuck reconciling. Once again, dependent on information over which they have no control, accounts payable managers find themselves in the delicate situation of trying to get another department to do a better job so that their own life may be a little less hectic.

Again, it is necessary to impress upon the receiving department the absolute necessity of doing a thorough match of the goods received against the receiving documents. Otherwise, it is quite possible to pay for goods never received. If at all possible, insist on having the receiving practices reviewed during the planning phase for ERS. At that point, adequate controls can be installed if needed. Use EDI technology to record shipments whenever possible.

### (g) Audit Controls and Processing

Whenever a new process is introduced, you can count on hearing from both your internal and external auditors. It is not a bad idea to invite them in at the planning stage so they can voice their concerns and you can answer them. It is much easier to design a system taking these matters into account than it is to go back and jury-rig the system to handle them. It also makes them happier and less likely to try to find holes as well as alerting you to possible Internal Revenue Service issues.

Many who use ERS audit by exception and utilize sampling techniques. They claim that auditing is substantially reduced. This is a blessing to the accounts payable staff who end up spending untold hours pulling documentation for auditors. It is in the planning stages that parameters need to be established to detect major errors. The likelihood of duplicate payments is reduced with ERS as there is no invoice and possible duplicate invoice to pay.

### (h) Information Systems

Without a doubt, changes will have to be made to your information systems. It will not be possible to implement ERS without making system changes. Review your current procedures to determine what changes will need to be made in order to operate efficiently. This is another reason it is so important to have someone familiar with the intimate details of accounts payable involved with ERS implementation.

Accounts payable managers who want other modifications made might take this opportunity to try to slip them onto the list. This, of course, will only work if the additions are small.

While the decision to go with ERS is rarely made in the accounts payable department, virtually every step of the implementation process affects it. If it is to work well, the implementation team must include a representative from accounts payable who has in-depth knowledge of the way the department works when it comes to paying bills. Thus, accounts payable managers need to push themselves to the forefront, if they are not initially included, at those organizations planning to use ERS. Otherwise, instead of having a say in getting a workable system, they will be presented with a fait accompli that may not work at all.

The requirements of a successful ERS program include:

**An integration between the purchasing, receiving, and accounts payable systems**. Accuracy in each of these areas is imperative or ERS can bring chaos to the organization. So, departments that might not have gotten along will have to put their past differences aside to make this program work. ERS means that purchase orders must be correct and contain accurate terms—something that is almost nonexistent in some organizations. It also means that receiving will have to check incoming goods closely against packing slips. This is another area that is sometimes lax. To successfully implement ERS, both these departments may need to clean up their acts.

**Vendor-supplier trust and cooperation is a prerequisite**. ERS will not work between two companies that cannot rely on each other. If the employees at two companies always seem to be at each other's throats, it might be a good idea to try to smooth over these relationships before ERS is implemented. This may be easier said than done since quite frequently the mandate to use ERS comes from the very top levels. However, the accounts payable manager in this situation doesn't have to sit back and do nothing. He or she can take the first step by extending a hand in friendship (or, perhaps an invitation to lunch) to try to establish smoother working relationships with the enemy. An in-person meeting can often do a lot to alleviate bad feelings.

**Establish and agree on certain information with trading partners**. This should, at a minimum, include: the identity of the trading partners who will use ERS; part descriptions and numbers; prices and rates (which must be accurate and allow for updates); payment terms; and shipping terms—if they are standard.

**Dynamic charges should be handled outside of the ERS program**. An ERS program can work even if the shipping terms are typically taken from the invoice. Most experts recommend taking the shipping terms out of the program and billing for them separately on a monthly basis. This would allow a company to still accrue most of the benefits of an ERS program. Other charges such as fees for returnable containers etc. can be handled much the same way.

**Discipline in ordering and receiving must be rigorous**. Since there is no invoice, the accounts payable manager must rely quite heavily on the information provided by purchasing and receiving. This matter must be discussed with these departments and should be handled gingerly. In fact, since the directive to use ERS usually comes from senior management, it might not be a bad idea to try to get them to raise this issue with the departments. The accounts payable manager might try pointing out that in order for ERS to work, more information will be needed from purchasing and receiving. This should get the ball rolling on a very delicate issue.

**Participating vendors must ship high-quality goods with minimal material rejects**. With ERS, resolving discrepancies can be a nightmare. The program works well only when there are very few disputes to settle so a vendor who ships inferior merchandise makes a poor candidate for this program. To be successful, the seller must impose the same strict discipline being required of the purchasing and receiving departments.

The consequences of implementing ERS without strict discipline in pricing, ordering and receiving are significant incidences of exceptions that will negate the benefits gained by eliminating the invoice. The implementation of a successful ERS program depends on the development and maintenance of rate databases, as well as discipline in the ordering and receiving process.

### (i) Barriers to Implementation

As with any new procedure, ERS will not be initiated without difficulties. By reviewing some common problems, accounts payable managers planning to begin ERS can anticipate obstacles and prepare for them. In-house resistance to change is the first roadblock most encounter. It is inevitable that people are comfortable with what they know and view change as disruptive and threatening. Some oppose it out of a misguided sense of protecting their turf.

Without invoices, the onus falls back on others to ensure that the company gets all the money it is due. To make ERS work smoothly, order purchasing and receiving must have as few errors as possible. In many companies, these departments are not used to this level of responsibility. If the concerns of these departments are addressed in the planning stages, ERS has a much better chance of succeeding. Enhanced bar-coding capabilities will help meet some concerns of the receiving department. Work hard to overcome sloppy practices in the receiving department.

### (j) Best ERS Practices Identified

Most ERS experts identify the following best practices for any company wishing to begin using ERS.

> For starters, a cross-functional team should be formed. This should include representatives from the finance, billing, accounts payable, accounts receivable, MIS, and customer service.
>
> All internal procedures associated with the process need to be identified and evaluated.
>
> All suppliers should be advised of the new bar code label requirements, if that is applicable to the industry.
>
> Once the program is worked out, conduct a beta site with several understanding companies before "going live." Remember, nothing ever works as smoothly in real life as it does on paper. Don't consider rolling out the program until all the bugs are worked out.
>
> When the beta site has been run successfully and all the kinks have been ironed out, roll out the formal plan with explicit presentations to all whom you wish to use ERS.

As more industries follow the lead of the automotive industry, more accounts payable professionals will find themselves in the position of being forced to use ERS, either at the request of their own management or that of one of their largest suppliers. Those who take the time to investigate what's involved may find they like it. While we don't expect to ever get away from invoices completely, we do see a trend toward a paperless society. ERS is one technique that will help get us on the road.

Soltec not only consults on ERS matters, but periodically offers seminars on the topic. To learn more about its services, it can be contacted at (810) 689-9299.

# Part Four

# Travel and Entertainment

Reimbursing employees for expenses incurred while traveling and/or entertaining on company business is not as simple as it might appear at first glance. However, many innovations are taking place in this arena. Companies are evaluating their travel and entertainment processes and many are coming to what others consider startling conclusions. Some are not checking receipts and others no longer require pretravel authorizations.

Given the cumbersome nature of the entire process, there has been a big move to handle the process electronically. Once again, technology comes to the rescue. Depending on the corporate commitment and the technological sophistication, this move can span a wide variety of applications and techniques. These chapters take a look at some of the best practices leading edge companies are using to make this process more efficient.

Finally, the more sophisticated companies whose employees travel overseas on company business are reclaiming their VAT and GST payments. Services to handle this unique function are discussed in this section.

# 15

# Handling Employee Travel and Entertainment Reports

One of the biggest time stealers and ulcer inducers for accounts payable managers is the handling of employee travel and expense reports and reimbursements. Most would gladly give the function away if they could. Traditionally employees who traveled would:

Obtain written authorization from their supervisor.

Get a cash advance.

Complete a detailed report including all receipts upon the completion of the trip.

Give that report to the immediate supervisor for approval.

Perhaps get a second authorization.

Send the approved report down to accounts payable for reimbursement.

## 15.1 THE PROBLEM

When the report arrived in accounts payable, a clerk would check the report to make sure the math was correct, the necessary approvals had been obtained, and the entire report conformed to company policy. If anything was amiss, the report would be sent back to the originating party for correction. If the report got held up at any one of the junctures mentioned above, and reports inevitably do get held up when so many different parties are involved, the reimbursement would be delayed. In more cases than not, employees would receive the bill from their charge account provider before they had been reimbursed by their employer. Since these bills tend to be hefty, especially if airfare and hotel charges were included, many employees would then call accounts payable demanding their money—often before the report had wended its way through the system to accounts payable. The issue was compounded by the fact that many companies used preprinted forms that employees filled in by hand—often making mathematical mistakes and more than occasionally using poor penmanship.

The conversations in these cases often get ugly, and the accounts payable staff ends up taking the brunt of it, even though the staff had nothing to do with causing the problem. Due to the inherent flaws in such a system, many travel and entertainment reimbursements would end up being written as manual checks—not the most productive approach for accounts payable. Adding insult to injury, often times the delay was caused by the employee demanding reimbursement. Let's face it, completing a T&E expense report is no one's idea of fun and many put it off until the last possible moment—then expect everyone else to jump through hoops to get the check issued. While this is unfair to those who toil in accounts payable, it is a sad fact of life. Given all the problems, it is only to be expected that the T&E function is one that comes under scrutiny and has undergone some major improvements in many companies.

## 15.2 SOLUTIONS

Companies typically approach their T&E problems from two fronts: they look at their policies and procedures and they let technology take a whack at the problem. The next chapter will take an in-depth look at how companies are using technology to solve this problem. This chapter will examine the best practices used by today's leading edge companies. It should be noted that not all approaches will work at all companies. Some will have a corporate culture that will not permit certain techniques. Others will not have the systems capabilities or will not be able to get the technical support they need from the company's IT department. Whatever the case, some of the following best practices can be used in most companies, although some will require policy changes and approval from upper management.

**Authorizations.** Most experts recommend eliminating the formal up-front authorizations. Why? For starters most employees don't take it upon themselves to plan and book a trip without their boss's approval. Most experts feel this step is a waste of time and adds no value. Those that are concerned about unauthorized travel can use monthly management reports to ensure that no unauthorized trips were taken at company expense.

**Cash Advances.** Nothing will get an employee to complete an expense report quicker than being out-of-pocket for company expenses. Many companies no longer offer cash advances to traveling employees. They feel that combined with the use of credit cards, employees will have to lay out their own money for only a few low-dollar items and this minor inconvenience is more than offset by the productivity saving.

**Technology.** Use as much technology as possible to automate the process. As mentioned above, this will be discussed in detail in the next chapter.

**Receipts.** Never give them to the manager. The only thing that happens when all receipts are attached to an expense report is that the receipts get lost. They should be placed in an envelope and sent along to accounts payable.

**Checking.** Let's face it, most employees are honest. Detailed checking of expense reports adds little value to a company. If the reports have been automated, it is unlikely that there will be any mathematical errors. Additionally, the errors caught tend to be small-dollar items. A company would be better advised to pay an employee an extra $25 once in a while than to hire a full-time employee to check every expense report. Spot checking based on dollars spent in various categories makes much better use of a company's limited accounts payable resources. Of course, a company that goes the spot checking route has to make it perfectly clear to all employees that anyone caught cheating on a T&E report will be fired immediately. This may sound a little harsh, but cheating on a T&E is fraud. To enforce such a policy, the company needs to come down hard on anything that is amiss on T&Es. While a company may not wish to terminate someone who requests reimbursement for a questionable item, it can make a big deal about it. And of course, employees who have any questions should be encouraged to ask them before submitting a report.

**Corporate T&E cards.** Employees should be required to use company T&E cards. Although the cards are corporate cards, the liability should be with the employee. That way, if they are tempted to use the card for personal expenses, they will be responsible for them. Some companies will act as a backup guarantor for those employees who do not qualify for the card. This generally happens to those who employee new graduates. Expect some resistance to this requirement. Why? Because for years many employees have become accustomed to accumulating free points for travel and other things based on their company travel. By requiring the use of a corporate card, many will feel they have had a benefit taken away from them. The insistence on the corporate card gives the company some cashflow advantages that can be readily understood when the reimbursing techniques are discussed.

**Payments for expenses made on corporate cards.** These payments should be made directly to the credit card company. This will give the company use of the money until the payment date. Some companies have found that changes such as this pay for a new electronic T&E system.

**Payments to employees.** These payments should be made electronically to the employee's checking account either with the normal paycheck or as a separate transaction. The employee can be notified by e-mail. For those employees who do not wish to use an electronic form of reimbursement, the payment should be included with the normal paycheck. Some companies insist on electronic reimbursement, but others are reluctant to take such a hard-line approach.

**Reimbursement by check.** If an employee cannot take the reimbursement electronically, the check should be mailed to the employee's home. No exceptions should be made to this policy as it is extremely time consuming and inefficient to have employees coming to the accounts payable department to pick up their checks.

**Reports.** If electronic reporting is used, take advantage of the data capabilities and prepare some management reports looking at where the money is being spent. Some companies have used such reports to see where they are spending the largest amounts of money for hotels and airlines. By aggregating use, they have then been able to negotiate lower corporate rates. The experts that do this recommend focusing on hotel bills and airline charges as these represent the largest amounts of money. However, many focus on car rentals, which tend not to be as much. Car rentals can be addressed after the bigger ones.

## 15.3 HOW MUCH CHECKING IS ENOUGH?

Of all the practices recommended above, the one that draws the most controversy is the suggestion to only spot-check. Many are aghast at the thought. In IOMA's benchmarking survey, respondents were asked about the policy at their companies regarding T&E report checking. Half the replies indicated that in-depth checking was the norm in their organizations, while one-third report moderate checking. Only 16% spot-check the reports. However, the concept of spot-checking has been gaining acceptance in certain circles over the last few years. The debate over what method is the most effective continues to rage and will probably do so for years to come.

The prospect of not checking every dollar on an employee's T&E report makes some managers cringe. They fear that if it becomes known that reports are not reviewed in detail, employees will take advantage. These individuals also believe that a certain percentage of employees are dishonest and will include expenses they should not. Stepping back and looking at the big picture often helps to put this issue in perspective. The following questions will help in planning a policy that will work effectively in any organization.

How much time is spent checking T&Es, and what does this cost the company?

In any given year, what is the total dollar value of unauthorized items entered on expense reports?

What is the additional amount of unauthorized entries that will likely be entered on T&Es if employees learn that the company is not doing a thorough review?

The truth of the matter: there is a limit as to how much anyone can enter inappropriately on a T&E. A figure such as $1,200 worth of travel expenses could be increased by $100 or $200 without raising too much suspicion, but that amount could not be inflated to $12,000 without causing a stir. The exposure in this area is somewhat limited. Those concerned about theft or fraud could check every report over a given amount, say $2,500. There are ways to design a spot-check program to address whatever safety issues are raised. Additionally, it has to be widely known that anyone caught cheating on an expense report will be dealt with severely.

### (a) The Compromise

There is a halfway position between in-depth checking and spot-checking. A moderate amount of checking will give the anxious some level of comfort. Firms that take this road often devise plans that will allay some of management's concerns. Many companies take this approach as a first step when trying to move toward a spot-check approach. After moderate checking has been in use for some period of time, often as long as a year or two, the amount of checking is gradually reduced.

Another approach some companies use is to let employees know that the amount of checking will be minimal and repercussions for fudging will be severe. However, not all executives are willing to take such a harsh approach.

### (b) The Norm

The level of T&E checking has a lot to do with corporate culture. Company size does not seem to have much of an impact on the amount of T&E review required, with one exception. A full 28% of large companies (those with more than 5,000 employees) permit spot-checking; a much higher rate than companies with fewer employees. While moderate checking for large companies seems to be in use in line with companies of all sizes, in-depth checking is significantly lower. To see the statistics by size of company, see Exhibit 15.1.

Looking at the statistics on an industry-wide basis, there are no startling trends readily apparent. The education industry uses spot-checking sparsely, while those in utilities and transportation use it more than any other industry. For full details of your industry's usage, see Exhibit 15.2.

***Exhibit 15.1*** **T&E Checking by Size of Company**

| *Number of Employees* | *Spot-Checking* | *Moderate Checking* | *In-depth Checking* |
|---|---|---|---|
| up to 99 | 11.8% | 35.3% | 52.9% |
| 100—249 | 13.2 | 33.0 | 53.8 |
| 250—499 | 12.2 | 41.5 | 46.3 |
| 500—999 | 17.9 | 29.8 | 52.4 |
| 1,000—4,999 | 12.9 | 31.6 | 55.5 |
| over 5,000 | 28.6 | 34.5 | 36.9 |

(Source: IOMA's 1997 Benchmarking Survey)

***Exhibit* 15.2 Amount of T&E Checking by Industry**

| | *Spot-Checking* | *Moderate Checking* | *In-depth Checking* |
|---|---|---|---|
| Manufacturing | 16.4% | 38.4% | 45.2% |
| Finance | 13.0 | 27.8 | 59.3 |
| Utilities and transportation | 28.9 | 35.6 | 35.6 |
| Private practice | 12.5 | 22.9 | 64.6 |
| Nonprofit | 14.8 | 25.9 | 59.3 |
| Wholesale/retail and distribution | 15.1 | 34.0 | 50.9 |
| Health care | 15.4 | 32.7 | 51.9 |
| Education | 4.2 | 45.8 | 50.0 |
| Communications | 20.7 | 37.9 | 41.4 |
| Construction | 13.3 | 26.7 | 60.0 |
| Other | 10.7 | 28.6 | 60.7 |

(Source: IOMA's 1997 Benchmarking Survey)

### (c) What If Management Resists

If there is resistance to the proposal to spot-check, review the work for the last six months and calculate how many T&Es were bounced back. How many charges were actually not paid? Compare this with the cost of auditing all the reports. If these figures are not accessible, start a log and keep track of this information for the next few months. Then the figures will be available to back such a recommendation—should the numbers warrant it.

### (d) Recommending Spot Checking

While spot-checking is clearly the easiest approach for those in the accounts payable department, it is not necessarily appropriate at every company. Depending on the corporate culture, management may or may not view it favorably. Before suggesting it, gauge the opposition carefully. This issue may not be worth alienating management over. However, if management asks for cost-cutting or productivity-increasing suggestions, this one is ideal. And don't forget that the amount of T&E checking can change over a period of time.

## 15.4 T&E MANUAL

Some companies do not have formal travel and entertainment policies, while others have policies that have not been updated in years and are largely ignored. For starters, companies need to have formal written policies that are freely communicated to every employee affected. This includes those who travel and those who enforce the travel policy, that is the accounts payable staff. Adrienne Glasgow, The American Red Cross in Greater New York's CFO, shared the following insights regarding the setting up of a workable T&E manual. Basically the manual should:

Be direct. Make no assumptions as these only lead to problems down the road. These translate into "loopholes" that only lead to trouble.

Detail everything—even the obvious.

Have an index and examples. In this case, a picture is truly worth 1,000 words.

Keep in a three-ring binder for easy replacement of pages.

Do not become attached to the book resisting future changes to your masterpiece. Good policies change all the time to take advantage of the latest technology and to incorporate innovative practices that may not have been possible when the manual was first written.

### (a) Written Policy

The actual written policy should be well thought out and documented. To be most effective it should:

Detail each type and kind of activity.

Clearly set limits. Don't leave anything to employees' imagination or discretion.

Keep the corporate culture in mind when writing the policy.

Don't be petty. Keep in mind the best practices utilized in the industry. These can generally be obtained from industry associations.

Clearly state what is needed and/or expected.

Keep it simple. Use short simple sentences. This is not a work that is going to be submitted for a literary prize but rather one that will be used by employees at all levels. Make it easily understandable by all.

Include all forms to be used and review those documents to make sure they conform to the policy as written.

### (b) Making Sure the Manual Is Correct

Everyone needs an editor and this includes those writing T&E manuals. In this case, it is not only to ensure grammatical accuracy, but also to ensure that the manual is correct from all sides. This can be done by:

Having others read the first draft.

Expecting changes and not being hurt by those corrections.

Making sure that all superiors are in agreement with the policies that are presented in the manual.

Having someone from accounting review the manual to ensure accuracy on that front.

The most successful manuals are fluid and constantly changing. Those who understand this will not be offended when the manual is changed. Additionally, it is important that whenever there is a policy change, the change be included in the manual and updates sent to all affected parties. This is a good way to notify all of the new changes and hopefully obtain compliance with these new procedures.

## 15.5 POLICY AND PROCEDURES CHANGES

As companies progress and reengineer their processes, travel and entertainment policies and procedures often come up for review and improvement. Listed below are some techniques that have worked at companies of differing sizes. They include:

Communicate the company travel and reimbursement policy to all affected employees. This includes not only those who travel, but their support staff as well. It is imperative that the secretary responsible for doing the boss's T&E report knows your guidelines. When employees know what the policies are, they are more likely to abide by them, making accounts payables' job easier.

Coordinate T&E reimbursement to coincide with the pay periods. This makes cash-flow forecasting a tad easier.

Use the company e-mail system to communicate with other departments. It can be used to notify employees that checks are ready for pick-up, that deposits have been made to their accounts, or for a query.

Limit the number of expense reports that can be submitted by one employee. A number of accounts payable professionals report success in suggesting that only one report be accepted per month per employee. Depending on the other T&E policies, this period can even be longer.

Rather than accept expense reports that are bound by arbitrary time frames, usually monthly, ask employees to submit reports that contain entire trips. It makes it easier to audit and it helps with management reporting.

Consider an electronic T&E reporting system. This can be as simple as templates designed in one of the spreadsheet applications and then e-mailed for approvals and submission.

Require receipts only on those expenses that exceed $75, the IRS limit. This will eliminate much of the paperwork associated with T&Es—even if none of the other recommendations are followed.

Enter vouchers into the accounting system in batches that are then used as control groups. Common groups can be approved and posted. This has saved a number of accounts payable departments a good deal of time.

Consolidate all decentralized travel systems. The side benefit of such a system is that it will allow management to negotiate new and lower cost travel agreements with the one or two selected travel agencies.

## 15.6 WHAT ABOUT ELECTRONIC RECEIPTS?

The Internal Revenue Service recently indicated that the agency will accept electronic data as documentation for corporate T&E expenses charged to corporate cards that meet given security requirements. As this goes to press, the details are being worked out.

### (a) Does This Mean No More Saving Receipts?

Data from corporate card vendors who exercise reasonable controls to ensure integrity, accuracy, and reliability of the data, and to protect it from additions, alterations, or deletions will probably be considered acceptable alternatives to receipts.

Whether companies will require their employees to provide receipts depends on two things:

The company's policy—many will probably still insist that employees submit receipts.

The capabilities of their credit card issuer—it will have to meet the strict guidelines specified by the IRS in order for you to discard receipts.

### (b) Effect on Accounts Payable

The most immediate effect on accounts payable will be the possible elimination of paper and a possible reduction in clerical work. Possible because not every company will decide to use the new guidelines. Even those that decide not to save receipts may still insist that employees turn them in. The first issue will be a determination of company policy.

Every company will need to address this issue almost immediately. Even if the decision is not to change anything, it is necessary to let traveling employees know. This issue will get a certain amount of attention, and if employees are not informed of their company's policy, some will inevitably come to the wrong conclusion. Information can be disseminated to all employees in a timely fashion.

The other big change that is likely to affect accounts payable is the increased usage of automated T&E systems. With the reduced paper requirements, certain companies will find automated systems more attractive. Expect to see automated T&E systems used in a growing number of companies—lightening the load ever so slightly for accounts payable professionals.

Because so little press has been given to this issue, there is an opportunity to educate the more senior members in their departments who, in many cases, will be the ones ultimately deciding company policy. This is an opportunity to present them with the information and facts that will bolster the case.

## 15.7 FASTER EMPLOYEE REIMBURSEMENTS

Those in accounts payable are often plagued by requests from employees for faster reimbursement of travel and entertainment expenses. There are some ways to accomplish that goal:

> Pay employee travel expenses within 10 days of receipt of the report. To make such a policy work it may be necessary to add a disclaimer that any incomplete or improperly prepared expense reports will result in payment delay.

If checks are used they should be mailed to the employee's home.

Use Electronic Funds Transfers for employee reimbursement.

Use ACH transfers. Send all a notification of their deposit—ideally by e-mail.

In many companies, the whole area of travel and entertainment is ripe for reengineering. Changes can be made that not only make the accounts payable department more efficient, but save the company money as well.

# 16

# Electronic Travel and Entertainment Handling

Electronic T&E filing is one of the techniques recommended by most experts when looking to reengineer the process. Most companies that go that route, do so either by developing their own proprietary software or by purchasing a third-party system. The former tends to be less expensive but also tends to require more help from the IT department. Depending on the level of sophistication desired in the system, some have even had success developing a system from a simple spreadsheet program. But why go the electronic route?

## 16.1 ADVANTAGES

There are many things that can be done electronically that simply can't be done using a manual system. Some of the benefits include:

> Reports to management help enforce compliance with the company's T&E policies. Once again, this removes the stigma of being the bad guy who won't pay for unauthorized expenses from the accounts payable staff.
>
> Corporate charge cards are paid exactly when they are due. While most accounts payable managers are adept at this, it's one less headache, especially when these bills are large.

The T&E audit process is simpler and more efficient.

The efficient settlement leads to greater employee satisfaction.

Because of the timely reimbursements that are possible with such a system, some companies have eliminated advances for those who travel.

These systems allow a more efficient use of the accounts payable department's resources, moving the staff away from clerical tasks and toward more productive work.

## 16.2 HOMEGROWN SYSTEMS

Travel and expense reports can be a royal pain for payables managers at both large and small companies. They are often messy and submitted at the last minute. Then there are the employees who harass A/P for their reimbursement checks long before it is feasible to turn the report around. The handling and G/L coding of these items can eat up quite a bit of time as well. Most payables professionals will grasp at anything that makes the T&E matters easier to handle. To this end, many companies, and not just large ones, are beginning to handle their T&Es electronically. The following two case studies show how both a large company and a mid-size one were able to develop workable T&E systems.

### (a) Case Study 1

The company in this case went from doing employee travel and expense reports manually on a Xeroxed form to a sophisticated electronic system. Although this company was relatively small, with only 150 employees, half submitted T&E reports on a regular basis.

The company first went from the manual form to a Lotus spreadsheet before progressing to the electronic form on its mainframe. This is a good step for those just getting started and depending on the number of travelers, may work just fine for a smaller company. The spreadsheet worked well, but each time it was enhanced, the form would have to be e-mailed to all the end users. Inevitably, this led to questions and phone calls for help.

**(i) Making the Change.** Since the people using the system were comfortable with the Lotus system, it could have been difficult to get them to switch over to a new system. However, with the important key ingredient to any new venture—management support, it was not. If employees wished to be reimbursed for their travel, the reports had to be submitted on the new forms. While there may have been some behind-the-scenes grumbling, the only complaint received was that traveling employees cannot do their expense reports while on a plane. They have to wait until they check into their hotel room and can get a phone hook-up.

**(ii) How It Works.** With the new system, employees fill out their reports online and then print out the report. Receipts are attached as in the past, and a supervisor's signature is obtained. This is important as the supervisor at this company is held responsible for the report. It is then sent to A/P where it is audited. Should small changes be required, it is no longer necessary to get the submitting employee involved. The professional reviewing the report simply pulls the report up on the computer and makes the change. If numerous or large changes are required, the report is bounced back to the submitting employee.

Once the report is verified, it is released for payment automatically. All reports received by noon on Friday are included in the following Wednesday's weekly check run. There are no exceptions to this rule. Since employees pay their own AMEX bills and cash advances are kept to a minimum, this system encourages everyone involved to get their reports done on time.

Employees are reimbursed either through the ACH with an EDI payment, just like direct deposit, or with a check. The method of payment is determined in advance.

The system is user friendly and includes G/L codes so that it isn't necessary for A/P to code reports once submitted. This is a big timesaver.

### (b) Case Study 2

The second case involves a Fortune 500-type company where "the system sold itself." The improved turnaround time of reports submitted electronically helped tremendously in getting users to accept the new system. Those submitting electronically were able to reduce their turnaround time to 24 hours from two weeks. Upper management buy-in was key at this company as well.

**(i) The Process.** At this company no special login is required from those completing their electronic T&Es. Users access it from their local e-mail or system/platform. The company uses many different systems but the electronic T&Es can be accessed on anything from a PC to a dumb terminal. The system also contains online management expense guidelines, making usage easy even for computer novices.

The company has found that due to the quick turnaround of the system, use of cash advances has been reduced as well. If the report is entered by 2:00 P.M., the employee can receive an ACH deposit the next day. If they require a check, they are e-mailed when it is ready.

**(ii) How It Works.** The employee enters an electronic request into the system. The form is signed with a PIN (Personal Identification Number) and then forwarded to the appropriate manager for authorization. For tracking purposes, the system assigns this report a unique serial number.

The manager is able to view the report online and authorize it with his or her PIN. At this point, the request is forwarded to A/P and an automatic notification is sent to the employee at the same time. Employees not notified can follow up with slow supervisors.

But what about the receipts? Upon receiving notice that the report has been approved, the employee faxes copies of the receipts to A/P, making sure to reference the unique serial number assigned earlier. The receipts are then fed into an imaging system by the A/P staff. When A/P has verified that clean copies have been received, reimbursement is authorized. In no case will the report be processed without the receipt of the faxed documents. The employee is required to hold on to the original copies of the receipts for 90 days. After that time they can be destroyed.

**(iii) Success Factors.** Both conversions discussed above were successful because they had two key ingredients necessary for any change:

1. Each was backed by a management which agreed with the assessment that it was appropriate.
2. They were able to get the necessary MIS resources to develop the new system.

Accounts payable professionals, in companies of any size, who are able to obtain similar commitments will be able to emulate their successes.

## 16.3 THIRD PARTY ELECTRONIC SOFTWARE

Accounts payable professionals are always on the lookout for better ways to handle the cumbersome task of travel and entertainment expenditures. The best hope so far for taming the unwieldy T&E beast is automation, in the form of new software. While by no means complete, those discussed below are a sampling of what is available today.

QuickXpense from Portable Software;

GeMS (General Expense Management System); and

Gelco products.

### (a) QuickXpense

QuickXpense is a simple-to-use software tool designed for travelers looking for a quick and easy way to fill out T&E reports.

Xpense Management Solution (XMS) is the successor to QuickXpense. It is Portable Software's new flagship product that automates the entire T/E expense management with client/server capabilities, offering everything from expense-report processing to data analysis. For information on QuickXpense and Xpense Management Solution, call Portable Software, (800) 478-7411, or visit their Web site: http://www.xpense.com.

### (b) General Expense Management System

Another application getting plenty of attention in A/P departments around the nation is the General Expense Management System (GeMS). It's an Internet-based system with a wide array of intranet features. Visit GeMS at http://www.go-gems.com. For more information, call (800) 337-6489.

### (c) Gelco Products

This company offers a variety of services, including:

**Traveletter Service.** This original check-based product is used to authorize self-reimbursement. A customized expense report is linked to a check to create what Gelco calls a "Combo" form. By combining the two together, the company ensures that the reimbursement doesn't occur before all documentation is submitted.

**Traveletter Direct.** With a single phone call, Gelco captures all the relevant information needed to automate your expense reporting process. Traveletter Direct is available 24 hours a day, 365 days a year. Reimbursement is made to the employee through direct deposit and corporate charge payments are made when they are due. For accounting, auditing, and budget purposes, Gelco provides summaries of all transactions.

**TLink.** TLink is Gelco's PC-based expense report management service. Employees with access to a PC can enter their information into their computer offline at their convenience. TLink compiles the information into an expense report that meets the company's guidelines. Corporate charge payments are made electronically when they are due.

**Other Recent Features Available.** Those who use Gelco's Traveletter Direct expense report management service will now be able to use Microsoft Excel or Lotus 1-2-3 for data entry purposes. Gelco has also introduced a service that allows online interactive clients to make changes to their master file data in a real time environment. Those looking for additional information about these services or who would like an analysis of their expense report management system can call Gelco at (800) 444-6588. Its Internet site is located at http://www.gelconet.com.

The products discussed here are just a few of those currently available. Those interested in using one of them should ask for recomendations from the vendors. Also discuss with industry peers the products currently being used and any real or perceived flaws. And as with any other new computer software purchases, make sure they are Year 2000 compliant.

Those accounts payable professionals looking to make the T&E process run a little smoother will find that technology is the answer. And, as more executives become comfortable with e-mail, some of the systems that at one time seemed to be unthinkable, will now be viewed as a reasonable solution to a cumbersome problem.

# 17

# VAT Refunds

U.S. travelers to other countries, principally Europe and Canada, are eligible to reclaim certain taxes paid while traveling abroad. These taxes are generally paid as part of various bills, such as hotel, conference charges, and so on. While these individuals are entitled to reclaim these amounts, doing so is not so simple. It generally falls upon the shoulders of the accounts payable manager who is responsible for T&E reimbursements to make sure the company gets its money back. Many companies are not even aware that they are entitled to get this money back and others have no idea how to go about doing so.

What is reclaimable varies by country and the rules for doing so are not consistent. Needless to say, the instructions are not all that clear either. Anyone who has ever tried to collect value-added tax (VAT) payments made while traveling overseas knows that it can be a frustrating, paper-intensive, and annoying process. Many get so disgusted, they give up and never claim the money they are entitled to—which might be what the VAT authorities have in mind when they make the process so difficult.

## 17.1 WHAT IS VAT?

VAT is a consumer-oriented tax imposed on goods and services sold. Meridian, a company operating a VAT reclaim service, explains that a taxable entity incurring VAT for business purposes may be entitled to a VAT refund in many European countries and Canada. To obtain a refund, an original invoice together with an application form and other supporting documentation must be submitted to the VAT authorities in the country where the expenditure was incurred.

In theory, this sounds simple enough, but it is not. Different countries have different rates. The VAT is recoverable on different items in different countries. For example, the VAT on hotel rooms is recoverable in the United Kingdom, but not in Belgium.

## 17.2 ASSISTANCE AVAILABLE

There are a few companies capable of reclaiming their VAT payments. However, these entities are few and far between. Most companies need help and this help can come in one of two forms. There are companies, generally referred to as VAT reclaim companies, that will handle the process for you. There is also a company that sells reasonably priced software to companies that wish to do it for themselves. Which approach is taken will depend on the resources available and the corporate culture.

### (a) VAT Reclaim Companies

Because of the difficulties involved with obtaining VAT refunds, a number of companies have made a business of handling these claims for other firms. The fees these companies earn are typically a percentage of the amount recovered. It can be a flat 10%, in the case of The VAT Clearing House, or a sliding scale depending on what has been collected, as with Meridian. Generally, there is no fee if the company does not recover the VAT, but it is important to discuss this before entering into a contract. There may be a minimum fee: in one instance, it is £ 75 per claim. Exhibit 17.1 lists three companies offering these services, along with contact information.

*Exhibit 17.1* **Companies Offering VAT Services**

| *The VAT Clearing House* | *Meridian* | *FEXCO* |
|---|---|---|
| Old Lion Court<br>High Street<br>Marlborough<br>Wiltshire SN8 1HQ<br>England<br>Contact: Freddy Vos, Gen. Mgr.<br>Tel: 011 44 1672 541 004<br>Fax: 011 44 1672 541 008<br>e-mail: freddy.vos@thevat-clearinghouse.com | Atlanta, GA: 404-880-4114<br>Chicago, IL: 847-291-6935<br>Houston, TX: 713-975-9887<br>Los Angeles, CA: 909-981-4775<br>New York, NY: 212-554-6600<br>San Jose, CA: 408-453-1300<br>Toronto, Ontario: 905-771-6044 | The Manager<br>FEXCO Tax Reclaim<br>FEXCO Centre<br>Iveragh Road<br>Killorglin<br>Kerry KHQ 100<br>Ireland<br>Tel: 800-865-4561<br>e-mail: ftr@iol.ie-house.com |

(Source: IOMA)

## (b) Software

Not all accounts payable managers are comfortable turning over their claims for VAT refunds to a third party. Some don't like releasing sensitive financial information to an outside firm; others don't like paying commission fees that average 20% to 40%. For those professionals, a resource now exists that makes this task much easier.

Auto VAT, from Corporate VAT Management, is fully automated VAT refund software that helps accounts payable managers manage the process of reclaiming VAT paid on travel expenses in Europe. It simplifies filing for reclaims by computerizing the task and filling in the forms in the required languages.

## (c) What Does It Cost?

The software is not expensive. It costs $995 for a company planning to use it for its own account only. Service providers are charged $9,950, with the caveat that the system can be used to process an unlimited number of client refunds.

## (d) Canadian GST

Like the Europeans, Canadians have their own tax—a goods and services tax (GST) that can be recaptured on accommodation expenses if the right forms are filed. Corporate VAT Management has a service for this (GST Simple Refund Services), as well. It provides postage-paid envelopes in which the receipts are put and mailed to Corporate VAT Management, who process the claim for 15% of the refund, with a minimum fee of $5.

For additional information, contact Mark A. Kotzer, director of sales and marketing, at (206) 292-0300 or markkotzer@corporatevat.com. Point your browser to http://www.corporatevat.com to visit the company's Web site.

## 17.3 TIME LIMITATIONS

VAT refund claims must be processed in a timely manner. Claims for the fiscal year ending June 30, 1998, must be filed by December 31, 1998. This is the date that the claims must reach the VAT authorities, not the reclaim service. Accounts payable managers who wish to take advantage of this service will need to get their companies' information for this time period to one of these service providers quickly in order to have the claim processed.

Those who are not certain if their company is entitled to such refunds, consider whether any of the company's executives travel to Europe. If they do, take a quick look at the applicable expense reports and compare them to Exhibit 17.2, which shows the allowable percentages for each country. There may be gold hidden in the company's files.

If time runs out, all is not lost. While it will not be possible to obtain refunds for prior periods, prepare for future claims. It should be noted that it is not necessary to hire a VAT reclaim service to do this work: It can be done in-house. However, most accounts payable professionals find it easier and more productive to let those who have the expertise handle it for them.

## 17.4 FOCUS ON VAT-FRIENDLY COUNTRIES

Companies who wish to handle some of the work themselves should focus on the Big Four; the countries providing the biggest refunds with the least amount of headaches: Germany, the Nether-

*Exhibit 17.2* **T&E VAT Chart[a]**

| *Country* | *Hotel* | *Meals* | *Car Rental[b]* | *Petrol* | *Transport[c]* | *Prof. Fees* | *Trade Shows* | *Leased Lines* |
|---|---|---|---|---|---|---|---|---|
| Austria | 10 | 10 | NO | NO | 10 | 20 | 20 | 20 |
| Belgium | NO | NO | 21[e] | 21[e] | 6 | 21 | 21 | 21 |
| Canada | 7[h] | NO | NO | NO | NO | na | na | na |
| Denmark | 25[f] | 25[f,g] | NO | NO | NO | 25 | 25 | 25 |
| Finland | 6 | NO | 22 | 22 | 6 | 22 | 22 | 22 |
| France | na | na | na | na | na | 20.6 | 20.6 | 20.6 |
| Germany | 15 | 15[g] | 15 | NO | 15 or 7 | 15 | 15 | 15 |
| Iceland | 14 | NO | 24.5 | 24.5 | 24.5 | 24.5 | 24.5 | 24.5 |
| Ireland | na | na | na | na | na | 21 | 21 | 21 |
| Liechtenstein | 3[d] | 6.5[d,e] | 6.5[d] | 6.5[d] | NO | 6.5 | 6.5 | 6.5 |
| Netherlands | 6 | NO | 17.5 | 17.5 | 6 | 17.5 | 17.5 | 17.5 |
| Norway | na | na | na | na | na | 23 | 23 | 23 |
| Sweden | 12 | 25 | 25[e] | 25[e] | 12 | 25 | 25 | 25 |
| Switzerland | 3[d] | 6.5[d,e] | 6.5[d] | 6.5[d] | NO | 6.5 | 6.5 | 6.5 |
| UK | 17.5 | 17.5 | 17.5 | 17.5 | 17.5 | 17.5 | 17.5 | 17.5 |

[a]Table correct as of July 1997.
[b]Car rental agreements are not eligible for reclaim. Must submit final invoice.
[c]Receipts over US $50.
[d]Proof of payment required for every invoice.
[e]1/2 of VAT is eligible for reclaim.
[f]1/4 of VAT is eligible for reclaim.
[g]Entertainment eligible with details of who was entertained and business purpose. German receipts must be over 300DEM.
[h]PST is recoverable in Quebec (6.5%) and Manitoba (7%).
(Source: Meridian VAT Reclaim Inc. N.A.)

lands, Sweden, and the United Kingdom. Corporate VAT Management suggests either ignoring or allowing a third party to handle the difficult countries, such as France, which requires an in-country agent, or Italy, where it traditionally has taken as long as five years to see any money.

## 17.5 FOCUS ON VAT-VALUABLE EXPENSES

The biggest return for most companies will be in the refunds garnered by hotel bill, car rental, conference attendance, and trade show participation. Focusing on these expenses in the four countries discussed before will enable most accounts payable managers to generate the largest refunds. Corporate VAT Management estimates that 90% of all travel-related refunds come from these categories. Non–travel-related expenses, such as telecommunication charges and legal and other professional fees, are also often eligible for refunds.

## 17.6 CONCLUSION

The process of reclaiming VAT is ugly and cumbersome, especially for those unaccustomed to such transactions. Those with a limited number of transactions will fare well by letting a third party service provider handle the issue for them. Also, those with difficult or unusual situations will do well to work with third party service providers, who are often willing to push the envelope and have contacts that most U.S. accounting professionals do not.

# Part Five

# High Tech Applications

Gone from accounts payable offices across the nation are the green shades, big ledger books, and worn pencils. Technology is invading accounts payable departments in ways never imagined just a few short years ago. While EDI still faces an uphill battle in many organizations, it is gradually gaining a foothold. Some experts expect EDI to receive a big boost as a side benefit from e-mail, which is invading corporate America at a phenomenal speed. Similarly, as corporate executives become comfortable with the Internet and imaging, the reluctance to EDI should further diminish. The final push will come as corporate America begins to use EDI-capable accounting software and it becomes easier to implement.

The chapters in this part take a look at some of these new high tech applications that are becoming more commonplace in accounts payable departments.

# 18

# Electronic Data Interchange

Mention Electronic Data Interchange (EDI) and watch eyes begin to glaze over and heads begin to nod. So right up front, here's an admission: This is not the most interesting topic in this book; however, it may be one of the most important! It involves the electronic transmission of data usually between a buyer and a seller. While this chapter will provide a basic understanding of EDI, it is by no means an exhaustive study of the topic.

## 18.1 WHAT IS EDI?

The National Automated Clearing House Association (NACHA) defines Financial EDI (FEDI) as the electronic movement of payments and payment-related information through the banking system in a standard format between two parties. EDI is the application-to-application exchange of business information in a standard format.

## 18.2 TECHNICAL BASICS: INTRODUCTION

There are several types of transactions that can be done using EDI. Each has its own set of instructions known in the EDI world as transaction sets. Each transaction set is broken into three areas:

1. The header, which contains data that pertain to the whole transaction.
2. The detail, which contains information that is applicable to one line item.
3. The summary, which is a small piece containing summary and control details.

As might be expected, the detail section can have many lines, each containing relevant information. The information within each area is called a segment and certain segments may be used in more than one area. All transaction sets begin with a header, called a transaction set header, and end with a trailer known as a transaction set trailer.

In order that everyone understands what everyone else is saying when talking about EDI, standards were developed. The most commonly accepted are those conforming to the American National Standards Institute (ANSI). ANSI uses the term X12 to denote standards that cross industry, function, and company lines. It is not uncommon to hear discussions about ANSI X12 standards.

One of the most common transmission is that of the purchase order from the buyer to the seller. In EDI, this is referred to as an 850 transaction set. The other two transaction sets that accounts payable professionals are apt to run into are the 810s, which represent invoices and 820s, which involve payment orders/remittance advices.

While many companies are happy to transmit information electronically, many will dig in when it comes to sending money in that manner. Corporate America is still far too attached to float and stretching payments to use Financial EDI to any great extent.

While large companies may have big technology staffs to help get EDI programs up and running, many mid-size (and in fact, a few larger) companies do not. These companies may not have the technical resources to devote to an EDI project or may simply not have enough transactions to justify hiring an individual qualified to handle EDI. Seeing a market need, a number of companies have jumped in to provide such an intermediary service for those who need it. These services were initially known as VANs, value-added networks. Not to be undone in their own backyard, the banks quickly entered the fray offering intermediary services of their own. When a bank offers the service it is known as a VAB. These third-party service providers will expedite your EDI transactions and many offer additional related services.

Many such service providers advertise and are listed in the magazine, *EC World*. Call the publication at (305) 925-5900 or access its web site at www.ecworld.com.

## 18.3 WHY EDI?

Competitive pressures have forced many accounts payable managers to take a hard look at not only their costs, but also their entire accounts payable process and how it relates to other systems in the company. In this challenging environment, innovative payable professionals often become corporate leaders in recommending and educating their companies about EDI.

Companies are turning to EDI for a variety of reasons, with cost reduction heading the list. The current reengineering craze, along with the downsizing that many have undergone in the last few years, is forcing many managers to turn to EDI as a way of handling increased workloads with smaller staffs. And to their amazement, they have found themselves mostly pleased with the results. The inefficiencies of a paper-based system combined with the fact that EDI allows for more timely invoicing is helping to overcome resistance to the concept.

Perhaps the biggest reason for turning to EDI in the first place is that trading partners demand it. And once they've tried it, many companies find they like it and expand their use of it. FEDI also helps reduce check fraud.

## (a) Opportunities for Saving

The typical manual accounts payable system is a labor-intensive process with many chances for error. One place where substantial savings can be achieved is by altering the three-way matching process that's typical in many companies. In this method, before an invoice is paid, it is usually matched against a purchase order and the receiving documents from the material management system. Consider this: If the purchase order is matched against the receiving documents, why is an invoice necessary? What if matching the purchase order against the receiving documents were sufficient to pay a bill?

## (b) Is the Purchase Order Adequate?

In order for this two-way matching to work, cooperation from the purchasing people and the materials management people will be needed. For starters, determine whether the current purchase order system is adequate. Does it generate electronic copies? If it doesn't, using EDI will be problematic.

Assuming that the electronic copy is available, is it available to the accounts payable department in an electronic format? Find out whether materials management's output is available in electronic form and available in this form to the accounts payable department. And finally, does the accounts payable department have the ability to match the purchase orders with the output from the materials management department electronically?

In all likelihood, if EDI isn't already being used, one or more of the areas described above will be lacking, and programmers will be needed in order to complete the necessary matching. Once this is accomplished, electronically match and pay suppliers through the ACH—or by check if financial EDI is not being used. For items without purchase orders, such as employee travel reimbursements, have an electronic invoice generated and fed through the accounts payable system.

### (c) External Requirements

Once the internal requirements are in place, work with external participants, that is, the suppliers you wish to pay electronically. The first step is to build a secured vendor file. This file should contain the vendor's name, its bank's name, ABA, and routing number, and the supplier's checking account number. Some suppliers will resist handing over account numbers, and they will have to be paid by check. The vendor file will also need to contain some indication by item as to the method of payment—ACH, wire, or check.

Also put in this file the invoice number, purchase order number, and adjustment reason data and codification, information typically on the payment stub.

Now you're ready for the second step—selecting suppliers for your EDI program. Start with those who are already EDI-capable. Try to sign up a few that will be "easy wins" so that your organization will have some early successes. Then when the company is a bit more experienced with EDI, it can tackle those vendors that are resistant.

## 18.4 GETTING STARTED

It is imperative that a sponsor or "champion" of the EDI concept be identified within the company. This needs to be a fairly high-level person who has the clout to see that the project comes to fruition. The sponsor needs to be educated and convinced of the long-term importance of EDI to the company. Without this support, it is likely that the EDI project will be relegated to the back burner when something that others view as more pressing appears. This seemingly simple requirement can mean the difference between the success and failure of a project.

Don't try to convert a large portion of your payments to EDI right away. Start slowly, waiting until the company has built up some confidence and expertise with what it's doing before expanding. That way, if something goes wrong, and when doesn't something go wrong, fixing it will be relatively easily. Also, if an error entails contacting outside parties, it will only have to be done with a few companies.

Once you become involved with EDI, it is very easy to get caught up in the technical aspects of the process. But remember, the reason for using EDI is for business purposes. Don't get waylaid by technical questions. At all times, maintain this business focus.

Ideally, start the program with someone who has some EDI experience. Try not to start with another novice. By starting with a company with experience, the company will dodge the bullet when it comes to making the obvious mistakes. That's not to say that mistakes won't be made—just that the easily avoidable ones will be missed.

## 18.5 BUSINESS INFRASTRUCTURE REQUIREMENTS

Once the decision has been made to go ahead, it will be necessary to get certain infrastructure changes in place in the accounts payable department. It will be necessary for the manager of the accounts payable department to see that the rest of the department recognizes the importance of their role in the transformation. Accounts payable plays a crucial part in the implementation and success of any financial EDI program at any company. Unfortunately they are often not brought in until the last minute. Once the team realizes this and "steps up to the plate," half the EDI battle will have been won.

Having accepted their role in this effort, it will be necessary to provide the staff with adequate training about EDI. This will help ensure the success of the program. Without adequate training, the program will flounder, increasing its odds of failure.

Next, it is usually advisable to appoint one person as the "EDI coordinator." Give this person the overall responsibility, not only for the program, but to become the departmental expert. By having one individual as the focal point for the process, it is less likely that it will become nobody's baby.

Inevitably, the introduction of financial EDI means that the existing work process will have to be redesigned to accommodate the new methodology. This is not necessarily bad and some take it as an opportunity to review their entire work flow process.

Typically, the accounts payable department in an EDI environment has three components: it handles vendor relations, it acts as the disbursement facilitator, and it also serves as the control point. This is not that different from the way many corporations run accounts payable without EDI. However, some (rightly or wrongly) view that final check signer as a control feature and that is gone with EDI. Tight up-front controls are essential for a successful EDI program or duplicate and erroneous payments will multiply.

## 18.6 MANAGING ACCOUNTS PAYABLE EDI

Once the company has completed all the work necessary to get itself EDI-ready, the lion's share of the ongoing work falls on accounts payable's shoulders. To have a productive ongoing program, it will be necessary to:

Train the EDI coordinator to read EDI data.

Educate others who will have to deal with a lack of paper invoices.

Use Trading Partner Agreements.

Manage the EDI vendors.

Advertise the company's EDI readiness.

Develop and maintain a plan and goals for the EDI efforts.

Perform a vendor analysis looking for those with whom a high volume of transactions is done, not necessarily high-dollar transactions.

Stay current with ANSI X12 standards.

Maintain a dialogue with trading partners.

Measure productivity.

Create a cumulative EDI transaction log.

Test, test, . . . test.

## 18.7 ACCOUNTS PAYABLE EDI OPPORTUNITIES

"But is it worth the effort?" you ask. There are many advantages, including continued business viability; automated data entry; fewer error corrections due to improved accuracy of data; increased velocity of accurate information throughout the organization; improved trading partner relationships; reduction in postage costs; decreased cost of paper supplies; fewer late payment charges; fewer lost discounts; comprehensive audit trail; and decreased product costs.

Even if these issues aren't enough to make a company think about EDI, there is another, often compelling reason to start to move in that direction. Many large companies, most notably in the auto industry, are insisting their suppliers use it if they wish to continue to do business with them. Thus, some companies that thought they would never go down the EDI trail were forced down it. And a remarkable thing often happens in these cases. These reluctant Jennies are finding out that using EDI is making their lives easier. These companies then begin to expand their own use of EDI, often demanding that their suppliers convert or else.

## 18.8 ACCOUNTS PAYABLE EDI SUCCESS FACTORS

It is easy for an EDI program to fall off the track and turn into a disaster. However, there are certain strategies that can be employed to limit the likelihood of that happening. Those wanting an EDI success story should:

Identify a champion and seek out a sponsor.

Identify and communicate to all stakeholders.

Continually educate not only themselves but all affected parties. This stuff changes constantly so it requires constant education to keep from getting left in the dust.

Join and attend EDI user groups and conferences. This will greatly help in the education department.

Maintain at all times a business focus. Communicate with the executives of the company on a business level that they will understand.

View EDI as one of many solutions to the ongoing business concerns.

Market the fact that the company is EDI-ready.

Following these guidelines will greatly improve the chances of hitting an "EDI home run."

## 18.9 SYSTEMS REQUIREMENTS

When deciding whether to implement Financial EDI (FEDI), senior management sometimes forgets that the accounts payable systems will have to be modified and, in many cases, strengthened to meet new requirements. If this is not done in the planning stages, the company may discover at the eleventh hour that the existing computer systems will not accommodate this new technology. But accounts payable managers responsible for the implementation process are aware that the systems will need to be updated. And the sooner this is recognized and investigated, the more likely it is that the FEDI program will be successful.

Those turning to Financial EDI expand the methods by which they pay their bills. They can now use a check, a wire transfer, an ACH credit, an EDI transfer and, most recently, corporate procurement cards. Thus, getting bills paid no longer means just having a check run. In order to successfully implement a Financial EDI program, managers must enhance the following aspects of their systems: modify the remit to address field, include a payment method indicator, review trade terms, produce an electronic output file, and improve the system flexibility. But before any of these items are changed, the entire accounts payable production cycle needs to be reviewed.

### (a) Production Cycle

An examination of the accounts payable production cycle will help identify areas that need to be strengthened when FEDI is implemented. Since no two companies do things exactly alike, weaknesses in this cycle will not be identical. There are a few areas of commonality, however. Companies that place much of the emphasis on checking and control after a check has been produced will need to modify their procedure. EDI payments will be completed before this stage is reached and the control and checking will not take place at all.

Controls over repetitive payments also need to be reviewed. This is especially important if the repetitive payments are to be stopped at some point—say if a loan is completely repaid. Document control and storage procedures along with retrieval processes may also need to be changed.

### (b) Remit to Address

For starters, the field for the remit to address will need to be modified to cope with a variety of formats. It will need to handle not only addresses where checks should be sent, but also bank transit and routing numbers and account number information. That's the only way that a payment will be able to reach a bank account electronically. Not all systems are set up to deal with this, and early detection of the deficiency is vital.

### (c) Payment Method Indicator

In most systems, it will be necessary to add a field to indicate the method of payment desired. That way the system will know whether to generate a wire, a check, an ACH credit, an EDI item, or even a credit card payment (still a rarity today, but in the future possibly a big player). Then, when the accounts payable system is run, it will know not only what payment method to use, but also what type of information to look for in the remit-to-address field. These first two items should be preset for payments made to the same vendor for the same type of goods. Once the system is set up correctly, it never needs to be modified except for changes relating to operations.

### (d) Review Trade Terms

The first thing to consider is what terms are actually used. While the invoice may say 2/10 net 30, is the check mailed on the tenth or eleventh day? Are the terms really 2/14 net 30? And then there's the question of what the vendor thinks the terms really are. Most companies who consider FEDI will try to renegotiate terms. Even with vendors who insist that the check be in their lockbox on the tenth day, there is the matter of when the funds become available. Giving up the float and renegotiating the terms are the two main reasons that FEDI has not been as successful as nonfinancial EDI.

The matter of terms needs to be evaluated internally and a decision made. Either renegotiate with the suppliers or adjust the terms within the system to reflect what is the reality. Thus 2/10 30 might be entered in your system as 2/14 net 30. A company that wants to take the discount but not give up the float might try adjusting their system in this way for a few smaller invoices. If the supplier doesn't complain, go full speed ahead with the larger ones.

### (e) Electronic Output File

In order to use FEDI, an electronic output file will be needed to be sent to the bank. Is the company's system set up to do this? If not, can it be modified so such a file can be produced? Many banks will take this information online from a PC or by magnetic tape. Check with the FEDI bank to determine what options are available. Once it is known what the bank can handle, it will be easier to determine how to meet its requirements.

By talking to the bank early in the process, some time and much aggravation will be saved. The bank may have other customers using the same systems as the company. These customers may be able to save the company some trouble by showing how they modified their system to meet the bank's requirements. Why reinvent the wheel?

### (f) System Flexibility

One thing is apparent: the system will need to be flexible to meet all the demands of the suppliers—especially dealing with the 800-pound gorillas. Even when paying them, they are in the driver's seat requiring their customers to do things their way. And there's one thing for certain—no two of the big suppliers will do things the same way. So in this game, once again, flexibility is key.

Paradoxical as it may seem, at many companies the accounts payable managers are not involved in the planning stages for the implementation of an FEDI program. They're typically informed at the last minute and left to deal with the problems that ensue because all the little changes needed to make the program work smoothly were overlooked.

Accounts payable managers whose companies are considering such a program need to demand to be included in the planning stages. This will ensure that none of the crucial day-to-day details will be forgotten—that is, until the program fails. Accounts payable professionals who are involved from the beginning will give their company a much better chance for success with their FEDI programs.

## 18.10 TRADING PARTNER DIRECTORY

One of the biggest complaints of many wishing to use EDI is the fact that it's difficult to determine which companies have the capability to receive EDI payments. It is often difficult for those wishing to use EDI to find trading partners who are willing and able to work with them. Likewise, those sticking their toes into the EDI waters for the first time need to start with a partner who has had some EDI success before. But how does an accounts payable manager find such companies? In recognition of this problem, the National Automated Clearing House Association's Bankers EDI Council has developed a list of Corporate Payment Key Contacts. This listing can be used to determine whether a trading partner originates or receives financial EDI, to identify the name of the contact for that trading partner, and to discover its financial capabilities. The list is broken into two categories: those companies that can receive and those that can originate. Many companies are in both categories. To obtain a copy of this list, contact NACHA at (703) 742-9190, or fax them at (703) 787-0996. The list is updated three times a year.

Companies that are EDI-capable and are not included on the list are urged to contact NACHA at the above numbers and ask for a Corporate Payment Key Contacts update form.

## 18.11 EDI STANDARDS

One of the many issues that hangs like a cloud over EDI is the existence of more than one set of standards. As those who use it are only too well aware, there are multiple settlement systems (ACH and Chips), multiple data transmission mechanisms (including VANs, VABs, and the Internet), and multiple data format standards (most notably, ANSI X12 and EDIFACT). So what's a company to do? Which standard should it choose? The answer is not as complicated as it might appear at first glance. Choose standards based on what your trading partners are using, advise most experts. It is likely that ANSI will remain the U.S. standard. Thus, if you are dealing domestically only, the choice is simple: ANSI. However, if your company is global, then some decisions will have to be made in this regard.

## 18.12 EFFECT ON SUPPLIER PARTNERSHIPS

Accounts payable professionals who are looking for ways to improve their relationship with purchasing can do so by enhancing supplier relationships—something that is usually out of the realm of most accounts payable managers. The most successful EDI programs are those that identify the benefits for both sides. By pointing out these benefits and making the EDI program as flexible as possible, the accounts payable manager can accomplish this. Flexibility is not an attribute normally associated with EDI programs.

## 18.13 TOP-TEN RECOMMENDATIONS: A REALISTIC VIEW

In an imitation of David Letterman, George White presented his top-ten EDI pointers, which he says are more sad than humorous:

10. Ignore large growth estimates for financial EDI volume. This expert who has followed electronic commerce of all sorts for many years calls for continued modest growth in this arena. To those still not convinced, he suggests they look at the forecasts made just a few short years ago.
9. Never make a commitment of anticipated financial EDI volume expectation to your management and/or the press unless you want to be held to it. He has seen more than one career torpedoed because of optimistic projections that came back to haunt the individual.
8. Avoid large commercial banks charging $50 or more per month for EDI accounts, regardless of volume. He cites cases of companies with one EDI transaction per month being forced to pay a high fee for account maintenance. He urges such companies to shop around for a bank offering a more reasonable fee. He also suggests trying to negotiate the fee downward—sometimes all you have to do is ask.
7. Beware of EDI if others in your industry are laggards in participation. He gives the examples of the grocery industry, a major EDI but not Financial EDI participant, and the chemical industry, which has major participants in Financial EDI.
6. Be cautious of those proposing or requiring trading-partner agreements when other commerce is not covered by legal contracts. White, who sometimes serves as a payments expert in legal cases, says he has seen overly detailed contracts that actually open participants to increased legal problems. He indicates that half the companies in the chemical industry operate with no agreements. In other industries a one- or two-page agreement is sometimes used.

5. Encourage financial institutions to use inexpensive financial EDI software. He says that the New York ACH makes its basic software free to member financial institutions, but few use it because of limited corporate interest.
4. Use vendors that translate input rather than installing expensive software before it is justified by volume growth. "Don't make it too complicated," he says. "Learn from the U.S. government's problems from designing its Vendor Express addenda records." Most financial institutions still cannot handle addenda records.
3. Be alert to the fact that legacy systems may be a deterrent that needs to be overcome before financial EDI can be implemented. White offers the same caution about outdated purchased software. "It is incredible," he says, "that major software firms continue to sell software unable to handle electronic payments."
2. Monitor innovative uses of the Internet and other approaches, including ways to simplify ordering. Certain companies already have Web pages for simplified ordering and subsequent payments. White points out that Chase Manhattan Bank has such a program for its corporate customers.
1. Participate in all applicable pilots, industry efforts, and so on, to standardize and/or test or implement more efficient and effective processes.

White, president of White Papers, runs conferences several times a year that address electronic topics. He can be reached at (201) 746-5456.

## 18.14 CONVINCING MANAGEMENT

Most accounts payable professionals know the benefits of using EDI and FEDI in the accounts payable department, but convincing upper management can be another story. However, if the advantages are presented in a clear and concise manner, it may just be possible to hold their attention long enough. If you can show management how to increase their net profit margin by 33%, you'll have them riveted. The greatest benefits from EDI come when there is a full cycle implementation, starting with the purchase order (PO), through the delivery/invoice stage, and ending with the payment.

### (a) The Benefits

Many companies take the opportunity to reengineer their work cycles as they implement EDI. When done simultaneously, the benefits increase exponentially. Some of the cost savings that result directly from implementing FEDI include postage costs, check stock, labor, reconciliation costs, and check fees.

But this is only the beginning. There are other benefits that may not be directly attributable to FEDI, but would not be possible without it. These include:

Inventory reduction.

Improved cash forecasting and accuracy.

A reduction in accounts payable fraud.

Errors are reduced and, consequently less time is spent resolving discrepancies.

Sophisticated technology makes it harder for those intent on committing fraud and, at the same time, implements controls at lower costs. And, with no checks around, there is no concern that someone, either in the department or mailroom or elsewhere, will walk off with a handful of checks—either written or blank.

## 18.15 FEDI APPLICATIONS

Most companies are already using FEDI, and they don't even realize it. Any company that has a direct deposit payroll program has already begun to use FEDI. The other big application is vendor payments. But there are a variety of other applications—tax payments, pension fund payments, child support withholding, utility payments, and healthcare payments. Insurance companies also use it to make annuity payments.

### (a) Cost Justifying FEDI

Sometimes small savings can make a big difference. For example, a company with $200 million in sales and $160 million in sales costs has a gross margin of $40 million. If variable expenses are $16.4 million and fixed expenses are another $20 million, there is a net profit of $3.6 million, or a net profit margin of 1.8%.

With the implementation of FEDI, the company in this example was able to decrease the cost of sales by $^1/_2$% and variable expenses by 1%. On the face of it, these savings don't seem earth shattering. The net profit margin increases 33% to 2.4%. These numbers will get management's attention. Keep in mind these increases represent only the quantifiable improvements. It is difficult to quantify the effects of improved customer service, greater accuracy, and more accurate cash-flow forecasting.

Accounts payable professionals who are able to present the benefits of FEDI and back them up with attention grabbing numbers will be well on their way to winning over an initially uninterested management team.

## 18.16 GETTING UP THE EDI LEARNING CURVE

Most professionals, regardless of their training, know very little about EDI. So, the accounts payable professional who falls into this category should not feel second-rate. There is much they can do to get themselves up the learning curve. By doing this, and doing it before the rest of the company catches on, the accounts payable professional may put themselves in the unique position of becoming the FEDI authority within their companies. Becoming the company resource for anything can not be a bad career move. Here's what accounts payable professionals can do to become this expert:

Develop a network.

Read, read, read.

Keep informed as to what's available.

Gain exposure.

## (a) Develop a Network

Meet with other people knowledgeable about EDI. This can be done under the auspice of attending trade shows, professional meetings, conferences and seminars. Some that might be useful include:

Local EDI/EC user groups. These can be found by looking in the excellent magazine, *EDI World*. The magazine can be reached at (305) 925-5900. The dues for these groups are usually minimal.

Industry/trade associations.

Treasury Management Association, which can be reached at (301) 907-2862.

NACHA affiliate groups. NACHA can be reached at (703) 742-9190.

Software vendor steering committees.

ANSI ASC X12. This group meets three times a year with workgroups meeting more frequently.

## (b) Read, Read, Read

Education can be the key to success in any endeavor, and the EDI field is no exception. Much of this learning can be done in spare time by reading relevant publications. Several useful publications that include EDI information are:

*Corporate Financial EDI User Guide.*

*TMA Journal.*

*EC World.*

*EDI News.*

*Corporate EFT Report.*

IOMA's Report on Managing Accounts Payable.

Vendors are also a wonderful source of information. Ask the salespeople who call to add your name to the vendor newsletter mailing list. Also visit the vendor's website regularly if one exists.

When attending conferences and trade shows, buy tapes and obtain handouts from as many sessions as possible.

### (c) Keep Informed As To What's Available

Knowing what's available is crucial to the accounts payable professional who wants to stay on top. Even if your organization already has an EDI program in place, or falls into the category of "never gonna happen here," it is still important to know what's available. You may change jobs or your company may change its focus. It's amazing how things can change when a new boss comes in or when a big supplier says "Jump!" Shrewd accounts payable managers are informed before their companies get ready to move.

The EDI areas that need to be investigated include: hardware, software, VANs, VABs, models, applications, and best-in-class practices. By identifying companies with best-in-class practices, you can approach them and ask how and why they did what they did. This will be less difficult if you already know someone at the company from your networking.

### (d) Gain Exposure

Professionals who have accumulated a wealth of EDI information are in a position to become a resource for others. This will enhance their reputations and is not as hard as it may seem at first glance. Some ways to do this are:

Speak at industry meetings and/or conferences.

Publish articles. Most trade magazines are happy to get contributions from practitioners who have successfully implemented some new EDI technique.

Volunteer.

Get involved in the relevant organizations.

## 18.17 INTERNET EDI

Although the technocrats have been singing the praises of EDI for years, corporate America's acceptance has been painfully slow. Many find the topic excruciatingly boring, difficult to understand, and occasionally, expensive to implement. The standards issues have not been resolved to all participants' satisfaction, further hurtling EDI into the abyss for many corporations. All that is about to change as the Internet invades the EDI world, just as it has many other facets of everyday life. The Internet levels the playing field by allowing small companies to play for the same cost as their much bigger cousins. It lowers costs and decreases processing time for all participants—regardless of size or technical know-how.

Yet, few companies have stepped up to the plate and begun to play. *EC World* estimates that less than 200 companies are now using Internet EDI. It theorizes that the reason for this is corporate fears regarding security. However, as companies become comfortable with the various methodologies now available for handling a secure transaction, this will change. Additionally, as executives become comfortable with e-mail and continue to look for ways to reduce costs and improve productivity, EDI will look even more attractive than it already does. Thus, it is imperative that those accounts payable professionals who have largely ignored the topic begin to get themselves up on the EDI learning curve. Despite the fact that the topic is becoming increasingly important, it still makes great bedtime reading for insomniacs.

## 18.18 SECURITY AND STANDARDS ISSUES

Those concerned about the possibility of interlopers viewing corporate secrets, manipulating private data, or worse still, diverting funds, have long steered away from the Internet. These issues are made all the worse as each group tries to force its own standard as the market standard. To date, such strategies have only resulted in less-than-optimal usage as corporate America throws up its collective hands and waits to see which company and standard emerges as the winner. Recognizing that no one wins in these circumstances, several groups have taken a different tack and are dealing with these concerns.

## 18.19 WHY THE INTERNET?

As these issues are addressed, the ease of the Internet will make it the ideal medium for transmitting information. Already, EDI documents are being translated into HTML format, the Internet standard, and from HTML format, as well. The Web servers that host these networks typically handle e-mail, encryption, and digital signatures, as well. As most reading this are well aware, the Internet can be accessed from almost any PC that is properly (and relatively inexpensively) equipped. Thus, even the smallest of companies can complete a transaction, from purchase order to the payment stage, online. This capability opens the EDI world up to anyone with a PC.

Accounts payable professionals who have seen the Internet and EDI beginning to trickle into their everyday workplace will soon find it bursting into their departments and infiltrating many of their transactions. It's only a matter of time.

## 18.20 SPECIAL APPLICATION: ACH DEBITS—FOR TAX PAYMENTS

Any accounts payable manager recommending the use of an ACH debit is likely to receive scowls, or worse, from management. Just the idea of letting another party debit a company's bank account can raise questions about the manager's business judgement. "Are you crazy?" was the response one such professional received when she mentioned the idea to her boss. Now, take this notion one step further and imagine suggesting that the party you'd like to allow to access your account is none other than the Federal government. In quite a few organizations this would be considered lunacy.

But this is exactly what a small but growing number of companies are doing. In some companies, the consequential damage issue regarding nonpayment or late payment of taxes has also helped management reconsider its position on this issue. Several banks have developed products to allay some of management's fears.

### (a) Background

Before delving into this topic in detail, it is necessary to take a look at a few related issues, including:

> Almost every organization has some experience with the ACH, although many don't associate the most common usage with the ACH. Any company that has a direct deposit payroll program is using ACH credits.
>
> Not everyone realizes that anyone can initiate an ACH debit against a bank account. Unless a company has specifically advised its bank that no ACH debits against its accounts are to be honored, any and all such transactions will be accepted. Most companies have never given this matter much thought and so have not apprised their banks to reject such exchanges. So, if management's first reaction is that they would never allow such an action, you might cautiously suggest that, by virtue of their inaction, they already have.
>
> The Federal government and many state governments are already requiring certain categories of companies to make all tax payments electronically. The current Federal guidelines, for example, state that any company paying the Federal government over $50,000 in taxes must make those payments electronically.

### (b) EFTPS Regulations

Basically, corporations are offered the option of paying through an ACH credit or an ACH debit, with the Federal government—big surprise—much preferring the ACH debit method. Firms can also use a Fed wire, but there is a debate as to whether one can be used in anything but emergency situations. The Federal government has made it clear that it prefers the ACH. Companies going the Fed wire route do so at some minimal risk if the payment doesn't make it.

The credit method has been perceived to be the less risky model by most. But is it really less risky? By using the credit method, only the account user has access to the account and, thus, is the only party that can release the funds for payment. However, if something unforeseen occurs with the payment/transfer, the business (tax payor) is liable and may be subject to interest penalties or fines.

When moving in uncharted waters, it is always possible to imagine the worst, and that is exactly what happens when the topic of ACH debits arises. Everyone envisions a decimal point being shifted or a zero or two added, or worse. The concerns of businesses regarding ACH debits can be broken down into three main areas:

The issue of letting anyone debit a firm's bank account.

The need for control over the timing of the debit to make sure there are adequate funds in the account to cover the transaction.

The need to regulate the amount of the debit.

Several banks have developed a service that mitigates both the real and perceived risks associated with the debits. The product allows a company to tell the bank when to expect the debit transaction and how much it should be for while still giving the Federal or state government the responsibility for initiating the transaction as it prefers. This completely removes the liability for late payment from the shoulders of the company.

By working with its customers, the banks have developed a

method of allowing the government to debit the business account by sending an 820 file to the bank to ensure that only authorized payments are made for the proper amounts within a pre-specified time period for a pre-specified amount. Some of these products introduce a much-needed flexibility into the process. By setting tolerance levels, a company avoids the problem that might be encountered if the dollar amount or date is off slightly. These variances may be as little as a dollar or one or two days.

### (c) Making the Most of ACH Debits

Whether or not most companies will allow ACH debits for tax payments, it is becoming increasingly clear that electronic-payment mechanisms will become a standard way of operating for some portion of payments made by virtually all U.S. companies within the next few years. Within that time period, accounts payable professionals will need to become conversant with all the options. In the short run, however, there is a more pressing concern: deciding whether to stick your neck out and recommend ACH debits.

# 19

# Software

Few accounts payable managers have any input into the accounting software used in their departments. Typically, they must make do with whatever general package was selected by the controller or some other high-level executive. Rarely is their input requested when new software is being purchased. Thus, they are often left to deal with a package that might be great for general ledger purposes but barely adequate for the needs of accounts payable.

An even bigger issue in this regard pertains to the nature of the systems in place today. Many are homegrown legacy systems that have been patched many times over to either fix various flaws or handle certain issues peculiar to an industry or company. While many have gotten by with such systems for years, the issue is being brought to the forefront from an unlikely source: the programming decisions made years ago by programmers looking to save a few dollars. The major problem now facing most companies is referred to as "The Year 2000 (Y2K) Problem" or the Millennium Problem. Simply put, the issue is that most computers use two digits for all calculations involving the year part of the date. Because of the above mentioned programming savings, computers recognize the year 2000 as the year 1900. This will cause all sorts of glitches in virtually every course of life.

Rather than put another bandage on already antiquated systems, many companies are choosing to deal with this issue by ignoring it. They are finally installing a new software package that is Y2K compliant. Whether this will solve the problem remains to be seen at the time this book is being published. To get a handle on the software issue, IOMA included several questions about software in its benchmarking survey.

## 19.1 SOFTWARE CURRENTLY IN USE

When accounts payable professionals were asked about the software used in their departments, they were not shy in their commentary. No one software package emerges as dominant, with the largest group of respondents (44%) falling into the "other" category. Other represents all software applications receiving less than one percent of the votes! Homegrown software is a distant second, with 15.5% of the respondents saying they used a system that was entirely designed in-house.

The only programs used by more than a tiny percentage of the accounts payable audience were Dun & Bradstreet, with 8.6% of the market, Oracle with 6.4%, and JD Edwards with just under 5%. For a complete breakdown, see Exhibit 19.1.

### (a) Massive Modifications

Respondents were quite vocal about the amount of customization that was done even on the more popular applications. "We started with a software program and then changed it to meet the needs of our business," says the accounts payable manager of a wholesale/retail company. "No package was able to accommodate all our requirements," she adds. Her comments were typical.

"We actually started with a canned accounting package and modified it to fit our company's needs," comments an accounting supervisor, mirroring the earlier comments. "Ongoing improvements are made," she continues, remarking on a phenomenon found at many companies.

*Exhibit 19.1* **Software Used by Organizations for Vendor Payments**

| | |
|---|---|
| Own homegrown software | 15.5% |
| Dun & Bradstreet | 8.6 |
| Oracle | 6.4 |
| Walker | 1.0 |
| JD Edwards | 4.7 |
| Software 2000 | 3.2 |
| Ask Man | 2.9 |
| American Software | 1.3 |
| Integral | 1.5 |
| SAP | 1.0 |
| Legacy | 0.6 |
| AS 400 | 1.8 |
| BPCS | 2.0 |
| Lawson | 2.8 |
| Platinum | 2.0 |
| Other | 44.5 |

(Source: IOMA's 1997 Benchmarking Survey)

Despite all the tinkering, however, not many of the respondents were thrilled with the results. "We use a customized accounting system designed for support by one programmer," explains an accounts payable manager from the West Coast. "It does not meet the quality standards set by upper management." She is not alone. "We created our software in-house for cost reasons," says a manager of administrative services, "and it leaves a lot to be desired."

## (b) Why Choose Homegrown?

Many of the respondents were quite definite about why they chose to develop their own applications instead of buying an off-the-shelf application. Their reasons broke down into three categories:

1. Management felt it would be less expensive to develop an in-house application than to buy software and modi-fy it.

2. Existing software could not provide the particular features needed by the company.
3. Industry-specific concerns were not addressed in the software on the market at the time of the purchase.

Virtually all these applications will either have to be scrapped completely or extensively modified in the next few years as the Year 2000 problem is rarely, if ever, addressed. Even if a company wishes to modify these systems, it may not be possible. "Our 'homegrown' program was created 10 years ago and has been upgraded and refined and improved up until three years ago," says the accounts payable manager of a software company. "Now, it is too complex for further improvement." This company is not alone in this experience. Unfortunately, these systems tend to be quite old, and, in many instances, the programmers who created the original code are long gone. In many cases, no one is available who fully understands the programming logic.

### (c) Antiquated Software Still in Use

The average software application used in accounts payable departments has been used for 6.4 years. While this might seem reasonable, keep in mind that this is an average. Several respondents report using software for as long as 30 years. Systems that old are barely being held together. Interestingly, the larger the company, the older its accounts payable system is likely to be. Companies with over 5,000 employees are using accounts payable software that has an average age of 8.3 years (see Exhibit 19.2 for a complete breakdown of age by company size and industry). Several companies indicated that they were in the process of implementing a new system. "Our old system died under heavy-volume processing," was a familiar complaint.

### (d) Where Accounts Payable Systems Reside

Respondents were asked whether the program was PC based, LAN based, or resided on the mainframe. Just over two-thirds of

*Exhibit 19.2* **Age of Accounts Payable Software**

| | *Years* |
|---|---|
| *Average age* | 6.4 |
| **Average by company size** | |
| Up to 99 | 5.3 |
| 100 to 249 | 5.9 |
| 250 to 499 | 5.8 |
| 500 to 999 | 6.2 |
| 1,000 to 4,999 | 7.0 |
| Over 5,000 | 8.3 |
| **Industry average** | |
| Manufacturing | 7.0 |
| Finance | 6.1 |
| Utilities, transportation | 5.8 |
| Private practice | 4.4 |
| Nonprofit | 6.0 |
| Wholesale/retail distribution | 7.2 |
| Health care | 6.6 |
| Education | 7.0 |
| Communications | 5.7 |
| Construction | 6.7 |
| Other | 5.6 |

(Source: IOMA's 1997 Benchmarking Survey)

all respondents have a mainframe-based accounting system, with slightly less than 13% using a system residing on a stand-alone PC. As might be expected, the larger the company, the more apt it was to have a mainframe-based system and the less likely it was to have a PC-based one. With the exception of large companies, those with over 1,000 employees, roughly one-quarter used a LAN system. To see how your company compares to others in the same industry or of similar size, see Exhibit 19.3.

## 19.2 MAKING SOFTWARE WORK

Accounts payable professionals are stuck with whatever software management has selected for the company and must de-

*Exhibit 19.3* **Where Accounts Payable Software Resides**

| | *PC* 12.9% | *LAN* 20.2% | *Mainframe* 66.9% |
|---|---|---|---|
| **Program by company size** | | | |
| Up to 99 | 41.7 | 25.0 | 33.3 |
| 100 to 249 | 23.2 | 23.3 | 53.5 |
| 250 to 499 | 10.6 | 22.8 | 66.7 |
| 500 to 999 | 14.3 | 22.1 | 63.6 |
| 1,000 to 4,999 | 8.8 | 15.6 | 75.5 |
| Over 5,000 | 1.1 | 12.6 | 86.2 |
| **Program by industry** | | | |
| Manufacturing | 10.4 | 20.8 | 68.9 |
| Finance | 16.7 | 25.0 | 58.3 |
| Utilities, transportation | 10.9 | 17.4 | 71.7 |
| Private practice | 28.9 | 22.2 | 48.9 |
| Nonprofit | 20.8 | 25.0 | 54.2 |
| Wholesale/retail dist. | 11.1 | 15.2 | 73.7 |
| Health care | 8.3 | 14.6 | 77.1 |
| Education | 4.3 | 13.0 | 82.6 |
| Communications | 7.7 | 34.6 | 57.7 |
| Construction | 20.0 | 20.0 | 60.0 |
| Other | 10.3 | 24.1 | 65.5 |

(Source: IOMA's 1997 Benchmarking Survey)

vise ways to "make it work." The following list shows how some accounts payable professionals are using their inflexible accounting programs to produce the reports management requires:

Report/statement generation.

Customization.

Word processing and spreadsheet.

Utilize features in current programs.

Integration with vendor systems.

### (a) Report/Statement Generation

Many complain that the programs do not even offer the report formats management demands. This is a common complaint from users of SAP software, which has powerful report-generating capabilities but no standard reports. In order to get the most out of this program, it is necessary to use someone who knows the built-in language—one that is not used for other applications and is notoriously "user unfriendly." While the worst complaints on this front are directed at SAP, both MAS90 and Solomon III receive their fair share of criticism.

Regardless of the software used, the solutions are the same. Accounts payable professionals report success by:

Learning—and using another program such as Lotus, Access, or Excel. While this means that some of the most powerful features of the accounting software may not be used, it still gets the job done.

Getting help from a third party. This can either be an outside consultant, who will probably be quite expensive, or in-house support. Don't overlook the information technology department, which may have some resident experts. Also, try nosing around in other departments to determine if they have had success getting reports out of the system. Occasionally, a techie in another department will be quite adept at pulling special reports. Perhaps this individual can be borrowed for a few days to develop reports for accounts payable.

Build "macros" for special reports.

Use "highlights" reports more frequently. If Solomon's response to a query of account status is a 250-page tome, reduce the data to a one-page summary of exceptions or highlights. The data will be easier to manage—and easier to communicate to senior managers.

### (b) Customization

Even more annoying than an application that offers no standard reports, is the one that offers a wide range of report formats, none of which are usable by the accounts payable department. Several might be close, but each needs to be tweaked a bit to make it suitable. There are two solutions to this irritating problem. As suggested above, a consultant proficient in the program can be hired to make the reports meet departmental requirements. Also look for help in-house.

The other solution is definitely low-tech. "Pray for an upgrade," suggests one user facing such a problem. Others might call this a "Sticking Your Head in the Sand" approach. Unfortunately, waiting for divine intervention can be chancy and is obviously *not* a workable solution. But before spending a lot of money customizing a report, evaluate the feasibility of just living with the problem for the short term, or just using some interim reports generated by Lotus or Excel while waiting for the manufacturer to fix the problem.

### (c) Word Processing and Spreadsheets

There are many things that computer literate payables professionals can do—even if their companies won't, or can't, spring for the big bucks required to purchase some of the more sophisticated accounting programs. Many companies have begun their electronic T&E programs using spreadsheets and e-mail as the platform. In fact, this is the total extent of many such programs. Use WordPerfect (or other word processing program) and Excel's (or other spreadsheet) capabilities to perform duties such as summaries of expenses, employee expense-report tracking, structural charts, memos, and other documents.

### (d) Utilize Features in Current Programs

Many accounts payable professionals have improved departmental productivity simply by reviewing all the features of their existing programs and finding new ways to use them. These include:

Use of default and model journal entry accounts.

Use of e-mail to generate a form for invoice approvals and send these requests on to the designated approver. For example, the system might automatically generate the pertinent information (invoice number, vendor name, PO number, and description), thereby improving efficiency.

Look-up features are available in many systems and can save accounts payable professionals much time and aggravation.

On-demand checks can be produced by certain software packages. These can be used to replace rush checks that are manually written and tend to lead to a large percentage of check related errors. Many also have the system automatically generate G/L entries.

Interfaces with other company systems.

### (e) Integration with Vendor Systems

Several accounts payable managers have reported partnering with vendors and others to produce some unique methods to increase productivity. Advances in computer technology combined with rapidly decreasing costs have made possible techniques not feasible just a few years ago. Both AmEx and FedEx have worked with their customers' accounts payable departments to help improve operations. Two simple techniques that have helped some companies when dealing with these two large entities are:

1. Have these two transmit information electronically to the accounts payable department rather than inundate it with paper.
2. Some have developed a process to read their AmEx airline bill (diskette) into a PC program that sorts the items to determine which tickets have been paid for but not received.

## 19.3 THE Y2K ISSUE

This is a very real issue facing companies of all sizes. At the time this book is being written, no one knows the true extent of the problem and whether it can and will be fixed in time in most companies. While some of the stories circulating about Y2K problems are amusing (a batch of cheese being destroyed because it was too old), the very real problems that will face professionals in all walks of life are not so funny. There are a few strategies that accounts payable professionals can utilize in order to minimize the fallout from this debacle.

For starters, insist that any new software be Y2K compliant. This, of course, is easier said than done. At a minimum, the software vendor should give a statement to that effect. But be careful. The second step would be to talk to existing software vendors to see if the software already in place is Y2K compliant and if it is, to obtain some sort of written statement to that effect. But, be forewarned, few will be willing to give such a statement.

Some experts predict that rather than fix the Y2K problem, certain software vendors, mostly the smaller ones, will go out of business. Generally, it is believed this will be done if the cost of the fix is too high. There is not much that can be done about such a solution since it is unlikely such vendors will give notice to their customers.

Those with homegrown legacy systems that are currently being patched, once again, to fix this problem, stand the most risk. The likelihood that every line of code will be altered and that it will be done so in a manner that does not affect other calculations is slim. Those who find themselves in this situation should try and establish some contingency plans. Of course, accounts payable is unlikely to be in the lead at most companies in solving this problem since it is a management technology concern that affects the whole company. However, it is important to think about the issue and make some contingency plans in case the company's systems disintegrate in the year 2000.

## 19.3 The Y2K Issue

Software can be used to help accounts payable improve productivity even if at times it seems like the software in use hampers that process. By being a little innovative and taking a close look at what's currently available and what can be done with other resources, most will find ways to make their software work for them—rather than the other way around.

# 20

# Imaging

With technology prices dropping and the push for higher productivity and lower operating costs, imaging systems are beginning to appeal to a growing number of companies. Imaging is the comprehensive capture, storage, retrieval, and management of digitized paper documents and/or computer-generated data files. Initially it was used in concert with high-capacity optical storage subsystems, digital scanning devices, and modified laser printers. However, this does not always have to be the case. Imaging helps accounts payable departments in the following ways:

Reduces storage costs due to less need for filing cabinets.

Improves accuracy because information is not rekeyed, but entered once.

Reduces clerical time on filing and retrieving documentation.

Reduces time and frustration related to routing invoices for approval, which you can do electronically.

## 20.1 POOR MAN'S IMAGING

At a recent accounts payable conference, one of the speakers mentioned putting a $175 scanner on all clerks' desks. Clerks needing to send copies of invoices or checks run the document through the scanner, download it into the software, and fax it to the appropriate party. This poor man's version of imaging saves the staff time spent at the copier and fax machine.

## 20.2 PLANNING FOR FULL-SCALE IMAGING

The most successful imaging programs, such as the one used at a very large construction company, take into account the needs of all affected departments. The accounts payable manager describes the process as follows: "We spent last year meeting with all departments involved directly (purchasing and accounts payable) and indirectly (billing, cost engineers, etc.), working out ways to easily accommodate everyone's needs to access information. The advance work paid off within a month of the imaging system installation. Everyone felt comfortable and appreciated its convenience.

"Accounts payable has especially benefited. The department can bring up purchase orders immediately for review with invoices. We no longer have to wait until they are printed, distributed, and filed before we can access them. Accounts payable no longer has to maintain paper files for each fiscal year, and lost and misfiled check copies are no longer a concern. We have seen a great savings timewise: we are able to process more invoices quickly and have more time to spend processing invoices as opposed to filing all the paper."

## 20.3 USING FULL-SCALE IMAGING WITH E-MAIL . . .

When married with e-mail, productivity savings can be impressive. The manager of disbursement services of a large utility company explains how it works in his shop: "During the last year, we have implemented an online approval process for our service-related invoices. This has eliminated as much as five days' mail time each way throughout the company. Approvers have the option of requesting, at the click of a button, a fax copy of the invoice, which has been scanned.

"Imaging invoices and the associated online approval process has greatly reduced the amount of paper the processors must work with, while ensuring that the authorized employee performs the approval." This system completely eliminates the chance of the paperwork getting lost in the mail. Of course, using any of these large-scale systems will work best at larger companies, which are willing to make the financial investment necessary to obtain imaging equipment.

## 20.4 ... WITHOUT SPENDING HUGE SUMS OF MONEY

Although at first glance it might appear that imaging will work only in organizations willing to invest large sums of money, this is not true. As indicated earlier, imaging equipment is not cheap. However, there are several options for those looking to make a smaller investment. These include:

*Outsourcing the imaging work to a third party.* Even some large companies are taking this as a first step to gauge whether using imaged documents is a big productivity-saver.

*Using imaged documents that others provide.* The most notable example is getting the paid check file back from the bank on a CD-ROM. You can then load this onto the network and allow any party with a need or interest in this information to access it. If your company is reluctant to use imaging, this is a good first step. As people become familiar and comfortable with this process, they may grow willing to look at additional applications.

Some accounts payable professionals who image their checks report the ability to go into the file, find the check copy, and "copy and paste" the information into a letter. This is great when writing to a vendor who claims not to have received payment. Since most banks will image both the front and back of the check, you will be able to include the vendor's endorsement showing where the item was deposited and when the check cleared the bank.

Sending information in that manner makes the communication almost instantaneous. Compare this to the old method of digging out the check, making a photocopy, and mailing or faxing it. Mail has the inherent time delays, and fax copies are often of such poor quality that the endorsement and dates are almost impossible to read. Today, relatively inexpensive technology is within the reach of virtually every company—even if it is not planning to use full-scale imaging.

Imaging is here to stay. Those who find ways to use it—be it full-blast or as a supplemental response—will improve the departmental productivity while eliminating some of the more tedious work for accounts payable.

## 20.5 OVERVIEW

The imaging process consists of the following:

Capture and index.

Delivery.

Storage (both online and archived).

Retrieval.

The most critical step in the procedure is the capture and indexing phase, since the other steps depend on it. Most companies who use imaging do so for a variety of reasons. They tend to see benefits in the following areas:

Improved processing.

Improved security.

Integration.

Customer service.

Document storage.

However, as with any new technology, there are some issues that need to be resolved. They include:

*Index structure.* This is not standardized, and those purchasing imaging systems should make sure that the index structure offered is one that will meet all their requirements.

*Cost.* Although prices have dropped, this technology is still expensive by certain standards. Make sure you understand all the costs before purchasing a system. This is also important if you do not purchase your own equipment but go with the services of a third-party service provider.

*Lack of standards.* Many experts believe that although there is no conformity between manufacturers currently, standards will emerge within the next few years. It is in the best interests of the manufacturers—especially since there does not appear to be any Microsoft-size imaging providers.

*Legal acceptance.* Some professionals are concerned about not having an original document in case of legal action. Currently most professionals feel confident that the best evidence rule will hold up, but it has not been tested at the state level in all locales yet. Needless to say, no one is anxious to be the test case.

*Disaster recovery.* The issues in this arena are virtually the same as in a paper-based environment.

## 20.6 REAL LIFE COMPLAINTS: CHECKS

As with any new process, there are growing pains. Implementation of imaging systems do not always go smoothly. The companies that allow their banks to image paid checks for them typically also allow them to destroy the checks. This policy, known as truncation, can cause concern in auditing and legal circles. Examples of how some have handled the issue are:

> The checks written at one company using this approach were not of a size to cause significant discomfort. The company decided that even though it was not comfortable with the current rulings regarding the legal acceptance of imaged copies in the event of court action, it was willing to take a chance. In this instance the company did not feel it

had a large financial exposure. The firm involved is an insurance company, and it does not use this process for claims checks.

Another company's internal auditors were not happy about the process. This firm turned to an outside law firm who researched the issues regarding rules of best evidence. The company received a satisfactory opinion from their attorneys and decided to move ahead.

Because the checks are destroyed, certain costs are eliminated. One accounts payable professional revealed that his company no longer paid check-sorting fees. A move to imaging can save some bank fees—but it still isn't free. Another participant revealed that imaging costs between one and two cents per check more than microfilm. Of course, the time saved not having to deal with microfilm (or microfiche) is not factored into the cost.

The good news regarding imaging far outweighs the few problems discussed earlier. The benefits include:

The ability to have information at people's fingertips. No longer do they have to write down information, pull a check from the file, make a copy, then mail or fax it to whoever needs it, and finally refile the original check—hopefully correctly. Instead, the phone call can be taken and without even getting up from the desk, a copy can be retrieved on the computer and with a few clicks faxed to whoever needs it. And, of course, this eliminates all cases of misfiling.

Clerical personnel who never had access to a PC at work were thrilled to be given the chance to learn. Sure, it took a little bit of time for some of them to get the hang of using a mouse, but this issue only lasts for a very short period of time (usually less than a few hours). Morale was lifted by this job-enrichment feature. In most operations, this side benefit came as a complete surprise.

By using cut-and-paste features in conjunction with e-mail and computer faxing, internal requests for information can be turned around very quickly.

Efficiency and storage savings is important. Since imaged information is saved on CD-ROMs, the amount of space needed for storage is significantly reduced.

## 20.7 REAL LIFE ADVANTAGES: CHECKS

A number of banks are now offering services whereby cancelled checks are imaged at the bank and then, instead of returning the cancelled checks to the writer, the bank sends a CD-ROM with copies of the checks. Usually, but not always, both the front and back of the check are imaged. Some accounts payable managers think this service is only for firms with huge imaging operations, but this is far from the case. Even organizations with no imaging operations of their own can take advantage of such services.

For starters, there is the space issue: Copies of approximately 25,000 checks can fit on one CD-ROM. By keeping the information on a CD-ROM instead of needing to allocate storage space for the checks, substantial filing room can be saved.

Additionally, if the CD-ROM is placed in a tower, many people can have access to the information from their computers. This improves the productivity of the department, as time is not lost pulling checks and then copying and refiling them—hopefully correctly!

### (a) Day-to-Day Uses

From a practical standpoint, there are a number of occasions when the accounts payable staff will find having cancelled checks on a CD-ROM very helpful. Some examples are:

When a supplier calls and says a payment was not received, the accounts payable clerk usually goes to the files, pulls the check, makes a photocopy, and then either mails or faxes it to the vendor. The check must then be refiled. This assumes, of course, that no one else has pulled that particular check and that it has been refiled. If it hasn't, the clerk must then go and find the unfiled checks. With the information on CD-ROM, the clerk is able to access the information with a few clicks of the mouse and print it. If the company has supplied a fax modem for the employee's computer, the copy can be automatically faxed. The employee never has to leave their desk and can handle this type of request in a few seconds.

The image of the check can also be copied onto the clipboard and then pasted into a memo, if that is what is required.

Sometimes, it is not necessary to provide a copy of the check, but only to ascertain if it has been presented for payment. In these instances, it is possible to check the information as indicated above and then pass on the information verbally.

## 20.8 FUTURE DEVELOPMENTS

It is expected that this imaged information will be available on the Internet in the near future. Of course, there will need to be security built in, so that only those authorized will be able to view your checks. Rumors are that the following banks will offer this service: Harris Bank, First Union, Wachovia, Crestar, Chase, Citibank, and Bank of New York also offer or plan to offer similar products in the near future. Others will soon follow. Those interested in using imaged checks should check with their banks. One phone call could ultimately save your staff hours and hours of time.

## 20.9 ELECTRONIC COMMERCE AND OBSOLESCENCE

Obsolescence has to weigh on the mind of any professional contemplating recommending a big technology purchase. No manager wants to be known as the individual who recommended the technological dinosaur. While this initial concern is understandable, it is not accurate when it comes to imaging.

EDI and Electronic Funds Transfer (EFT) might pose the biggest threats in this area. Use of EDI, while growing rapidly, still accounts for only a very small percentage of all information and payments exchanged between corporations. We expect its use to continue to expand but not to the point where an imaging system will become obsolete. Additionally, many people take information produced electronically and marry it with information that is scanned. The two forms of input are then utilized to produce images that can be accessed by a number of people within the company.

The other "threat" is EFT. While we all would like to get away from that paper check, it just doesn't appear to be a reality that any of us will see in our lifetimes. Thus, while EFT activity may be increasing, it will not make a dent in the number of checks written for quite a long time—if ever! A hard look at the technology reveals that it should not be a big concern.

## 20.10 LEGAL ACCEPTANCE

Companies using imaging do not keep original documents. That's one of the advantages of using this new and dynamic technology. However, as most accounts payable managers are well aware, original documents are usually required in those unpleasant situations when a legal matter develops. And, with imaging, the original is long gone by the time the lawsuit unfolds. This issue has some "Nervous Nellies" worried, but their concern, while worth considering, is probably overblown.

Although the matter has not been tested in every state, it is believed that the imaged document or check will be accepted by the courts. "How's that?" you ask. By demonstrating that it is your standard business practice to use imaging, most legal experts believe that the courts will accept the imaged document. Helping the cause is the fact that the IRS and the Federal Reserve have been leaders in the move to accept imaging—a fact that might be used with management if they are dragging their feet when it comes to imaging.

In legal cases, it is also important to show that the imaged document is stored in a manner that prevents alteration. It also believes that the issue will fade in importance as the use of this technology becomes more widespread and accepted. Finally, microfilm and ASCII files have been accorded "circumstantial trustworthiness" in federal courts since 1975. Many believe that this extends to other electronically archived documents also.

## 20.11 LACK OF STANDARDS

If there's any imaging issue that will drive an accounts payable manager to distraction, it is the standards or the lack thereof. It is imperative that the products of one vendor work with the products of the next. Otherwise, the company is tied to one company for every aspect of their imaging systems and very few will stand for that anymore. Nor should they. Most experts do not believe that this will be an issue for long. The vendors realize that if they do not get together and set some standards, corporations will shy away from the whole technology.

## 20.12 DISASTER RECOVERY

Every professional worries about disasters—both manmade and acts of nature. Whether a system crashes or is attacked by a virus or a fire or flood destroys files, the result is the same. The information is lost. This is an issue regardless of whether a paper-based or imaging system is used. Most companies have addressed this issue for paper systems. However, those contemplating imaging need to think it through. The simple solution is to have duplicate images stored offsite. By discussing the matter with both your vendor and your peers at other companies, you will be able to come up with a workable plan for your company.

By evaluating these matters carefully, accounts payable managers will be able to integrate these concerns into the operations of their own company and decide which, if any, are really problems. You just may be surprised when your study is complete to discover that the concerns that once stood in the way of implementing an imaging system at your company have evaporated.

## 20.13 FREQUENTLY ASKED QUESTIONS ABOUT IMAGING

**Who needs imaging?** Any organization in which paper plays a central role in the day-to-day success of the enterprise. Accounts payable departments certainly meet this criteria. According to *Computerworld*, 95% of all documents are in file cabinets. The cost of owning and maintaining a standard file cabinet is $880 per year. Executives spend more than 150 hours a year looking for information that was misplaced, misfiled, mislabeled or lost. The cost of each misfile averages $120.

**What is imaging?** The comprehensive capture, storage, retrieval, and management of digitized paper documents and/or computer-generated data files. It is normally used in concert with high capacity optical storage subsystems, digital scanning devices, and modified laser printers.

**How does imaging work?** Documents are fed into a scanner that digitizes the information and then indexes it. This allows the end user to later retrieve the actual image of the document if needed.

**Isn't imaging just for big companies?** Absolutely not. There are a number of low cost products on the market today. Of course, these are generic imaging software packages that would need to be customized for accounts payable applications. Alternatively, software customized for A/P can be purchased.

**Don't you need a lot of expensive equipment?** Not necessarily. According to Dataquest Inc., 42.5 million personal computers were shipped in 1994. Most professionals have them sitting on their desks. These PCs can be used to access scanned information if the right software has been installed. The cost of this equipment varies. It can be had for as little as $1,000 depending on the volume and speed needed. Some Fortune 500 companies with huge applications have spent as much as several hundred thousand dollars.

**What about the software? Will the staff have to forgo raises in order to pay for it?** Again, the cost will depend on how many users you will have and what bells and whistles are added to your system. To put the software question in perspective, Optika indicates that its average, not smallest, order is for $25,000 and this includes five users.

**Is it difficult to learn to use?** That all depends on the computer sophistication of those using the imaging system. According to Optika Imaging Systems, Inc., many find that it actually enhances the computer skills of their staff.

**What is COLD?** The other terminology frequently associated with imaging is COLD (computer output to laser disc). COLD is a microfiche and green-bar-paper replacement solution to process, retrieve, display, and search report information produced from any host computer using optical disk as the primary storage mechanism. Most accounts payable managers welcome any technology that keeps them from having to deal with microfiche or search through those horrible computer runs on green-and-white paper.

## 20.14 TYPICAL ACCOUNTS PAYABLE IMAGING PROCESS FOR FULL-BLOWN IMAGING

The accounts payable process when using imaging is not that different than without it. The big difference is that most of the work is done online rather than with stacks of paper. A typical accounts payable work process in an imaging environment would go as follows:

When invoices are received at the company, they are scanned and automatically indexed. This step, of course, can only be done in an imaging environment.

Purchase orders that have been previously stored via COLD are also retrieved.

The accounts payable professional responsible for matching the invoices and purchase orders then completes this match online.

If receiving documents are also matched, they, too, can be scanned into the system and incorporated into the match.

When using a Windows-based system, it is possible to have several documents open at the same time. If the match is satisfactory, the invoice is approved for payment and the next transaction is processed.

If there is no match, the invoice is forwarded to the appropriate management person for approval.

If information is missing, it is possible to attach a yellow sticky, just as you might in real life, asking for the missing information. This is then forwarded to the appropriate person. Most systems allow other manual entries to the imaged documents.

The information is entered into the corporate accounting system so that the appropriate accounts and general ledger entries can be updated as needed.

The system will allow for the bill to be paid immediately or scheduled for a later date. It also allows for automated business decisions depending upon credit terms.

When the process is completed, the invoice and associated documents are moved to a closed accounts payable file.

## 20.15 IMAGING BENEFITS OTHER DEPARTMENTS

Once an accounts payable department uses imaging, other departments benefit as well. Since all this information is online and the whole process is completed electronically, all data is available to everyone who needs it at any time. Thus if a vendor calls looking for payment, customer service can have access to the same information as the accounts payable department. They will be able to provide the vendor with the information they need without ever leaving their desk. And, there's no need to return a phone call. Customer service can also have immediate access to old records that are not normally kept in an office. For large organizations document storage costs are greatly reduced.

Many companies that undertake to install an imaging system do it as part of a reengineering effort. In the process, the existing work flow of the department gets reviewed and pared down, eliminating extraneous steps that were once vital but no longer have any meaning or use. One organization undertaking an imaging installation was able to reduce the work flow time frame from 22 days to 3. While some of it was attributable to the improved work flow, much of it was due to imaging.

## 20.16 OTHER TECHNICAL CONSIDERATIONS

When imaging is used and the two- or three-way match is done online, it usually entails having several screens or windows open at the same time. Keep this in mind when purchasing monitors for your staff. Consider spending a few extra bucks and buying a higher quality monitor with a larger screen to make life easier on the staff's eyes. Nineteen- or twenty-inch screens would be more appropriate than the standard ones bought for office use today. These can be hooked up to a 386 or 486 computer which are used by many accounts payable professionals.

Some large-scale imaging operations are incorporating the use of bar coding into their process. At one company, a staff member places a pregenerated sticker with a bar code and voucher number on all incoming documents. Their bar-coding software integrates with their imaging software and uses these voucher numbers to create empty folders where scanned documents will be stored. This level of imaging sophistication is presently used only by very large companies.

## 20.17 PREP CONSIDERATIONS

While it is true that imaging systems can be incredibly fast, there is a caveat to these claims. Many who use such systems report that the fast speeds reported work only if all the papers fed into the imaging system are in perfect condition. This is rarely, if ever, the case. Most do not take into account the amount of time that will be necessary to prep documents before they are imaged. This might include tasks such as removing staples and paper clips, copying poorly printed documents, smoothing out wrinkles and reducing or enlarging documents that are either too small or too large to image easily. It is imperative that adequate considerations be given to these details when planning to use a full-blown imaging system.

Only a few years ago, imaging was the province of the very

large, technologically sophisticated companies. And it was rather expensive. With costs dropping and the capabilities of computers growing exponentially, imaging is now within the reach of leading edge companies of all sizes. As these trends accelerate, more companies will turn to imaging as management continues to expect staff to do more with less.

# 21

# Internet and E-mail

Technology has given accounts payable professionals two resources that did not exist just a few short years ago: the Internet and e-mail. Those who are successful are not only learning all about these new technologies but are finding ways to integrate them into their everyday jobs, thus making themselves and their departments more productive. Not all companies have embraced these technologies. This lack of complete acceptance puts the accounts payable professional who learns about them in the driver's seat. Here's why: Eventually all companies will use e-mail and almost all will give employees Internet access. The question is when? Professionals who sits around waiting for the company to educate them have missed a golden opportunity. This is the time to be a leader rather than a follower.

Get on the Internet at home and get an e-mail account. Those who learn on their own can do two things that will help them careerwise:

> They can become an advocate or missionary within their own company pushing for the company to use these new technologies. When the company finally acquiesces, they will be

in the position of being the company expert. This will give them visability and the opportunity to shine.

Those not willing to push for the use of this new technology—perhaps because the corporate culture does not permit it—should still learn on their own. When the company finally does adopt the technology, they will be ready to step up as an expert and offer their expertise in helping set up and use the technology.

The great thing about both the Internet and e-mail is that they are both relatively easy to use and the financial investment required to get online is not out of the reach of most professionals. For $1,000 a computer with the necessary hardware and software can be purchased—although, by the time this book is published, the figure will probably be lower. Access to the Internet can be had in most locations for $20 a month although there are a few services that charge an even lower fee.

So, what can accounts payable professionals do with these two technologies?

## 21.1 E-MAIL

Without a doubt, the hottest application is e-mail. A few ways that the technology is being used in leading edge accounts payable departments includes:

To notify individual employees that their T&E reimbursement has been electronically deposited in their bank accounts.

To send follow-up messages to invoice approvers when invoices can not be located.

To contact a vendor with a question or discrepancy.

To broadcast a message to the entire company regarding month-end cutoff closing dates.

To broadcast a message to the entire company regarding a change in any accounts payable process or procedure.

To communicate with those in different time zones.

To communicate with those whose spoken English is difficult to understand.

To send copies of purchase orders, cancelled checks, or any other document that has been imaged.

It should be obvious that e-mail can be used in any situation where a phone call would be used. However, it doesn't matter whether the other party is available at the same time and games of telephone tag are eliminated. It also makes accounts payable professionals more productive because it is no longer necessary to spend time chatting for a few minutes with every single person called.

When e-mail is tied into an imaging system, it is also possible to copy and paste, or attach a copy of a document. No more running to the copy machine to make a copy and then to the fax machine to send the copy. E-mail makes the lives of those who use it a little easier—and it's great for adding a little humor to the workplace as many circulate jokes, unfortunately often of questionable taste.

### (a) Dealing with Unnecessary E-mail

Like any new technology, e-mail can bring its own headaches. Some people feel they must respond to every message they receive, regardless of whether it calls for a response. This is a needless waste of time for not only the recipient, but also the sender. Cut this practice off at the pass. For example, when sending a companywide e-mail directing that all check requests must be received by the twenty-seventh in order to have a check dated within the month, include a message at the end to the effect of, "There is no need to let me know you've received this message."

However, there are times when it is important to know that the recipient received the message. This is especially true in cases of timely or important requests. Inevitably, these are the people who don't bother to respond—so ask them to. At the end of the message, add, "Please send a reply to let me know this message was received." This also puts the recipient on notice that you know exactly when the message was received. Some e-mail systems have an automatic reply notification, but most work only marginally well when going out of system.

### (b) E-mail Etiquette

Try to keep your messages short and to the point. Any run-on sentences should be divided into two or more. Use the header section to clearly state the topic of your message. Most important, never respond quickly in anger to an e-mail message. Wait a few hours and review the response. Many an executive has come to regret a response made in haste while a temper was flaring.

## 21.2 INTERNET

While the uses for e-mail are quite obvious, the applicability of the rest of the Internet is not as clear. Some use it for research purposes to find product or legal information. Some companies have gone so far as to set up a site that vendors can access to find out the status of a payment. This greatly reduces the number of calls coming into the accounts payable department. However, recruitment is turning out to be one of the largest reasons accounts payable professionals are turning to the Internet.

### (a) For Recruitment Purposes

Recruiting for the most skilled employees in today's tight labor markets makes the Internet a perfect tool. When looking to hire someone who is computer and Internet proficient, what better place to start than the Internet.

"But where should we start?" many ask. With a profusion of new job banks, applicant Web sites and Internet employment services, it's difficult to know how best to use these new tools—or which of the new services are the most cost effective. In essence, there are several ways to recruit on the Internet. Many experts predict that use of the Internet will cut the time and cost of recruiting by 50% within three to five years. Examples of how it is being done today include:

**Postings on the Company's Web Site.** This requires asking the Webmaster to put the job listings on the company's Web site. While this is certainly one important avenue to explore for recruiting, it is not necessarily the easiest route. The first and perhaps most difficult aspect of this approach is getting time from the Webmaster to put up what in a growing mid-size company can amount to 10 to 20 jobs per month. The Webmaster has a dozen other departments to deal with in addition to your single request. So, getting his or her attention may take more time and effort than it's worth. Then there's the problem of handling the resumes that come back—from the Russian Nuclear Science Commission, for example, or in hard-to-read formats like ASCII text. One easy way to deal with some of this is to simply state that only U.S. domestic English-speaking candidates need apply.

**Newspapers that Post on the Internet.** Nearly two dozen newspapers from *The Wall Street Journal* to the *Houston Chronicle* now automatically post their classified adds on one or more of the large online databases of current jobs, like Careerpath.com or Online Career Center. Both sites are easy and fast to use, with searching by region, keywords, and job descriptions. And each offers a wide variety of professions, not just computer and engineering.

**Trade Journals that Offer Banner Ads.** One good example is *ComputerWorld*. A classified banner ad on their Web site costs roughly $150 with an ad in their print publication, or $400 to $500 without. Check with your marketing and advertising departments to see what publications your company is advertising in and to help you secure the best deal.

**Internet Resume Databases.** There are now eight major databases where job seekers are posting resumes. Monsterboard.com is one of the largest, followed by Careermosaic.com. Monster Board's resume-posting feature is free for applicants and allows them to change a resume as needed and to send it along to the human resource department at a company when they see a job they are interested in. For a company to advertise on Monster Board costs roughly $500 per month and allows the posting of 20 to 30 jobs. Additional features of this Web site are a database of some 4,000 companies to which you can add your own company's profile for applicants to scan, and a service job hunters can sign up for that will automatically prompt them when a job that meets their criteria comes up.

Additional sites of use include:

Careermosaic.com is also a great resource for accounts payable managers, since it contains some 36,000 resumes at last count. Of course, only a small percentage will be related to the accounts payable profession. It also contains over 250 links to other resources, career descriptions, listings of professional organizations, and salary information.

America's Job Bank, or ajb.dni.us, from the U.S. Department of Labor, is free to both job seekers and employers since it is funded by federal unemployment-insurance fees. It contains a wealth of information on low- and mid-level positions and allows sorting by job, state, type, or keyword.

Espan.com currently contains some 10,000 resumes. It is oriented more toward browsing by company than by other methods of searching. It also has a fairly unique Special Needs resource section for the disabled job applicant.

Jobtrak.com offers direct access to the graduating job seekers of more than 500 colleges and universities. This site reports that over 250,000 employers have used the database. It might be a good place to start if entry-level personnel are required.

### (b) Push Technology and Smart Agents

Push Technology involves a database of people who are found to fit a set criterion for the job opening. The job posting is pushed to them for a fee. Alternatively, when searching for a job, so-called Smart Agents will submit a resume automatically to jobs when the criteria match.

**(i) Special A/P Sites.** Many sites developed just for accounts payable professionals have job listings as well, and some will list positions for free. Another option is to place a listing on one of the growing number of discussion groups. The big advantage of placing the listing on such a site is that the candidate replying is Internet savvy. Be suspicious of any faxed resume received in response to an Internet ad if Internet knowledge is a strong requirement. If the individual can't respond via the Internet, he or she may not have the technical skills required. The information about the listing may have come from a friend who is Internet knowledgeable.

Ultimately, perhaps the best advice for the accounts payable professional who must decide which Internet service or route to take is not to rely on only one site. There is not likely to be one single best resource, so plan to use two or three major sites as well as your own. There is not currently, nor is there ever likely to be, a single list, network, or resource that will contain all of the information you want for an effective on-line job search.

### (c) Accounts Payable Discussion Groups

It is not possible to finish a chapter on accounts payable and the Internet without mentioning the IOMA accounts payable discussion group. At this site, professionals pose questions and their peers respond based on personal experience. The advice offered is quite good and many add their e-mail addresses and occasionally a phone number so there can be further in-depth discussion. Only occasionally does a question go unanswered. Whether someone needs help with a particular software application, dealing with an unproductive staff or other question, the assistance offered is outstanding. The site can be visited at www.ioma.com.

This is not the only site where help can be obtained. RECAP's Ask the Experts can be visited at www.recapinc.com. However, questions and answers are not posted but the company responds on an individual basis—at least for the time being. Both sites offer a valuable resource to accounts payable professionals.

### (d) Internet as a Source of Information

Many companies do not have procedures manuals but as accounts payable comes under greater scrutiny, seek to develop one. This can be a time-consuming task if starting from scratch. But why reinvent the wheel if this is not necessary. Most companies would be able to jump start the process if it were possible to get a manual from another company—but how to get that manual to use as a starting point? The Internet will help in this regard. Many colleges and universities have extensive web sites that include tons of information—including the operating policy and procedures for the institution. By doing very little sleuthing, most accounts payable professionals will be able to find more than one such manual online. Review several and select the sections that fit the company best. Then simply modify to meet the company's unique requirements. A process such as this is much easier than starting from the beginning with a blank piece of paper.

As time goes on, the applications available through the Internet will grow and the accounts payable professional who is Internet savvy will be in a position to take the most advantage.

# Part Six

# New Accounts Payable Topics

Just a few short years ago, benchmarking the accounts payable department was something few, if any, companies did. Today, companies of all sizes seek good benchmarking data to measure the effectiveness of their operations, and reliable benchmarking information is hard to find. The chapter on this topic will get those interested in the issue started.

Similarly, only a smattering of accounts payable professionals had heard of P-cards (also known as corporate procurement cards or simply purchasing cards) a few years ago. Now companies across the board are dipping their toes in the P-card waters—and looking for information on getting their programs going. The chapter on this topic will get them launched.

Although payment recovery firms have been used in accounts payable longer than benchmarking or P-cards, they are one of the best kept secrets in the field. Some experts say there are 30 such firms. Others estimate their number at 50. Whatever the number more companies are hiring these pros and reaping the benefits. The chapter will guide the reader in selecting the right firm and provide the names and numbers for some of the larger service providers in this field.

# 22

# Purchasing Card

If asked to identify the hottest trend to hit accounts payable in the last few years, most experts would pick the purchasing card. It is also referred to as a P-card or a corporate procurement card and is being used in companies of all sizes. The impetus for the card may come from purchasing or treasury or accounts payable itself. Regardless of where the original idea originates, the P-card is making the lives of accounts payable professionals easier in the companies that use them. For starters, they reduce the number of small-dollar invoices flowing through the department. If this were the only benefit, it would be enough, but there is more.

Use of the card greatly reduces the friction between purchasing and payables. It reduces the paperwork, the storage space necessary for that paperwork and probably even has an impact on the number of duplicate payments a company makes but never discovers. With procurement cards, the payment is effectively made at the time the purchase is made, completely eliminating the invoice. If there is no invoice to be paid, there can be no chance that it will be paid twice.

Companies using the card have discovered that they also boost morale as employees who are given the cards feel empowered to make certain decisions on their own and thus better about themselves.

Some companies are reluctant to give cards to employees fearing the worst—an employee will go shopping "on the company" or commit some sort of fraud. There are controls that can be put in place that will be discussed later in the chapter. However, most companies have one big control factor working in their favor: FEAR. Most require employees to sign a statement saying they understand they can be fired on the spot if the card is misused. That seems to work with most people as they are not willing to risk their jobs in exchange for a few trinkets. Combine this with the fact that most people are honest and most companies have instituted extensive controls and the fact that little fraud has been committed with these cards will come as no surprise.

## 22.1 WHAT IS A PURCHASING CARD?

It is a specialized type of corporate card that has sometimes been referred to as the "Poor Man's EDI." Experts estimate that the potential payment market for this card is in excess of $500 billion annually. Those who have used it successfully see it as a tool to reduce purchasing costs. And, it also drastically reduces the expenses related to making the payments for those purchases.

Users of the card also report that it is a wonderful employee empowerment mechanism. And, despite skeptics' concerns about abuse, next to none have been reported.

## 22.2 HOW IS A PURCHASING CARD DIFFERENT FROM A CONSUMER OR CORPORATE CARD?

The differences can be broken into three categories that are of the utmost importance to payables professionals: controls, accounting information, and reporting. None of these features are available with traditional credit cards. Individual transactions can have a dollar limit set. These limits can be as low as a few hundred dollars. This will ensure that the card is used only for the low-dollar items for which it is intended. Then, limits can be set for the individuals on a monthly basis. Finally, limits are also set on the types of merchants where the card can be used. This prevents anyone from taking a trip to Tahiti at the company's expense.

Some managers have expressed concern about the accounting information. Default accounting distributions are set up when the cards are first issued. Additionally, the information can be automated and for those with EDI capabilities, it can be transmitted electronically.

Finally, all the required detailed reporting is created through the billing statement. This doesn't mean that all accounting issues are adequately addressed. It is a well-known fact that they are not. However, many who use the card feel the minor inconveniences are more than offset by significant advantages and cost savings. And remember, the card is generally used for low-dollar purchases.

## 22.3 WHY USE A PURCHASING CARD?

At most companies, orders for less than $1,000 make up more than 50% of transactions processed. At some companies, this percentage is significantly higher than 50%. These very same orders account for less than 5% of the total payment dollars. Given that processing costs typically range from $50 to $150 per transaction, significant processing costs can be saved by moving as many of these small transactions to a purchasing card requiring only one payment.

Many experts estimate that, on average, it costs up to $150 to process one purchase order. Users of the purchasing card report that savings of up to 90% of processing costs can be realized. Lastly, those using the card say it greatly simplifies the procurement to payables process.

## 22.4 HOW DOES THE PURCHASING CARD WORK WITHIN THE COMPANY?

The manager sets guidelines and monitors the transactions as they come through monthly. The employee uses the card to order goods from the supplier. The receipts are saved by the employee who then verifies the charges on the monthly bill. The supplier receives payment from the card issuer typically within three days of the purchase. This is attractive to most suppliers since it effectively improves their payment terms dramatically. Some companies have used this fact to go back and renegotiate better pricing from their suppliers.

## 22.5 FOR WHAT OTHER APPLICATIONS CAN THE CARD BE USED?

Smart payables professionals realize that purchasing cards have enormous potential beyond their current uses. To date these cards have been mainly used by purchasing executives. But the presenters suggested that the cards could also be used for employee merchandise programs, cellular phone bill payments, small equipment rentals, legal services, fuel purchase programs, and minor service work contracts. Those reading this will probably have a few additional suggestions themselves.

## 22.6 WHAT ENHANCEMENTS CAN BE EXPECTED IN THE FUTURE?

As said earlier, there are still some accounting issues that professionals would like to see addressed. The major complaint has been the lack of adequate sales tax reporting. Most experts, along with the presenters, expect to see this matter resolved in the next year or two. Additionally, they see the following improvements: 1099 reporting, minority/women-owned business reporting, hazardous material reporting, variable data capture, and vendor incentives.

## 22.7 A PLAN ADMINISTRATOR

Some programs get bogged down because end users don't know exactly what to do, how to use the card correctly, or when to use it. A plan administrator is necessary to ensure the success of a program and see that the program doesn't fail when it should succeed. The plan administrator is the person responsible for answering the numerous questions participants in such programs seem to have. This person can keep the users from getting frustrated when nothing seems to go right and they are tempted not to use the card. If the program at a particular company is not large enough to warrant a full-time employee devoted to the topic, someone should be assigned the responsibility on a part-time basis. After all, if no one uses the card, the program becomes worthless.

## 22.8 USER FEEDBACK

To make sure the program is working according to plan, solicit user feedback. This is the only way to determine problems. Some users report that the card is extremely useful in emergency situations and with new vendors. Using the card eliminates the time lag that many experience as a new vendor goes through the credit checking routine. If a P-card is used, there is no need to establish a credit line and no delay. However, this can be costly, as will be discussed in the next section.

Since the card is so new, not all vendors accept them. Thus, users may experience some problems when they go out with the card. As use of P-cards becomes more accepted, this problem should lessen, although it will probably never completely disappear.

Once people begin to use the P-card, they often fall in love with it. It is much more convenient that filling out POs and dealing with accounts payable when a disbursement is not made on a timely basis. Some accounts payable managers report that this can even become a problem with those who try to use the P-card for everything. Some report that occasionally they have to rein in those active users who use it where other payment mechanisms are preferable.

## 22.9 VENDOR FEEDBACK

In the beginning of any program, it is also important to solicit vendor feedback. This is especially important if there is trouble signing up new suppliers for the card program. Most vendors like the card because they receive payment faster and the billing and receivable process is simplified. Both of these attributes are welcomed by vendors. However, there is one serious drawback from the vendor's standpoint: Use of these cards is costly on any large transaction.

Most P-card vendors must pay somewhere between 1.75% and 5.0% on any balance charged on a P-card. On a $50 balance, most vendors are happy to pay a dollar or two for the service. They do not have to check credit, print and mail an invoice, set up a receivable on their ledger, deposit a check, and apply cash. All this is costly. However, as the dollar amount of the receivable increases, so does the fee, since the fees are based on the value of the transaction.

On the face of it, this should not be a major issue for the customer. But it is. Eventually, all costs get passed back to the customer. If it costs your vendor an unrealistic amount to process your payment, it is only a matter of time before the vendor will incorporate those charges into its pricing scheme and pass exorbitant costs back to the end user. Don't add to vendor costs, since increases will only get passed back to the customer.

## 22.10 CONTROL FEATURES

One of the most frequent objections to P-card use is the concern that the cards will not be used properly and put the company at risk. In actuality, there has been little reported improper card use and the risk objection can be easily overcome by ensuring that the proper controls are in place. These controls include:

**Choose whom is empowered.** By only giving the card to trusted employees, employers can give themselves some level of comfort. Many have great success by having employees who are authorized to use the card sign a statement saying that the employee understands that any misuse of the card will result in automatic termination. This can serve as a powerful deterrent.

**Set card guidelines and procedures.** When a procurement card program is begun, detailed guidelines and procedures should be established. Copies of these regulations should be distributed to all affected. While this seems obvious, it is not always done.

**Limit the dollar amount of each transaction.** This is certainly a good way to minimize losses should fraud occur. The dollar limit can vary by employee and is usually related not only to the level of trust but the actual need the employee might be expected to have. These limits can always be changed if it is determined that the original level was not high enough.

**Limit the dollar amount that can be spent each month by each employee.** In addition to the dollar amount each employee can spend per transaction, it is also possible to give each a monthly allowance. This, too, can vary by employee and area of responsibility. This control device limits the amount of risk a company has with the card. Most who use the card establish per charge and monthly limits.

**Use standard industrial code (SIC) block outs.** Companies concerned that an employee will take the card and go Christmas shopping or take a trip to Tahiti can use SIC block outs. By disallowing charges at certain SIC codes, a company mitigates this issue. Of course, this matter can be resolved by the dollar limits placed on the employee for each transaction and for each month. If an employee would charge a vacation on a company credit card, the company has other, bigger, issues with this person.

**Set a departmental budget.** Another fear associated with corporate procurement cards is that everyone will go out and charge their little hearts out, buying things for the office that are *not* absolutely necessary. This, of course, rarely happens, but by setting budget levels at the departmental level, management has control over the big picture.

**Insist on a monthly review of all charge card statements and have a supervisor's signature on each statement.** This after-the-fact review will uncover any spending that might be slightly off base. It also assures management that the proper oversight is being given to all expenditures and improper spending not otherwise detected might turn up. In one of the rare cases where the card was abused, an employee was buying a computer for himself—piece-by-piece. One month a hard drive was purchased, the next a printer, then the CPU, and so on. Without the supervisory review, these items might have slipped through since they fell within the dollar amount and SIC codes allowed.

**Reserve the right to review.** At any point in time, senior management should be able to come in and review the statements for the entire company or any one department or individual. It is not a bad idea to have internal auditors, and perhaps even the external auditors, periodically spot-check the statements.

**Set up workable dispute resolution procedures with vendors.** One of the advantages of receiving an invoice that doesn't need to be paid for 30 or more days is the leverage it gives to the purchaser. If the goods turn out to be substandard or defective in any way, the purchaser can withhold all or part of the payment. This can then force the supplier to negotiate in good faith. If the supplier has been paid, it has less incentive to resolve disputes. In fact the only incentive it has is the promise of future business. By establishing dispute procedures in advance, the purchaser avoids this issue. Now some reading this might think that the vendor might have little interest in developing such a mechanism. But, remember two things. First, the vendor wants to do additional business and thus needs to placate its customers. Second, the vendor is also interested in using the procurement card. It lowers costs on both sides of the table. If a customer is dissatisfied with the service received when the procurement card is used, it will stop using it—forcing the vendor back to more costly billing and collection procedures.

**Set supplier guidelines.** This will guard against the card being used inappropriately. It will also put the vendors on notice as to what is expected. Remember, in most cases both the buyer and the seller benefit from the use of the procurement card.

**Institute card cancellation procedures.** This puts everyone on notice that the card can be revoked at any time the corporation sees fit. This is especially important in the instance of employee termination. Regardless of the reason, the accounts payable manager will want the ability to immediately cancel the card. This should be done even if the parting is amicable or the employee has left of his own volition. Not canceling a card under these circumstances is begging for trouble. Most card issuers will be able to handle this requirement.

All these controls are aimed at ensuring that a company is not put at risk by instituting a corporate procurement card program. The reality is that a company is always at risk. An employee can submit a phony invoice, steal a check meant for another, or filch a blank check. So, in many ways a procurement card program, if handled correctly, will actually reduce risk as the amounts that can be swindled are limited. Many who use the card report a side benefit not anticipated was instituted. Employees given the card often experience an increase in morale. They are pleased that the company would trust them with the card and take their responsibility for it quite seriously.

If after pointing out all the controls and all the benefits, management is still reluctant, there is another aspect to consider. When procurement cards are used, the number of small invoices drops, often dramatically. The money saved by not having to process those invoices, print checks, and then mail those checks is often quite staggering. When this figure is compared with the small amount that might be lost due to the use of the procurement card, many who were originally reluctant change their tune.

## 22.11 MAXIMIZING COST SAVINGS

While most accounts payable professionals are well aware of the cost savings potential associated with corporate procurement card programs, many do not realize that this is only the beginning. There are ways to make the purchasing card program generate some money for the company. However, the card issuer won't reveal these techniques without being asked. Examples of what innovative accounts payable managers are doing to squeeze a few more dollars out of their P-card programs include:

**Negotiating favorable terms** for the payment of the P-card bill. In most instances, payment on these cards is expected within seven days of receipt of the bill. A number of companies have succeeded in getting these terms extended to 14 and even 21 days. A company with an average bill of $1,000,000 each month might be able to add $25,000 to its bottom line by getting the card issuer to agree to accept payment on day 21 instead of day 7, assuming it invested the money at 5%. Those borrowing at higher rates would have an even greater savings. While this might not seem like an extravagant amount of money to many, it's not a bad return for the few conversations it might take to get the card issuer to agree to these terms. Those just setting up a program might make the payment terms one of the negotiating points, especially if several issuers are bidding for the business.

**Negotiating rebates from the card issuer.** This is a subject the card issuer will never initiate. However, conversations with numerous managers reveal this is going on at certain levels. In order to qualify for these rebates, your company will need to make purchases using the card at a reasonably high level. It has been suggested that the minimum program should be about $500,000 per month in expenditures on the card before the issuer will even entertain discussions about a rebate. Rebates are generally quoted in basis points with 100 basis points equaling 1%. At this level, a company might expect a rebate in the neighborhood of 5 basis points or $25,000 per month, or $300,000 on an annual basis. As programs get larger, the number of basis points the card issuer is willing to rebate grows. It has also been suggested that really big programs might be able to earn as many as 50 basis points in rebates. As with the terms, this issue can be used as a negotiating point when establishing a new program with several issuers bidding for the business.

**Rolling T&E programs into the purchasing card programs.** Why might enterprising accounts payable managers wish to take this action? There are several reasons. Obviously, it makes it easier to qualify for rebates as discussed above. Also, some of the cards will allow travelers to get cash advances on the cards. Finally, it lets the accounts payable department deal with one program rather than two. However, the main force behind such moves appears to be the desire to qualify for as large a rebate as possible.

**Using the P-card for larger dollar expenditures.** The purchasing card is typically used in organizations for small-dollar purchases. The initial idea was to get as many small-dollar invoices out of the accounts payable department as possible. That is still a motivating force. However, as these programs succeed, many are trying to push the envelope a little further. Initially certain merchants were reluctant to take the card because they did not want to give up the discount on larger items. While no one minded paying the card issuer $1 for a $50 transaction (assuming a 2% discount), many suppliers are not willing to give up that amount on larger transactions. On a $5,000 sale, this discount could be $100, again assuming a 2% discount fee. As accounts payable managers try to push the envelope on using the card, many run into the obvious stumbling block at their vendors—and who can blame these suppliers? There is some hope on this front. Certain card issuers are offering a special high dollar discount for larger invoices. Once again, this is not advertised and the company accepting the card will need to ask their servicer about it. Again, this is not a subject anyone wants to go on the record about. However, general indications are that it should be possible to get the discount reduced to somewhere around 1% for amounts over $4,000. Accounts payable managers who run into this complaint from their suppliers might suggest the vendor talk to its processor about getting such a discount reduction. While this will not be attractive to all vendors, it will definitely increase the number willing to accept purchasing cards. As the number of vendors accepting your cards grows, so will the amount of money running through the program. Not only will the number of invoices in the department be reduced, the company may qualify for those rebates nobody is talking about.

## 22.12 CONSIDERING A PROGRAM

Some readers may work at companies not considering a P-card program. If this is because the issue has not been put on the table, they are in an excellent position to become the "missionary." Begin by reading everything available about the card. Talk to peers using the card at other companies and find out how they have benefited; that is, reduced numbers of low-dollar invoices, etc. If they are willing to divulge the information, get real-dollar savings to share with management. The same strategies can be used by those employed at companies that are refusing to consider purchasing card programs. If the issues can be identified, it might be possible to find others who faced the same challenges and have overcome them. Others have overcome resistance by starting very small and gradually growing the programs. Additional information is available from these major issuers:

American Express: (800) 686-5493

MasterCard: (800) 219-1013

VISA: (800) 847-2221

Another good source of information about P-cards is the Internet.

# 23

# Post Audit Firms

As more and more CFOs focus on the bottom-line impact of payables, they are pushing accounts payable managers to wring the last cent out of their operations. These managers want to make sure that not one extra penny is paid out to vendors, suppliers, or freight companies. While accounts payable managers do their very best to make sure that the company's profits don't leak from their operation, this is often beyond their control. Duplicate payments get made and discounts are not taken. When this happens, it is up to the company making the mistake to take the necessary steps to get its money back. If the company waits for the receiving company to find the mistake, identify the cause and return it, they may be waiting a long, long time. To address this growing need, postaudit firms have emerged.

These companies, also referred to as payment or profit recovery firms, will come in after the fact, look at the payments a company has made, and then identify those payments that have been made more than once along with discounts that could have been taken and charges that were paid but should not have been. Typically, the firm works on a contingency basis collecting only if it can recover money on behalf of its clients. As might be expected, no one likes to admit to using one of these companies, but many do—including a large portion of the Fortune 500. Companies that don't use them, should. The simple reason for this is that it doesn't cost anything. If a company's controls are as good as it thinks, the profit recovery firm will find nothing. The best of these companies will also point out weaknesses in the controls of the company being audited so the client may tighten up and not continue to lose money.

## 23.1 WHY ARE ACCOUNTS PAYABLE AUDIT FIRMS NECESSARY?

An audit can rapidly uncover a number of problems. Poor controls, incomplete documentation, and rush exception checks are just a few examples. Other departments may not be providing all the information A/P needs to do its job. In some instances, businesses don't even realize they've paid twice or too much for goods or services—or paid for something the supplier was supposed to provide. Many believe that once the money's gone, it's gone. This is just not true. It's often possible to get money back, and that is exactly what astute A/P professionals do.

In order to address these problems, a growing number of corporations are turning to A/P audit firms to review their accounts payable systems, with the goal not only of discovering overpayments, but of identifying procedural weaknesses in the overall operation. Very often these weaknesses lie outside the accounts payable area. By cleaning house, not only does the company get some of its money back, it closes the loopholes that allowed the overpayments in the first place. This is not a case of locking the barn door after the horse is gone, but of actually getting the horse back!

## 23.2 HOW THEY WORK

It's really not very complicated. The audit firms come in and review your records. Since this is their area of expertise, they know where to look and which companies are the most likely to hold on to extra payments. Some companies believe that requesting statements from their vendors will allow them to identify all credits. What they don't realize is that not all vendors list credits on their statements. The audit firms know which companies are likely to omit credits from their statements even when asked to show *all* activity. They will look for:

- Duplicate payments.
- Missed discounts.
- Missed co-op funds.
- Incorrect invoices.
- Overlooked allowances.
- Excessive transportation costs.
- Purchase price variances.
- Overpayment.
- Sales tax errors.
- Real estate lease overcharges.
- Other lost opportunities.

## 23.3 ACCOUNTS PAYABLE BENEFITS

The first reaction of many accounts payable managers is to see these firms as a threat rather than a service. Nothing could be further from the truth. By identifying overpayments and their causes, these audit firms help the accounts payable manager tighten controls within his or her own organization, and crack the whip at other departments when required.

Many accounts payable managers experience great difficulty in getting other departments to change their mode of operation as it relates to accounts payable. However, when they go to these departments with data from a third party showing how the company lost money because of sloppy procedures, they have more clout within their organizations. Additionally, they will have the proposed changes recommended by the audit firm. The accounts payable manager who recommends such a service to management and then gets money back for the company will look like a real hero.

## 23.4 COSTS

Some accounts payable managers have expressed the concern that since their organizations are well run, they would be spending money needlessly for such a service. This fear is groundless, however, since these firms work on a contingency basis—they get nothing if they find nothing. And, if they only find a small amount, they only earn a small amount. In other words, the more they benefit, the more *you* benefit.

Depending on the volume and nature of your accounts payable, the auditors' fees can be as high as half of what they recover. This can be negotiated, but be aware that the fees tend to be high. Before getting outraged, remember that without their services, not only would your company get nothing, but in many instances the company wouldn't even know it was entitled to any payment. In addition, you are closing loopholes for the future.

Audits of average organizations generally show that between 0.1% and 0.2% of total payments made can be retrieved. To put this in perspective, a company that has $100 million in payables (not sales!) would recover between $100,000 and $200,000. Of course, some companies would receive more and some less. Such overpayment can plague any company. In one instance, an audit firm uncovered a duplicate payment to itself.

## 23.5 GETTING MONEY BACK

As you might expect, most vendors who are presented with a claim for a repayment or credit are not thrilled. Some are even embarrassed. Such repayments are typically made either by check, credit memo, or as a deduction against a future invoice.

Accounts payable professionals who suspect their organization might benefit from these services can recommend one of the firms profiled in the next section. What do you have to lose?

## 23.6 SELECTING THE BEST PROFIT RECOVERY FIRM

The number of profit recovery firms looking for your business is quite staggering. Some executives find it overwhelming and don't know where to start when it comes to identifying the best company to handle their companies' accounts. The following is a list of questions, supplied by RECAP, Inc., to help you make the determination:

> Does the company have experience in your industry? Familiarity with industry practices and vendors is essential to catch all erroneous payments and to avoid falsely identifying legitimate payments as erroneous.
>
> Do they obtain refunds from vendors or simply do charge backs, credits, and reversals? Some firms collect their fee after notifying the vendor that you will be taking a credit for an erroneous payment. The hiring company should be able to decide if it wants to accept a credit or insist on a refund, and the payment recovery firm should not receive its fee until the refund arrives or the credit is used.
>
> Do they pursue low-dollar recoveries? Since most of the payments are less than $500, a large pool of potential erroneous payments exists here. However, because of the difficulty involved in sifting through such a massive volume of data, some firms are reluctant to search for these items, preferring instead to concentrate on the big-dollar recoveries. A good payment recovery provider will pursue low-dollar items, thereby increasing the total amount recovered and providing a better understanding of what types of errors have occurred.
>
> How much of your staff's time and how much space at your site will be required? Some companies require desk space and telephones at your site or frequent use of your staff, systems, and equipment. Make sure that the disruptions to your operation will be minimal and that any use of your systems and equipment does not adversely impact you staff's productivity.

Will they maintain your confidentiality? Many firms do not want outsiders to know that payment recovery is outsourced. Be sure the payment recovery firm is invisible to your vendors and that your company name will not be included on advertising or promotional materials without permission.

Can the payment recovery firm accept electronic data in the format most convenient to the hiring company? The systems staff of the hiring company should not have to do any custom programming or conversion to provide files from the purchasing and accounts payable systems. The payment recovery firm should be able to accept recent backups of the files in the preferred media.

Will they suggest enhancements to the current process on an ongoing basis? The hiring company should not have to wait until the end of the project to receive an audit report. Within 60 days of providing the data for analysis, the payment recovery firms should give you suggestions specific to your operation in order to eliminate many types of erroneous payments.

Does their recovery process account for the sensitivity of the vendor relationships? Many of the vendors may also be customers or potential customers. Vendors should always be provided with substantiating documentation and given adequate time to resolve erroneous payments in a friendly manner.

Will the hiring company control the correspondence with the vendors? The hiring company should approve each claim before the vendor is notified and be aware of any contact made with the vendor on its behalf.

Ask for and CHECK at least three references. The references should be companies in your industry or related industries and of approximately similar size to the hiring company. Check with the references to see if they have had problems in any of the above nine areas.

## 23.7 OTHER CONSIDERATIONS

As alluded to in the questions in the last section, there may be times when a company chooses not to pursue an erroneous payment. Some of the reasons might include:

> The payment was made to a key vendor and the hiring company makes a decision not to pursue the reimbursement for fear that such action might hurt the relationship. This is especially important if the payment is small.
>
> Occasionally, there are political considerations. The company to whom the erroneous payment was made may be owned by a member of the board of directors and rather than taking the chance of bringing the matter to this person's attention, the payment is forgone.
>
> If there is any chance of negative backlash, a company may also choose to avoid pursuing repayment.

## 23.8 REACTION TO PROFIT RECOVERY FIRMS

While hiring companies love payment recovery firms, the accounts receivable managers on the other side of the fence are growing to hate them. They consider them a real nuisance since investigating such claims often require going back through records that have been shipped off to cold storage. Some companies, mostly the larger 800-pound gorillas are:

> Refusing to look at claims that are more than 24 months old.
>
> Refusing to look at large batches of claims but rather are insisting that each claim be sent individually.
>
> Writing clauses in sales contracts limiting reviews to 24 months.

These trends make it more imperative than ever that if a company intends to use a payment recovery service, it should be hired relatively quickly and frequently.

## 23.9 SELF-AUDITING

Some companies are reluctant to pay others for a task they feel they should be able to complete themselves. An approach that has been used successfully by several companies undertaking a self-audit is:

Use the invoice amount and the invoice date.

Take two to three years of payment history.

Create a program that uses that history and a subset of the accounts payable master and creates a report that is stratified in two or three different ways.

Have someone familiar with the company's payments review the results and then check against "hard copy" data (invoices and purchase orders).

When the information is verified, collect what's owed to the company.

## 23.10 CONCLUSION

Payment recovery firms offer a valuable service to the companies that hire them. Not only do they obtain money for the company that would never be obtained without them, but they also help uncover weakness in procedures that permit these payments to be made in the first place. The company that hires such an outfit should end up with a report that can be used to force other departments to change their processes and procedures that are causing these problems in the first place. A judicious use of payment recovery firms can help in more ways than is apparent at first glance.

# 24

# Benchmarking

Benchmarking has become a hot issue in virtually every department in corporate America. Accounts payable is no different. Ed Koch, the former New York City mayor, used to get away with asking constituents, "How am I doing?" but such an informal survey would not be adequate for most of the powers that be. It looks like everyone wants to measure themselves against something—and the amount of data available for accounts payable is quite small. However, when a meaningful measuring tool can be found, benchmarking can provide a wonderful resource for those who really do want to know how they are doing. As long as it is done carefully, everyone can benefit.

Benchmarking will reveal who is doing a good job and who needs some process improvements. It is also a wonderful way to identify inefficient processes. If other companies in the same industry can process double the number of invoices than at a particular company, then that company needs to do some investigating.

## 24.1 WHAT IS BENCHMARKING?

Benchmarking is the process by which a company measures its performance against the performance of a group of similar companies. Those who come out on top are typically referred to as world class or best in class. That's the group everyone wants to be in. But that is very difficult to do. For if it were easy and everyone could do it, then that performance would be considered average and not world class.

However wonderful benchmarking can be, it must be done carefully in order for it to be accurate. It is very easy to get off mark—especially in accounts payable where processes are not cut and dry and the same from organization to organization.

### (a) Benchmarking Caveats

What can go wrong? Just about everything under the sun. By carefully considering the following issues, accounts payable professionals can avoid some of the obvious benchmarking problems:

Are you comparing similar processes? Unfortunately, every company does things a little differently. This means that the process at one company will be different than the process at the next. For example, in preparing a check, some companies will have the checks computer signed at the time the check is printed while others will have the check signed by hand. Some will have only one signature and others will require two. Some will allow lower-level employees to sign checks while others will require relatively high-level (read that to say highly paid) employee signatures. All these issues will affect the number of checks a clerk can prepare and the cost for preparing the check.

Are you benchmarking the company against those in a similar industry and of similar size? Both these issues will affect processes and costs as discussed above. For example, invoices received in certain industries are rather straightforward and are relatively easy to process while others are difficult to read and may have many deductions and other adjustments. Where these issues are resolved will also affect the number of invoices an individual can process.

Are the benchmarking costs reported fully loaded? If they are, rents in different parts of the country can have a radical impact on costs. Depending on the part of the country where the company is located, a low rent can hide a myriad of problems while a high rent can make it look like problems exist where none actually do.

Are there any special circumstances surrounding your operations? If clerks are expected to perform special chores not normally performed in the accounts payable department, it will affect the outcome of the benchmarking. If petty cash is handled by one of the clerks, numbers will be lower than if 100% of the time were devoted to invoice handling.

All this is not meant to discourage those interested in benchmarking. It is a good practice—when used intelligently. Rather than look at the results as being etched in stone, it can be used to guide a department in looking for process and productivity improvements.

## 24.2 SOURCES OF BENCHMARKING DATA

There are a number of places that accounts payable professionals can get useful benchmarking data. They include:

Consultants such as KPMG periodically survey their clients. The results produced by these firms tend to be for large Fortune 500 companies and are not especially useful for middle-market companies

The IAPP periodically surveys its members and participants receive a copy. However, there is a charge for participating in the survey. Recently that charge was $100.

The IOMA Benchmarking Accounts Payable Survey. This undertaking is completed once a year. Subscribers to the newsletter, *Managing Accounts Payable,* are given the opportunity to participate in the survey. Respondents to the survey are given the results for free and IOMA sells the results to anyone else for $129. Call (212) 244-0360 for more information.

Salary information—several personal consultants, such as Watson Wyatt, tabulate average salary data for a wide variety of titles including those related to accounts payable titles. This data is extremely useful in determining whether departmental salaries are adequate.

## 24.3 SOME IOMA STATISTICS

Just under 700 companies responded to the first annual IOMA benchmarking survey, making it the largest such survey of its kind. The results provide the first in-depth look at how accounts payable departments operate at companies of all sizes, not just large ones, across the nation. Departmental statistics include:

Women hold just under two-thirds of managerial positions in accounts payable. Interestingly, there is virtually no difference between men and women in average age, years of work experience, or years of accounts payable experience.

The "average" accounts payable manager has a staff of 7.75 people. However, the greatest number, just over one-third of all respondents, have staffs of two or fewer members. Large accounts payable staffs are not the oddity that some might expect, however. Over 8% report having more than 20 staffers in their department.

Approximately one-third of the respondents have international dealings, either handling payments made by employees outside the United States or making payments in foreign currencies.

### (a) Payment Errors

There are two caveats to take into consideration when reviewing the data for payments with errors. The reported figures reflect only what people are willing to admit to and also only what they know about. By the very nature of the issue, the numbers given will be lower than the actual incidence. How can an error be included if no one is aware of the problem?

Also, many companies do not formally track the number of errors made in their payments. This was clear from the fact that almost 15% of those filling out the survey entered "less than one percent" on the line where the error rate was to be entered. This group was not included when calculating the average error rate. It should be noted that, with very few exceptions, everyone who entered less than 1% for vendor payment errors did so for T&E errors as well.

Overall, almost 2% of all vendor payments have errors and 1.32% of all vendor checks are destroyed and reissued. From this data, it can be concluded that the remainder of the errors are found after the payment has been made. While there is some variation in the numbers based on company size, it does not appear to be huge.

### (b) Payment Processing Costs

Once again, several caveats must be used when reviewing the data in this section. The steps included in processing an invoice for payment are different from company to company. Certain functions are sometimes handled in accounts payable, sometimes in purchasing, and sometimes in treasury. This is part of the reason that payment processing costs vary so much from one firm to the next.

On average, it costs an accounts payable department $16.54 to process a vendor payment and $14.51 to do the same for a T&E (see Exhibit 24.1). These figures may seem a little high. However, over 7% of the companies responding reported a check-processing cost of over $50. A close review of the data also revealed quite a few companies reporting amounts in excess of this amount. When the numbers were rerun, eliminating all who had entered $50 or higher, the average dropped to $10.55 for vendor payments and to $10.90 for T&Es.

The very largest companies, those with more than 5,000 employees, have the most success in keeping their costs to process a payment down. They are followed closely by those with fewer than 10 employees. Interestingly enough, those with between 100 and 249 workers have the highest costs.

## 24.3 Some IOMA Statistics

### *Exhibit 24.1* Payment Processing Costs

| | *Vendor Payments* | *T & Es* |
|---|---|---|
| **Average cost to process payments** | | |
| *Cost* | % | % |
| $0 to $5 | 52.9 | 49.0 |
| $6 to $10 | 13.5 | 16.6 |
| $11 to $15 | 3.7 | 7.3 |
| $16 to $20 | 5.1 | 4.2 |
| $21 to $25 | 8.4 | 5.4 |
| $26 to $50 | 9.4 | 10.4 |
| over $50 | 7.1 | 4.6 |
| *Average cost* | 16.5 | 14.5 |
| **Average cost to process by size of company** | | |
| *Number of employees* | | |
| 0 to 99 | $12.04 | $11.58 |
| 100 to 249 | 26.66 | 20.13 |
| 250 to 499 | 16.06 | 16.75 |
| 500 to 999 | 17.12 | 15.58 |
| 1,000 to 4,999 | 18.76 | 14.46 |
| Over 5,000 | 8.15 | 9.83 |
| **Average cost by number of invoices processed** | | |
| *Number of invoices* | | |
| 0 to 500 | $18.05 | $16.02 |
| 501 to 1,000 | 19.21 | 19.15 |
| 1,001 to 5,000 | 19.19 | 16.15 |
| 5,001 to 10,000 | 15.13 | 9.69 |
| Over 10,000 | 9.50 | 8.40 |
| **Average cost to process by industry** | | |
| *Industry* | | |
| Manufacturing | $18.64 | $14.73 |
| Finance | 12.79 | 11.69 |
| Utilites, trans. | 14.84 | 7.54 |
| Private practice | 17.12 | 18.34 |
| Nonprofit | 9.66 | 23.18 |
| Wholesale/retail/dist. | 16.91 | 16.66 |
| Health care | 7.09 | 8.86 |
| Education | 29.29 | 25.00 |
| Communications | 14.07 | 17.19 |
| Construction | 16.90 | 5.12 |
| Other | 22.44 | 15.17 |

(Source: IOMA's 1997 Benchmarking Survey)

Processing a large number of invoices also seems to have a positive impact on processing costs for both invoice payments and T&Es.

Industry also seems to have an impact on final costs. This might be due to special processes used in certain industries. Healthcare and nonprofit firms seem to have the best luck in keeping costs down, while education companies fail badly at doing so.

### (c) Processing Time

On average, it takes an accounts payable department 7.3 days to process an invoice for payment (see Exhibit 24.2). However, this number is pulled down by the small group that takes a long time to process. Almost two-thirds of those responding turn an invoice around in less than six days. This is offset by the 7.3% who take over 21 days to complete this task.

Neither the size of the company nor the number of invoices processed appear to have much impact on the speed at which an invoice is processed.

Not only do education companies have a hard time in keeping their processing costs down, they take the longest time to process an invoice for payment. Quickest are finance companies and the potpourri labeled "other."

## 24.4 BENCHMARKING APPLICATIONS

While most people think of using benchmarking to measure staff performance or costs, a growing number of accounts payable professionals are finding ways to use it to improve their operations. By thinking "outside the box" it is possible to develop methods of measuring for productivity improvements. Some of the nontraditional ways it can be used include:

Maximize vendor relationships.

Identify high-producing employees.

Measure customer service for problem resolution.

Identify problem makers.

Reduce duplicate payments.

## *Exhibit 24.2* Payment Processing Time

**Average time to process invoices**

| *Number of days* | *Percentage of Respondents* |
|---|---|
| 0 to 2.9 | 26.6% |
| 3 to 5.9 | 39.6 |
| 6 to 10.9 | 19.5 |
| 11 to 20.9 | 7.1 |
| over 21 | 7.3 |
| Average time | 7.3 |

**Average time by size of company**

| *Number of employees* | *Number of Days* |
|---|---|
| 0 to 99 | 6.6 |
| 100 to 249 | 8.5 |
| 250 to 499 | 6.5 |
| 500 to 999 | 8.1 |
| 1,000–4,999 | 6.6 |
| over 5,000 | 8.4 |

**Average time by number of invoices (combined PO and non-PO)**

| *Number of invoices* | *Number of Days* |
|---|---|
| 0 to 500 | 7.1 |
| 501 to 1,000 | 6.9 |
| 1,001 to 5,000 | 7.7 |
| 5,001 to 10,000 | 7.1 |
| over 10,000 | 8.0 |

**Average invoice processing time by industry**

| *Industry* | *Number of Days* |
|---|---|
| Manufacturing | 7.14 |
| Finance | 4.85 |
| Utilities, trans. | 7.80 |
| Private practice | 7.83 |
| Nonprofit | 6.28 |
| Wholesale/retail/dist. | 7.06 |
| Health care | 7.32 |
| Education | 13.21 |
| Communications | 9.27 |
| Construction | 10.20 |
| Other | 4.64 |

(Source: IOMA's 1997 Benchmarking Survey)

### (a) Maximize Vendor Relationships

Many have at their fingertips valuable vendor information that can be used to track the volume, both by dollar amount and items ordered, by vendor. Use these numbers to identify high-volume vendors and assign each to a particular staff member. This can help to smooth the relationship with key suppliers.

With this information, a savvy purchasing department can also negotiate quantity discounts, where applicable, and solidify relationships. Rather than order the same item from a dozen vendors, the company can limit its purchases of a particular article to two or three vendors. Limiting the number of vendors will result in a larger quantity being ordered from each, giving purchasing additional strength to negotiate discounts.

This information can typically be manipulated out of the accounts payable system—something most purchasing departments do not have access to. Teaming with purchasing to obtain this data and analyze it can enable both departments to come out winners.

### (b) Identify High-Producing Employees

Another way to look at the numbers is to see how many transactions are handled by each employee. Even if the system cannot calculate it, it is often possible to do this by hand with a little effort. Use these numbers to determine which staff members are producing the largest number of invoices. Are they more efficient because they are doing something different, or are they just more efficient? This is another place where it is important to make sure apples are being compared with apples. Sometimes an employee looks like he is processing a large number of invoices when in actuality the employee is simply handling the easy no-problem invoices.

### (c) Measure Customer Service for Problem Resolution

Track customer service inquires by type. This will help the department identify areas that should be changed or processes that need tightening. If a large number of calls are received because deductions are not clear, the company may want to include a note on the check stub identifying such deductions to help eliminate some phone calls. Of course, if the vendor does not view the deductions as legitimate, the problem will not be solved. Then determine whether these deductions should be taken or if they are actually costing more than they are saving.

Similarly, if an unduly large number of complaints revolve around the work of a certain staffer, a little retraining may be in order.

### (d) Identify Problem Makers

Track the quality of incoming work. In many companies, the accounts payable department "cleans up" the mistakes made by a variety of other departments. These errors are often made through carelessness, laziness, or sometimes just plain lack of knowledge. By identifying the culprit departments and then the cause of the errors, it is often possible to fix some of them. Once again, a little training may be called for.

If it is not, more aggressive action may be needed. Making it more trouble for the offending party to fix a mistake will slowly correct the problem. Initially, it will be more work for accounts payable, but ultimately the department will be rewarded with better incoming work.

For example, if the purchasing manager often forgets to code invoices before they are submitted for payment, send them back for coding. Many accounts payable professionals fall into the trap of simply looking up the code themselves: It's easier than sending it back. But, it does not encourage the purchasing manager to complete the form correctly the next time—why should he take the time to look up the correct code if accounts payable will do it for him?

### (e) Reduce Duplicate Payments

Keep a log of all duplicate payments, including who the offending party was. It is quite possible that a pattern will emerge and it will become clear who the culprit is. Again, it is imperative that offending parties be made aware of their errors.

As can be seen from the examples discussed earlier, benchmarking can lead to productivity improvements that will also make everyone in accounts payable's life just a little less stressful while possibly improving the company's bottom line.

# Part Seven

# Other Accounts Payable Topics

This section contains some commentary on an odd assortment of issues that may or may not land in accounts payable—depending on the company. Still, they should be discussed as they can make a serious impact if not handled correctly.

# 25

# 1099s

Employee or independent contractor? That is the question facing many accounts payable professionals. Often, there is simply no straightforward answer. However, the penalties for getting it wrong can be significant. The information provided here is intended to give the reader an overview of the subject. It is by no means complete as that is beyond the scope of this book. At the end of this chapter is a list of resources that will provide additional assistance to those who wish to learn more about this important issue.

## 25.1 BACKGROUND

Each year in January, companies must provide W-2s to all their employees so these individuals can complete their income tax reports. At the same time the W-2s are given to the employees, the information is provided to the Internal Revenue Service (IRS). Usually, that process is quite straightforward. However, there is a second part to this scenario and it involves those who are not employees. Companies making payments to independent contractors must report that income to the IRS as well. The information is reported to the recipient of the income on a form known as a 1099. Those receiving 1099s must include the amounts reported on the 1099 as income.

In order for a company to complete a 1099, it must have the

entity's tax identification number (TIN). If the entity is a person, it will probably be that individual's social security number. If the receiving entity is a business, it will be its TIN. This information is usually obtained by having a W-9 (which is similar to a W-4) filled out. While this might seem straightforward to those reading this chapter, it can turn into a nightmare for the accounts payable department. Why? For starters, getting W-9s filled out tends to fall through the cracks in many organizations. When year-end rolls around, the accounts payable staff is often faced with the unenviable task of not only identifying all those payments that will require 1099s, but also of obtaining all missing W-9s.

Getting those missing W-9s can be a nightmare as many individuals who received such income have no interest in having it reported to the IRS. If the social security number can not be identified, then the income can't be reported and that individual will not have to pay income tax on it. Thus, once the funds are received, the vendor has no incentive to provide the necessary TIN.

The second issue regarding W-9s revolves around the transient nature of many vendors. Many are long gone by the time year end arrives, even if they are willing to provide the TIN, and locating them can be frustrating. Even when these individuals can be located and are willing to provide the necessary information, the task is still a thankless waste of time.

## 25.2 BEST 1099 PRACTICE

Virtually every expert on this topic will recommend holding back the first payment until the W-9 has been received. When money is owed to someone they are most likely to provide whatever is asked. Once the funds have been paid, the strong bargaining chip has been removed and the vendor is now in control. No matter how many complaints come from the various powers that be, accounts payable professionals need to stick to their guns on this issue. If a vendor won't supply a TIN when it is owed money, why would they supply it later on when there is no incentive. It can not be emphasized strongly enough to hold off payment until the necessary information has been received.

## 25.3 WHAT IF THE 1099 IS NOT FILED?

For starters, there is a penalty of $50 for each 1099 not filed. Now many reading this may be thinking to themselves, "Well, that's not so bad," but that is just the beginning. The IRS can also require the 31% backup withholding of the amount distributed. Once the vendor is gone, so is the money. Now, if the payment is large, so will the 31%. Let's look at a $100,000 payment. The backup withholding would be $31,000. Thus, the penalties for not filing a 1099 can be substantial. Don't let anyone gloss over the issue as simply having a $50 penalty charge—that is just the beginning.

When the pressure comes from above to make a payment without having the information on file needed to complete the year-end 1099, calculate the costs to the company and ask if the company is prepared to pay the IRS the required amount should the W-9 not be forthcoming.

## 25.4 WHO SHOULD RECEIVE A 1099

Needless to say, this is not simple either. Independent contractors definitely receive 1099s. Generally, these are nonemployees who are recipients of payments subject to backup withholding taxes. 1099s are also given to directors. Many, but by no means all, people prefer to have the income reported on a 1099 instead of a W-2. This has to do with the fact that many expenses can be written off against 1099 income that cannot be written off against W-2 income.

Corporations typically do not get 1099s, with the exception of medical corporations. The rules relating to medical corporations and doctors are quite complicated and those dealing with those entities should get additional information.

### (a) Employees and 1099s

Employees generally do not get 1099s. Bonuses paid to employees should not be reported on a 1099. Only under very special circumstances would an individual be considered an employee, receive a W-2, and also receive payments that would be reported on a 1099.

The IRS will look very suspiciously at a company who pays someone as an employee on a W-2 and also on a 1099. Employee expenses also should not be reported on 1099s.

### (b) Documentation

Companies that do not wish to have trouble with the IRS over whether an individual is an employee or an independent contractor should take the trouble to document their files correctly. Some, including some that you would never expect, have run into trouble when it was concluded that the person working was actually an employee and not an independent contractor. Microsoft has had a rather lengthy battle over this issue. Ideally, a person would work for more than one company and report income from several sources. This helps make the independent contractor connection clear. However, this is clearly beyond the control of the hiring company. The hiring company should keep complete files documenting the independent contractor status of its hires. Each should contain:

A W-9.

A business card.

A contract detailing the agreement with the independent contractor.

Invoices from the independent contractor on its letterhead.

Anything else that will clearly indicate the independent contractor status.

These files should be kept as part of the vendor files and not as part of the employee files. After all, the independent contractors are vendors.

## 25.5 LETTERS INSTEAD OF W-9S

Occasionally someone will provide a letter with the TIN number instead of the W-9. This is acceptable if it contains a statement that says the document was signed under penalty of perjury and the information supplied is true and accurate.

## 25.6 B-NOTICES

Not everyone gets the TIN using a W-9. Some accounts payable professionals, especially those who are trying to get a large number of 1099s issued in January, will simply call the recipient and get the numbers over the phone. This approach is not a good idea as many mistakes are made this way. It is sloppy and no signed document exists. Someone is less likely to write down an incorrect number if they are signing the document than if they are giving the number over the phone. Even where no malice is intended, numbers transmitted orally are more apt to have a mistake in them.

When the IRS gets the information, it will send a B-Notice to those who issued incorrect 1099s, that is those documents where the recorded social security number does not match the recorded name. When such notices are received, a company has 30 days to correct them. If there is a signed W-9 in the file, it does not take much work to pull the file and make the necessary changes. However, if the information was gotten orally, there can be problems. Trying to track someone down long after the fact can be almost impossible if the individual has moved.

Don't ignore these notices as the IRS will assess the same penalties for incorrect 1099s that are not corrected as it would if none were filed. Thus, the 31% withholding could kick in. One company that ignored its B-notices found itself facing an IRS assessment for almost half a million dollars.

### (a) What if the Independent Contractor Can't Be Located

The IRS doesn't care. It wants its money and it is not too particular as to who pays it. Poor recordkeeping on the part of a company is not its problem.

## 25.7 TYPES OF PAYMENTS REFLECTED ON 1099S

There are several types of payments that must be reflected on 1099s. These include:

Payments of $600 or more.

Royalties or broker payments.

Certain sales of consumer products.

Payments subject to backup withholding.

## 25.8 TIMING AND DEADLINES

1099s must be provided to individuals by January 31. This is part of the reason for the January rush in many accounts payable departments. The information must be reported to the Internal Revenue Service no later than February 28. In both these cases the information provided is for the entire prior calendar year.

## 25.9 MORE HELP FROM THE IRS

The revised edition of the IRS's Worker Classification Training Manual, *Employee or Independent Contractor*, designed to provide guidance to IRS field agents for use in audits on income and payroll tax issues, was recently released. The document, which is more than 100 pages long, seeks to provide agents with both guidance and factors to consider in determining whether an individual providing services to a company is an employee (for whom the company should withhold income and payroll taxes and pay a share of payroll taxes) or an independent contractor (for whom the company has no such responsibility). Accounts payable managers confronted with the employee/independent contractor issue will find useful guidance in this manual.

The IRS also has released a revised "Classification Settlement Program" (CSP), under which the IRS will make a standardized settlement offer to an employer once it determines that the employer has classified its workers improperly.

The CSP is supposed to replicate what would have happened if the employer went through the entire process and obtained relief at the appeal or judicial level. Thus, the offer, if given, is expected to reduce costs for both the IRS and employers by jumping straight to the bottom line. This should also make life a little easier for those accounts payable professionals confronted with this issue.

## 25.10 OTHER RESOURCES

Keeping current on the IRS's thinking on independent contractors versus employees can be difficult for accounts payable professionals. To get the latest information on this difficult topic, contact IRS publications at (800) TAX-FORM to obtain your free copies of Publication 15-a—*Employee Supplemental Tax Guide* and Publication 1976—*Independent Contractor or Employee?* These publications offer industry-specific examples and discussion of how the IRS conceivably could classify individuals under similar circumstances as well as info on whether you are eligible to use the Section 530 safe harbor exception. And for good measure read what the IRS agents are reading—the training materials on worker classification.

Those looking for help with the issue of missing TINs can get help from the IRS website.

# 26

# Petty Cash

Petty cash is one of those pain-in-the-neck functions that the accounts payable department gets saddled with in many companies. This often happens despite the fact that any auditor worth his or her salt will tell you it doesn't belong there. Still, the responsibility is often given to the accounts payable department. Given that fact, it is important to take a look at the right way and the wrong way to handle the petty cash function.

## 26.1 PETTY CASH NO-NOS

Some companies are quite loose in the way their petty cash boxes are handled. Virtually everyone associated with the function has a horror story or two to tell. Embezzlements that began as short-term loans, funds used to pay for activities that most would consider questionable at best, and personal IOUs are just the tip of the iceberg.

While most accounts payable professionals given responsibility for the petty cash box are not in a position to set company policy regarding the funds, they usually have some freedom to make recommendations. Getting those ideas listened to, however, is another matter—particularly if their ideas might inconvenience a higher-up. It might be more difficult to promote change at privately held companies where some owners sometimes treat the firm's cash as though it were their own—which it technically is. A well-run petty cash system should not allow:

- Borrowing by any individual.
- Check-cashing privileges for employees.
- Access by anyone other than the individuals responsible for the box.
- Unapproved cash disbursements.

## 26.2 RECOMMENDED PROCEDURES

In an ideal world, there would be no petty cash boxes. However, the harsh truth is that most companies think they need them and so it is necessary to establish sound operating procedures. The petty cash fund should be kept in a secure place with limited access. Some security-conscious companies keep the money in a locked box, which is then placed in the company safe. As a basic precaution, personnel with access to the locked box shouldn't have the combination to the safe. Thus, at least two employees will be needed in order to get any money out of the box. At a minimum, the money should be kept in an envelope in a locked drawer. Other important security measures include:

- A reconciliation form either attached to the envelope or kept in the box. Every time a withdrawal is made, an entry should be made on the form. This should be initialed by the person disbursing the funds.
- The person getting the funds should have a request signed by someone empowered to authorize such disbursements.
- The reconciliation forms should have sequential control numbers and be used in numerical order.
- The fund should be reimbursed and audited on a regular basis.
- Surprise audits should be performed.

Disbursing funds from petty cash is one function where separation of duties is imperative. Only a limited number of individuals should have the ability to access the box. The only reason more than one person should be authorized is so there will be adequate coverage in case of absences and vacations. This is *not* a function where every officer should have access to the box.

Given the fact that petty cash funds are, in most cases, a necessary evil, astute accounts payable managers will establish procedures to ensure the safety of the funds while still meeting the company's needs for ready cash.

## 26.3 OTHER RECOMMENDED PROCEDURES

Handling petty cash for a company can eat up a good chunk of time unless procedures are set up and enforced to prevent that from happening. Use of petty cash should be held to a minimum, recognizing of course, that there will be emergency situations where the time frames will not be able to be enforced. However, an emergency must be just that—not that someone forgot to go to the bank or is too rushed to do so. If a company MUST have petty cash, the following procedures will help minimize the disruptions it causes:

- Set a predetermined time when cash will be disbursed.
- Ask for several days' notice if a large amount of cash is to be given to one or more individuals or if a large number will be making withdrawals at the same time. This might happen if the company is sending a large number of people to a conference or if it is holding an off-site meeting for executives. In these instances, the person coordinating the event should notify the person responsible for the petty cash.
- Actively discourage the use of petty cash. If the company gives travel advances, try and have those advances handled via check.
- Look for alternative procedures such as P-cards and perhaps, as many companies have done, move to a policy of giving no travel advances.
- Do not accept IOU notes in the box when staff members run a bit short of cash and don't have time to go to the bank. True story: one company did allow such a practice and the man-

ager handling the box found himself in an awkward position when the executive who had given the IOU had a heart attack and died suddenly. However, his discomfort was short lived as one of the deceased's friends came forward and bought the IOU back.

## 26.4 MAKING THE BEST OUT OF A BAD SITUATION

Once the petty cash function has been given to accounts payable and there is no way to get it out of the department, try and look at it as an opportunity. Generally speaking, petty cash is used by individuals high up in the organization—those executives who might be able to give the accounts payable professional a boost in his or her career. Therefore, once it becomes clear that the function will be in accounts payable, handle it like a professional. Provide courteous service always remembering that the individuals using the cash may one day be in a position to offer career assistance. This often gives the professional access to executives they might never meet otherwise.

Now often the requests for cash will come through the executive's secretary. Never underestimate the power of these individuals. Treat them poorly and they will go back and make sure their boss know of the shoddy behavior in the accounts payable department. Treat them like royalty and they will tout the praises of the department. Once it becomes clear that petty cash will remain in the domain of accounts payable, look at it as an opportunity rather than just another headache.

This, however, does not mean that the accounts payable professional should overlook any chance to get the function moved elsewhere. When the auditors come in for the annual review, make sure they are aware that petty cash is handled in the department. This might be the one time accounts payable might want to be in the management letter. Let the outside auditor note in its management letter that petty cash should be moved elsewhere—for control reasons, of course. If the suggestion comes from the auditor, it just might be accepted.

There is another way that a few accounts payable professionals have gotten rid of this disagreeable task. It is a bit devious and some might not feel right about using this approach. In most organizations there are one or more individuals who will take on any work—no matter how far from their normal responsibilities the task might be. Typically these individuals will dump the unglamorous work on their poor unsuspecting staff while basking in the glow of praise from the department manager who has managed to unload the undesirable task. These individuals also tend to think that more responsibility translates into more power—even when taking on tasks normally below their rank. If such an individual can be identified within the organization, find the right time to broach the topic of moving the function out of the department. Find a way to make it look glamorous rather than tedious, and the individual may jump at the opportunity.

Handling the petty cash function for a company is a thankless task. The best anyone stuck with the function can hope for is to break even or have the company eliminate the process. Following the procedures discussed in this chapter will help keep the issue under some sort of control.

# 27

# Making International Payments

Making international payments is very different from making domestic payments. For starters, it may be necessary to make those payments in another currency. This introduces a whole other element into the payment function, one that is alien to most who deal only with domestic transactions. The best source of information for those getting started is their local bank. Ask the banker for information about making such payments long before any live transaction is available. This will allow the accounts payable professional the time to make the necessary preparations and to discover the best method for the company given the nature of its business. Unfortunately, this is not always possible as these matters seem to rear their ugly heads at the last moment. Lack of time to prepare is just the beginning of the problems.

The cost of making an international payment can be staggering if attention is not paid to *all* the details involved. Yet quite often, especially at organizations that don't have many international payments each day, some of these details are overlooked. Some strategies to use to reduce international payment costs are:

Foreign exchange.

Bank account issues.

Payment mechanisms.

International payment service.

Benefits of international payment services.

## 27.1 FOREIGN EXCHANGE

Companies purchasing small amounts of foreign exchange at any time get slaughtered on the exchange rate. If you don't believe this, check the foreign exchange rates quoted in the *Wall Street Journal* the next time foreign exchange is purchased at your company. The reason for this is the small size of the purchase. To get around this problem, some companies use bank online systems to purchase foreign exchange. While this is not always possible, it's worth the effort.

When purchasing the foreign exchange deal directly with the traders. Do not go to a correspondent. Why? Because they will have to be paid. They'll tack on a spread to the price quoted by the trader and this spread will often be quite hefty. Ask for quotes for the amount needed. And, ask for quotes from several banks. Let them all know that several quotes are being gotten and that you intend to come back shortly for a live quote.

Now occasionally a great quote will be given when asking for an indicative quote, and then a lousy one when the trade goes live. Don't let this happen. The bank should give a quote that it can live with for a few minutes. If it seems out of whack, call back one of the other banks and ask them for a live quote. If the first institution was playing games, let them know in no uncertain terms that this is not acceptable and future deals will be in jeopardy if it ever happens again—and if it does, drop them forever.

## 27.2 BANK ACCOUNT ISSUES

If it is feasible, open an in-country account where balances in local currencies can be maintained. This works well if there are some receivables in the local currency. It also saves the spreads on round-trip foreign exchange transactions. While this suggestion will only work for a few companies, it is worthwhile considering if the foreign sales from the company happen to fall into this category.

## 27.3 PAYMENT MECHANISMS

If payments are made to the same institutions on a regular basis, not necessarily in the same amounts, try and make those payments repetitive transfers. Why? It is much less expensive this way, less prone to error, misrouting, and fraud.

Consider also reverse wires using SWIFT. This is similar to Fedwire and the debiting party's banker will confirm before sending the funds. If this is done, use the SWIFT MT-100 format.

## 27.4 INTERNATIONAL PAYMENT SERVICE

Technology has changed payment processing for international payments. Real-time foreign exchange trading is now available thanks to inexpensive automation. These real-time systems take advantage of personal computers and networks. They have made discount international payment services possible. Most are available through money center banks.

Ask a local bank if these services are offered. If they are, realize that an intermediary bank may be involved, so check. If the services aren't offered locally, try one of the money center banks.

## 27.5 BENEFITS OF INTERNATIONAL PAYMENT SERVICES

There are some very real benefits to be realized by using one of these services. These advantages come from both reduced costs and improved controls. For starters, the fees associated with these services tend to be fixed rather than variable. Soft costs and uncertainty are eliminated.

Use of such a service also transforms the relationship from what may have been adversarial to cooperative. If there were constant fights over the foreign exchange levels, it is not likely that the relationship was smooth. By eliminating the source of friction, the foreign exchange trading, the relationship has a much better chance of progressing smoothly.

The automated support and reporting capabilities of these systems minimizes errors, improves controls and allows 24 hour a day access. It no longer matters what part of the country the company is located in nor where the banker may be.

The systems also offer security features that, as fraud becomes a bigger issue, are becoming more and more important. This is done through a dual password and data encryption. These last two features will make the auditors happy.

These services are great for those making a few international payments a week, although some of the banks will be happy to sign you up as a client with even fewer payments. Should you have that number of payments or more, investigating these new services may solve more than one or two of your international payment issues.

## 27.6 PAYMENTS TO NAFTA PARTNERS

Canada and Mexico are not only the United States' NAFTA partners, but the largest and third-largest U.S. trading partners. Given these facts, it is likely that accounts payable professionals making international payments will do so to a company in one of these locales at some point in their career. Thus, it is important to understand the ways banking and payment systems in these two countries differ from those in the United States.

### (a) Canada

Canada is the easier of the two to understand, as it is similar in many ways to the United States. With the exception of Quebec, where French is spoken, the language and culture are the same as in this country. Payments are typically made in either Canadian or U.S. dollars and are primarily paper-based, although the country has a high usage of EFT/EDI. Canadians are most accustomed to checks, although on a percentage basis there are more EDI payments than in the United States.

Lockboxes are not as common as in the United States and the mail system is poor. This has an impact on cross-border transactions. Mail is generally delivered to company offices, not post office boxes. The big difference in Canada involves what many American companies view as their God-given right: float. In Canada, there is no bank float. Thus, the games that U.S. companies play when paying their vendors don't work in Canada, if the payment is made from a Canadian bank. Drawing a check on a bank located in Montreal to pay a vendor in Vancouver will gain the company nothing.

Because of this lack of float issue, there are no advantages of using remote locations for bank accounts. Controlled disbursement accounts do not exist, as there is immediate availability on Canadian dollar checks. Generally speaking, there is a one- to two-day availability on checks denominated in U.S. dollars. Again, partially because of the lack of float issue, wire transfers are used less frequently than in the United States.

However, there is one big similarity that accounts payable managers should be aware of: positive pay is offered by Canadian banks. Any company with bank accounts in Canada is advised to use it there, as well as in the United States.

### (b) Mexico

Unlike Canada, it is safe to say that banking and making payments in Mexico is quite different from in the United States. For starters, the different language and business culture present obstacles to those not familiar with the norms in that part of the world. While this may seem obvious, do not underestimate the importance of cultural differences. Payments are generally made in pesos or U.S. dollars. The big difference, however, occurs with the choice of payment mechanism. A full 92% of all transactions are made in cash, with 6% being made by check, and only 2% by EFT.

Mexican banks push EFT because check fraud is such a problem. According to many experts, check fraud in Mexico is several times worse than in the United States. This should give some indication of the magnitude of the problem in Mexico. The mail system in Mexico can best be described as inadequate—and this is probably a charitable characterization. Lockboxes are not used.

For those not familiar with accounts payable in Mexico, the tale is quite amusing. Typically, companies make payments once a week, with the most frequent time being 2:00 P.M. on Friday. These are usually picked up by *cobradores*—messengers who ride bicycles and travel the city picking up payments. Several experts believe that the 2:00 Friday time slot is used because it makes it difficult for the messengers to get the checks to the bank before closing time. If the messenger misses picking up a payment, the company must wait until the following week at the prescribed time.

As in Canada, there is no controlled disbursement. Additionally, banks don't offer account reconciliation services. A statement will be sent to the owner of a checking account, but the checks are not returned. However, it is possible to get positive pay on bank accounts at certain Mexican banks. Banamex and Bancomer both offer the service.

Between 80% and 85% of the population does not have bank accounts. Although most companies do have accounts, most experts strongly advise verifying this information before sending a check. The availability of checks drawn on U.S. banks is generally between two and four weeks.

## 27.7 CONCLUSION

When dealing in international matters, it is usually a good idea *not* to assume that everything will be the same as it is in this country. Things rarely are. Whether dealing with companies in Canada or Mexico, or another part of the world, become familiar with the in-country banking system. Similarly, get acquainted with both the accounts payable and accounts receivable practices and procedures.

The language issue needs to be managed. Whether calling a vendor in Mexico or one in Quebec, it is important to be able to communicate. If the vendor doesn't speak English, look for someone in the organization who speaks the vendor's language. If possible operate in-country bank accounts and, where possible, paying the vendor in its own currency. This issue, however, may have been negotiated between purchasing and the vendor's credit department. Thus, once again, it is important to work with other departments.

As in any unfamiliar situation, the best piece of advice is also the simplest. When in doubt, ASK QUESTIONS. The international waters are murky and it is very easy to make a mistake or handle a transaction in a manner that will ultimately cost the company much more than it should have. So, don't be afraid of looking foolish. Ask all questions.

# Part Eight

# Fraud

When most people think about accounts payable, fraud rarely comes to mind. Yet, it can be quite relevant since accounts payable is the department overseeing the release of a company's money. And, that is precisely what most crooks are interested in. The topic has been broken into three separate segments:

1. Check fraud.
2. Employee fraud.
3. Vendor fraud.

However, there is much overlap between the three chapters. While most check fraud does not involve employees, it occasionally does. After all, these are the people with the most intimate knowledge of a company's procedures regarding the release of its money. However, frequently, but not always, there will be some employee interaction when vendor fraud of any sizeable magnitude takes place. Typically, but not always, vendor fraud for small-dollar amounts will not require the collusion of an employee.

The information contained in these pages is not meant to frighten readers but rather open their eyes to the very real risks most companies face with regard to both internal and external fraud.

# 28

# Check Fraud

According to *Business Week*, check fraud carries a $10 billion price tag for businesses. These numbers are not meant to frighten the reader, but rather to draw attention to the seriousness of the problem. To put this issue in perspective, consider that while total check fraud losses are estimated at $10 billion (arising from 1.3 million cases), bank losses in 1993 were estimated to be a far smaller $813 million. Yet, many companies don't take this issue seriously—that is until it happens to them. They believe it won't happen to them, and until it does they continue to stick their head in the sand. However, banks, fed up with eating huge losses, are now forcing them to approach the whole check matter with more care. In the past, banks or retailers who accepted a fraudulent check generally had to eat the check loss, regardless of how careless the firm issuing the check was. This will no longer be the case.

## 28.1 GROWTH INDUSTRY

Some jokingly call check fraud the growth industry of the 1990s. And, unfortunately, they are correct. With the prices of technology plummeting, check fraud no longer requires a huge investment of money. Color copies and laser printers are now within the financial range of the common crook and the quality of the output fools all but the most seasoned experts. Combine this with the fact that even if the forger is caught, the likelihood of prosecution is small.

With limited police resources, most communities prefer to use their limited resources to prosecute criminals who commit crimes like murder, armed robbery, and other crimes where physical violence is involved.

And to a certain extent this makes sense. When this is combined with the fact that even if a crook is caught and prosecuted and convicted, the chances of serving time are small. Thus from the criminal's perspective, check fraud is the crime of choice—little risk, chance of detection, prosecution, or conviction. Why get involved with a messy dangerous act like robbing a bank, when you can forge a few checks in the comfort of your own home and come away with a lot more money than actually going out and risking bodily harm? Only an idiot would rob a bank.

## 28.2 LEGAL ISSUE OF REASONABLE CARE

Recent changes in the Uniform Commercial Code have introduced the concept of comparative culpability into the matter. Check issuers must exercise "ordinary care" in the handling of their checks. These changes have been enacted in virtually every state and allocate responsibility for check losses back to the company should the company fail to exercise "reasonable care."

The American Bankers Association defines check fraud as "the intentional negotiation of a check without the account holder's full authorization and approval. [This] includes altering an authorized check, forging the maker's signature, forging the payee's endorsement, creating unauthorized check stock, drawing a draft on an account but not delivering the goods or checks, and check kiting."

## 28.3 CORPORATE RESPONSIBILITY

Since companies will no longer be able to rely on others, namely their banks, to protect them against fraud, they will have to initiate certain practices to guard against big check losses. Companies wishing to avoid responsibility for check losses can do this by following a three-pronged approach.

Ordinary care must be exercised in managing check stock. This includes incorporating certain safety features into checks.

Companies should take precautions such as performing employee background checks, securing their check stock, and reconciling monthly bank statements promptly.

Most important, companies must report any check fraud to their banks as soon as it is uncovered.

Document company procedures and controls.

## 28.4 CONTROLS

Installing controls will make it even harder for the perpetrators of fraud to take advantage of the company. By making checks harder to duplicate, the likelihood of the company's checks being forged diminishes. These controls can be incorporated both into the checks and in the form of bank services.

Banks are continually on the lookout for new ways to prevent fraud. Professionals who stay up-to-date on these new products and technologies are in the best position to minimize the chances of check fraud at their companies.

## 28.5 IF PREPRINTED CHECK STOCK IS USED

In an attempt to reduce the threat of blank checks being stolen, and as it turns out to lower costs as well, many companies are doing away with preprinted check stock. Those who still use preprinted check stock, should implement the following security measures:

The check stock itself should be stored in a secure location under lock and key.

Control of the check stock should lie with an individual who is *not* an authorized signer.

If mechanical check signers are used, they should be physically stored in a secure location separate from the check stock.

If a signing machine is used, the signature plate should be stored in a separate secure location. The plate should always be removed after use.

Rubber signing stamps should never be used.

Adequate controls should be put in place to monitor the check stock and the number of times the check signing machine is used.

## 28.6 CHECK SECURITY FEATURES

Many are coming to the realization that use of preprinted check stock is not the way to go. Technology in the form of reasonably priced laser printers equipped with MICR capabilities has changed the way many issue checks. A growing number of companies are eliminating preprinted check stock and are using secure paper in a laser printer to produce their checks. While ordinary blank paper can be used, it is not recommended. Even if they keep preprinted stock, most companies include a number of the following security features in their checks:

Watermarks.

Ultrasensitive watermarks.

Holograms.

Foil strips.

Microprint lines.

Complex background.

Void pantograph.

Laid lines on back.

Warning banner.

If you look at your own personal checks, they contain some of the items listed above. Most of these features cost nothing, or next to nothing, to incorporate into the check production cycle. The purpose of these features is simply to make it harder for a thief to copy, scan, or alter a check. Failure to include a number of these features will result in the company being considered liable for any copied ar altered check.

Given the rapidly changing business environment, those who don't review their check production cycle, including the physical check itself, may find that their company is exposed to a liability that didn't exist just a few years ago. It is the obligation of accounts payable managers to bring these issues to the attention of senior management in those instances where such management appears uninformed about these changes.

## 28.7 DON'T HELP THE FORGER

Sometimes, corporations unwittingly give the forger the information needed to copy their checks. Some of the things they do are:

While many recommend putting a statement on checks that says "not valid for amounts over" a given amount, fraud experts urge against it. Why? The statement gives information to the teller at the bank cashing the check, but it also gives it to the forger. A better approach is to put this information in the deposit agreement with the bank. The check will still kick out of the system if it has been altered for too large an amount, but the forger will not know the level. Without this helpful information, it is unlikely that the crook will make the check small enough.

Similarly, putting a statement on the check that says two signatures required for checks over a certain amount ultimately helps the thief. Never put two signature lines on a check, especially if two signatures are required. This will only alert the swindler that two signatures are needed. Again, if the deposit

agreement stipulates two signatures and only one appears on the check, the bank should reject it. And, if they don't, it's their problem, not yours. Two signature lines provide the cheat with valuable information—intelligence you don't need to supply.

## 28.8 REASONABLE CARE

Recent changes in the Uniform Commercial Code (UCC) make sloppy check practices costly to the negligent party. Those contributing to the fraud through negligence are now liable for losses to the degree that the company's lack of controls contributed to the commission of the crime.

The revised code specifically refers to the use of checks that do not contain safety features. One of the easiest things a corporation can do to guard against check fraud is to make it difficult for potential thieves to duplicate or alter their checks. This is done through a variety of means.

### (a) Copy Protection

The development of sophisticated and relatively cheap duplicating machines and scanners has made counterfeiting relatively easy. To thwart such efforts, it is necessary to integrate features in your check that cannot be reproduced.

- The most common approach is to incorporate an artificial watermark into the design of the check. These emblems can be viewed only when the check is held at an angle. Thus they will not show up on a copy of a check made on a duplicating machine or on one that is scanned into a computer for alteration purposes. To make this technique effective, the check should contain a not-too-small statement that says, "Do not accept this check unless you can see an artificial watermark when held at an angle."
- Along the same lines, a microprinting border can be used. To the naked eye, it will appear as though the check merely has a border. Yet under a magnifying glass, there is some

verbiage in the line. When copied or scanned, the microprinting will appear as a line.

- Another design element being incorporated into checks prevents the checks from being copied. When a reproduction is made, the word VOID automatically appears on the copy. This, of course, makes it useless.

### (b) Protection Against Alterations

- Copying a check isn't the only method thieves use to defraud companies with checks. Some take perfectly good checks for small amounts and alter them. A favorite strategy against this type of thievery is the use of a chemical VOID. The beauty of this technique is that the thief does not know it has been incorporated into the check until he goes to "fix" it. When an attempt is made to eradicate some item on the check, the chemical treatment makes the word VOID appear. For an added sense of protection, some of these treatments make the word appear in more than one language.
- One of the favorite techniques of certain counterfeiters is to take a laser check, remove the pertinent features, usually dollar amount and/or payee, and replace them with their own information. This is done in a variety of not-very-difficult ways including the use of a very sophisticated tool—transparent tape. Coating checks produced on a laser printer with laser lock makes it impossible for the information to be removed or altered.
- Another common feature employed to prevent the alteration of checks is the use of laid lines. These prevent thieves from cutting out vital information and replacing it with their own new and improved version. While the swindler may be able to fix the front of the check with his new information, it will be difficult to match the wavy lines on the back of the check. Similarly, use of prismatic printing, that is, the use of a continuous tone of different ink colors for the dollar amount, makes it very difficult for the larcenist to change the check.

- Some have also found that giving the space for the dollar amount a different background than the rest of the check helps. Apparently alterations of the dollar amount are very obvious on checks with this feature.

### (c) Manual Inspection

- One of the best ways to prevent fraud is simply to have someone look at the check when it is presented for deposit. This is easier said than done, of course. But once crooks know that a check will be manually inspected, they are likely to cast their sights elsewhere. The warning banner discussed above instructing the teller to look for the watermark is one way to do this. Another is to have certain accounts, or perhaps just certain check stock, for smaller dollar items. In these instances, it is necessary to have a statement to that effect on the check. The statement might say something like "This check not valid for more than $500."

These are just some of the techniques that you can use to help ensure that your checks won't be tampered with. They are generally inexpensive. For the most part, check stock incorporating these and other safety features is available through your bank. Astute accounts payable professionals will recommend that some or all of these features be incorporated in their checks when new check stock is ordered.

## 28.9 POSITIVE PAY

Virtually every check fraud expert promotes positive pay as one of the easiest ways to reduce check fraud. Yet, amazingly, few companies use it. A side benefit of positive pay is that the daily reconciliation process associated with it leads to early identification and resolution of problems. Companies who use it find that activities associated with the month-end close usually go more quickly and smoothly.

### (a) How It Works

In its most basic form, a company transmits to its bank its check-issued file each time there is a check run. This file contains a list of all check numbers and the dollar amounts associated with each one. Any manually written checks must be added to this file. Each morning the company's bank matches all checks presented for payment against the company's outstanding-check file. If there's a match, the check is honored and the check number is removed from the outstanding file.

Thus, if a check is duplicated many times, it will be paid only once. If the dollar amount of the check is altered, it will kick out of the system. This review also gives the bank an opportunity to fix any encoding errors it may have made.

## 28.10 REVERSE POSITIVE PAY

Positive pay is great for those who have the capability to produce the tape in the format required by the banks, but not everyone has that ability or writes enough checks to warrant such a tape. Also, some institutions are not comfortable giving their banks a list of all the checks issued. Yet for many companies in this category, one big loss due to fraud could mean the difference between overall profit and loss.

A simpler version of this product is called reverse positive pay. In this case, the bank faxes the customer a list of all check numbers and the associated dollar amounts of the items presented for payment that day. This list is typically faxed by 2 P.M. The customer then reviews the list and lets the bank know by 5 P.M. if any of the checks should not be honored.

## 28.11 FRAUD PROBLEMS NOT ENTIRELY SOLVED YET

What these two products do not address is the problem of an altered payee. Under current law, companies have 21 days to catch an altered payee and have the check returned to the bank of first deposit. This period is not long enough for many companies, especially those whose reconciliations can't be completed within that time. Even if the reconciliation is completed, the altered payee may not be discovered, since the dollar amount and check numbers will match. Most companies discover that the payee has been altered only when the original payee comes looking for their money.

But never fear, your friendly bankers are developing a product to address this issue as well. A product called Image Positive Pay has been introduced by several banks, with others making ready to do the same. With this product the bank downloads images of your checks onto your PC. If you want, you can even view the back of the check. This tool can be used to view questionable items, large-dollar items, or all checks, depending on your requirements.

## 28.12 A TOTAL FRAUD PROTECTION PROGRAM

Adopting positive pay doesn't mean that you can ignore other fraud protection strategies. While it's true that checks that aren't on the outstanding check file can be bounced back, there are too many other ways around this safeguard to permit it to be your only fraud protection technique. Continue all other safeguard programs, including controlling check stock, segregating duties, and incorporating document controls in your checks.

Accounts payables managers who wish to ensure that their company doesn't get taken should incorporate one of the positive pay programs currently available from most banks. At a minimum, try reverse positive pay and verify all large-dollar amount checks. Ask your friendly banker for more details. These simple programs can save your company thousands of dollars, even if only one fraudulent check is caught. Remember, recent changes in UCC codes no longer hold a bank totally responsible for forged checks.

## 28.13 IDENTIFYING FRAUDULENT CHECKS QUICKLY

As most accounts payable professionals know only too well, recent changes in the Uniform Commercial Code require prompt bank-statement reconciliation in order to avoid responsibility for fraudulent checks. However, there are times when other work requirements make it difficult to get these reconciliations done. A few helpful techniques that detect obvious forgeries are:

> Fan through a group of returned checks, a counterfeit may stand out as having a slightly different color than the rest of the checks in the batch.
>
> The perforations, or lack thereof, may also give a counterfeit note away. Most checks produced by legitimate printers are perforated and have at least one rough edge. Those created by fraudsters generally do not have such imperfections. This once hard-and-fast rule must be used with some care. The checks generated by in-house laser printers, for example, tend to have micro-perforations that are more difficult to detect.

These techniques will not identify all fraudulent checks but will help uncover the obvious frauds.

## 28.14 SEGREGATION OF DUTIES

Check fraud often takes the cooperation of more than one person. While often difficult or time consuming to implement on a day-to-day basis, segregation of duties is one of the best ways to inhibit internal fraud. When related duties are handled by different individuals it makes collusion necessary in order for a theft to occur. Of course this happens all the time, but it makes fraud more difficult. Different individuals, independent of each other, should perform the following duties: check stock custody, check production and signing, bank statement reconciliation, and payment processing.

By incorporating as many checks and balances into procedures, it is possible to further reduce the risk of internal fraud. For example, have one person enter figures into a check log and a second verify and initial off on them.

It also helps to get individuals from other departments involved as well. That is why some companies will have the treasury department obtain signatures and mail checks. Many also recommend never returning checks to the person who submitted the invoice for payment. Rather, it is recommended that the check be mailed directly to the vendor. Why? This will partially prevent employees from submitting phony invoices for payment.

Segregation of duties won't make it impossible for employees to commit check fraud, it will just make it more difficult. For more information on employee fraud, see Chapter 29, Employee Fraud, on this topic.

## 28.15 ACCOUNT RECONCILIATION

Bank account reconciliations are often the point at which check fraud is discovered. The key, now more than ever given the changes to the Uniform Commercial Code, is to perform those reconciliations as quickly as possible. These reconciliations should be reviewed and any discrepancies investigated immediately. If the reconciliations are not done on a timely basis, and most take this to mean within 30 days of receipt, the bank may not be liable for any forged checks later discovered.

## 28.16 ACCOUNTS PAYABLE CONTROLS

While a company stands a good chance of having its bank cover its losses due to a forged check, there is no such safety net for checks written to phantom vendors. Unless the company wants to go to its insurance company—assuming it has such coverage—it will be totally liable for such losses. Thus, it is vital that good controls be put in place regarding vendor files. This not only includes how a new vendor is created but also how the vendor file is updated. (Unscrupulous employees have been known to go into a vendor file to temporarily change an address in order to divert a large payment.) Some produce reports showing all changes to the vendor file and who made such changes. In fact, one savvy manager uncovered an employee changing overtime and vacation records through use of such a report.

Good controls also need to be put in place with invoice procedures. Once an invoice has been paid it should be cancelled or marked paid—no matter how small the invoice. One iniquitous clerk squirreled away a small fortune by taking one or two small invoices from big batches and then resubmitting the "new" batch for payment. And what brilliant detective work uncovered his deception, which had gone on for years? There was no great work. He was only discovered after he bragged about his escapades one night after having a bit too much to drink. The company immediately started canceling all paid invoices.

Any accounts payable professional who has the opportunity to hear a fraud expert talk about check fraud should listen. As fast as banks and reputable companies devise solutions to known fraud techniques, the thiefs stand ready to develop new ones. The education process must be ongoing.

# 29

# Employee Fraud

Corporate America doesn't like to admit it, and in fact, rarely prosecutes, but employee fraud is an issue that many large and not-so-large companies have had to address. Unfortunately when it happens, the companies are usually so embarrassed, they simply fire the employee and try and hush the whole matter up. The reason for this is actually quite simple. It doesn't make the company look too good and usually indicates weak controls of some sort. When companies do nothing, the offending employee is then given the opportunity to repeat the fraud, eventually at another unsuspecting company. Unfortunately, this is what happens all too often.

## 29.1 BE AWARE OF TYPICAL CANDIDATES

The typical perpetrator is male, white, 45 years old, and good at what he does. However, as women enter the workplace in greater numbers, this is changing and we're starting to see women committing fraud.

## 29.2 EXERCISE PATIENCE

It's a company's worst nightmare. A trusted employee is committing fraud of some sort against the company. At least, the company suspects the employee of a fraudulent act. When this happens, do nothing at first. Experts recommend:

Never approaching and questioning the suspect directly. This can be quite difficult, to resist the impulse, but many supervisors try and they ruin the case. They simply don't know the right way to question a suspect. Patience is a virtue that will be rewarded in this case.

Not firing the individual immediately, either. If no proof of the crime exists, the chances of getting it will vanish with the employee.

## 29.3 CALL IN THE PROFESSIONALS

Whether the individual in question has stolen blank checks or checks meant for another person, submitted phony invoices for payment, or committed some other type of fraud, is irrelevant to this discussion. For the purposes of this discussion, just assume that an individual in your department is suspected of defrauding the company in some manner. Then take the following steps:

Alert management.

Confer with the company's legal counsel.

Any decisions on fraud issues are usually made at the management level. This is especially true at those firms that do not have their own in-house counsel. In those instances most will bring in a professional trained to handle those situations. A few attorneys may try to handle this themselves, but most will not. They will bring in a private investigator trained to handle such matters. Some believe that this is covered by attorney/client privilege. Should the matter ever go to trial, the private investigator then cannot be compelled to testify about matters the client might like to keep private.

Once professionals are hired, they usually do one of two things. They either help devise a situation where the individual can be caught in the act of committing the crime, or they will interview those involved to determine if a crime has been committed and, if so, who did it. Remember, until proof exists, extreme care should be taken. It may not be the person originally suspected. There have been many instances where the person first suspected by the company did *not* commit the crime.

Now, some readers may be thinking they are quite capable of handling the questioning themselves. But this is not true. For starters, those involved are not impartial, especially if they feel they have been duped along with the company. Private investigators are trained in interviewing techniques and can read body language. They will pick up clues novices miss.

## 29.4 WHEN FRAUD HAS BEEN IDENTIFIED

Whether the proof exists or the individual under suspicion confessed because he was caught in the act, the two scenarios will proceed identically. Bring the person into an office and present them with the facts. Again, it will be helpful to have a private investigator lead the discussion and ask the questions as this is something they are trained to do.

Once a verbal confession has been obtained, the private investigator can get the individual to write it out. Even if they are not successful in obtaining a written confession, a private investigator *can* surreptitiously tape the conversation in most states. It can then be used should the matter ever go to trial. Check individual state rulings on this matter. A lawyer can not do this nor can a lawyer obtain a written confession. In most states, either of these would be considered coercion if done by an attorney.

Bringing in an outside professional will also help in another area. They will be able to advise the company if the matter has to be reported to authorities. Most of the types of fraud committed by someone in accounts payable would probably not have to be reported. But there are exceptions, such as cases involving money laundering, which might have to be reported.

## 29.5 DEALING WITH THE AFTERMATH

The reporting issue can become very important in deciding how the matter will be handled both internally and externally. The company will have to make some hard decisions. The severity of the crime and possibly extenuating circumstances might lead a company to show clemency. But, if this is done, verify every last detail of the story presented by the thief. A company's actions will also depend on the public embarrassment a company is willing to expose itself to, the proof it has, the magnitude of the crime, and the amount of compassion it is willing to extend.

Usually, a company will fire the employee and try to get the individual to repay whatever was taken. Of course, without a job, it is difficult for anyone to make restitution. In one instance, the only way the individual was able to make restitution was to steal from the new company. Whether a company decides to press charges will also depend on the amount of public humiliation it is willing to experience and the amount taken. It is often difficult to get law enforcement to prosecute these cases, especially if the amount taken is not large. This can be infuriating to those who want to do the right thing. Some counties have threshold limits setting what they will prosecute. Before making any decision, find out what the limits are in your locale. This might dictate your actions.

Remember, if the issue is prosecuted, the matter will become public and in all likelihood the press will pick it up. For many this is enough to keep them from prosecuting. Inevitably, the fact that fraud occurred reflects poorly on the company and its management. If proper controls had been in place, the crime could have been prevented. Management at many companies prefer to keep this from their shareholders and boards of directors. For others, the compassion factor kicks in and they can't bear to prosecute the person involved.

Should you decide that restitution is the way to go, consult again with your attorney. In some locales, once you make such an agreement, and the employee makes one payment, you forfeit your right to prosecute—even if the individual never makes another payment.

## 29.6 PREVENTING FRAUD IN THE FUTURE

The old adage about an ounce of prevention is certainly appropriate. There are some actions that can be taken to reduce the chance of having employee fraud committed at your organization. Start by checking out those you hire. In the end, money will be saved. Anyone who handles money should be checked out before they are hired. Thorough background checks are appropriate but rarely done. Since white collar crime of this sort is rarely reported and almost never prosecuted, many of these crooks simply move to another company. Some learn their lesson but others inevitably return to their old ways. They lay low for a while but eventually are lured in again.

Once fraud has happened, focus on putting controls in place so it can not happen again. The last thing you need, or want, is to have a repetition of the crime. While no one likes to think they have an employee who would steal from them, it does happen from time to time. By knowing the proper way to handle the matter should it occur, accounts payable professionals can provide a valuable service to their firms.

Check the phone book for private investigators in your locale or call Claire H. Irving of Investigative Consultants International at (212) 685-8277 or David J. Levin (718) 428-8169, gumshoe@pipeline.com.

# 30

# Vendor Fraud

Vendor fraud comes in a variety of flavors. It ranges from the penny-ante stuff, discussed in more detail at the end of this chapter, to the serious big-dollar issues. There is a very gray area when it comes to duplicate payments. When a company pays a bill twice, it may or may not get its money back. If the duplicate payment is made to a utility of some sort, the payment is typically credited to the account and then applied to the following month's bill. While this is not the optimum use of cash, at least the company has not lost its money.

However, if a duplicate payment is made to a vendor, many simply issue a credit—and then never let the payee know about it. Even if statements are sent, many companies omit credits from such statements. If statements are requested from vendors it is imperative that the vendor understand it is to include all balances—both credit and debit. Unless this is spelled out to the vendor in no uncertain terms, the vendor may forget to tell the customer. This assumes that the vendor has been able to identify the correct account.

When the vendor is not able to identify the account, the money is put into a suspense account and the cash is applied whenever the vendor gets around to it. This tends to be a very low priority at many companies and ultimately, if the amount stays in the suspense account for six or more months, it may be written off. That's right, the vendor will simply keep the money. Is this really fraud? Probably not, under the strictest definition of fraud, but it still represents lost money.

## 30.1 THE MASTER VENDOR FILE

The master vendor file is a treasure trove to the fraudster intent on separating your company from some of its money. Yet many firms do nothing to either guard this valuable asset or make sure that phantom vendors can't creep in without proper authorization. Access to the master vendor file is often where corporate fraud begins. The criminal simply adds a phony vendor or alters the information on an existing entry that is already included in the master file. Consider the following scenarios. Would any of them cause you to think twice?

Employee John Doe has the exact same address as vendor JDL Services, Inc.

All the invoices from Vendor A are sequential.

You can never find all the paperwork for Vendor B's purchases.

### (a) Beware of the Phantom Vendor

Remember the most likely perpetrator of corporate fraud is the long-term, trusted employee. For most companies today, the probable existence of a phantom vendor looms large. Those interested in preventing vendor fraud can set up proactive fraud-detection systems that combine the data in your internal database with information derived from searches of external databases and directories in order to pinpoint possible fraud. These tools can assist accounts payable professionals in uncovering the real identity of suspicious vendors.

### (b) Giveaways in Company Records

Sometimes the information that can identify a phantom vendor is readily available to the accounts payable professional. If the company database is complete, the information needed to verify the existence of the vendor's company exists. From these files, it will be possible to:

- Compare vendors against approved vendor lists.
- Cross-check each vendor's address, phone number, and ZIP code against those of employees.
- Check the invoice sequences of each vendor.
- Identify payments made without purchase orders or receiving documents.

Software is available to make quick work of these tasks. Several packages include:

- ACL software, (604) 669-4225, facilitates internal data acquisition and analysis by auditors.
- IDEA (Audimation Services, Inc., [713] 623-0008) aids in fraud investigations and data transfer, among other features. It was created by the Canadian Institute of Chartered Accountants.

### (c) Use Standard Business Directories

Legitimate vendors can be found in standard business directories. Again, software is available to help. Several useful programs include:

- American Business Information, (800) 555-5666, offers a treasure chest of data on vendors, by both industry and owner. Its CD-ROM directories can be accessed by name, address, phone number, or SIC code. Use this directory to determine whether a vendor exists, to match vendor phone numbers or addresses to those of employees, and to generate a list of mail-drop addresses.
- Security Software Solutions, (800) 681-8933, allows the verification of Social Security numbers (often used as employer

ID numbers by small vendors) and to identify vendors at mail drops.

BRB Publications, (800) 929-3811, publisher of *The Public Record Research Library*, offers various directories of online resources. *The Sourcebook of Online Public Records Experts* features proprietary databases, gateway vendors, CD-ROM providers, national and regional public records search firms, and other resources. *Verify Those Credentials* is designed to provide the necessary tools to check on the representations people make in business. And *The Sourcebook of State Public Records* is a guide to searching for public record information at the state level.

### (d) Online Investigative Databases

Information obtained via these resources is valuable in assessing whether people are living beyond their means or have undisclosed outside businesses—or whether a vendor even exists. Two such software programs are:

CDB Infotek, (800) 427-3747, is one of the most complete online investigative databases.

IRSC, (800) 604-4772, provides similar services to Infotek. For example, IRSC's Business Locate search returns information compiled from the *Yellow Pages* and business white pages that is verified by phone before being added to the database.

Public records available through both Infotek's and IRSC's online databases include business filings, liens, judgments, bankruptcies, and other information.

Both CDB Infotek and IRSC charge monthly service fees ($25 for Infotek and $30 for IRSC) and have a menu of fees for specific inquiries and searches. For example, Infotek offers a single search of corporate records in 44 states for $16 (which also includes an identification of business affiliations for the principal officers).

### (e) Get a Complete Financial Picture

Several services can be used to gather financial information, locate bank and brokerage accounts and safe deposit boxes, or conduct asset checks, including:

Online Search (800) 858-5294.

US DataLink (800) 527-7930.

Lexis-Nexis (800) 858-5294.

### (f) Proper Controls

One of the best ways to guard against phantom vendors is to have strong controls over the master vendor file. Limit access to the file and have periodic reports printed and reviewed of all changes made to the file. These reports should be reviewed by some high-level manager and should show who made the various changes. Even seemingly innocuous changes such as change of address and change of contact should be included on the report.

For more information about Master Vendor files and the proper way to maintain and control them, see chapter 10, Master Vendor Files.

## 30.2 CON ARTIST VENDORS

There are a number of small scams that appear to continually attempt to extract a few dollars from legitimate businesses. Most, but not all, of these scams involve relatively small amounts of money. What these thieves are counting on is that it is too much trouble to verify and fight small invoices that appear to be inaccurate or even fraudulent. Rather than waste a whole lot of time, many companies pay small bills. After all, does it make sense for an accounts payable professional to spend two hours, plus involving someone in purchasing and maybe the controller simply to decide that the company shouldn't pay a $25 bill. This is precisely what these con artists are counting on. Here are some, but definitely not all, of the scams currently being used:

### (a) Sending Low-Quality, High-Priced Goods

This scam is quite simple. The company receives some very low-quality goods priced at an outrageous price. It never ordered these goods and it certainly would never use anything of this quality. Yet, the bills begin to arrive along with threatening and harassing phone calls. The most common goods for this type of service are paper and toner for the copier machine. Often, a representative from the fraudster will call the company and ask the receptionist for the brand and/or model number of the copy machine. Then, paper or toner "designed" for that machine will arrive. At first glance it will appear to be a legitimate order since it is for the company's machine. Occasionally, the phony vendor will even demand the goods back—which most companies would happily return, if they had any clue as to where the goods were. Frequently, they have been used as no one initially realized they hadn't ordered from that company.

### (b) The Advertising/Phone Book Scam

When a company places a classified add, whether in a newspaper or yellow pages type phone book, it will find an exact duplicate of that advertisement running in another obscure publication. It will find this duplicate attached to an invoice for payment. Since the ad belongs to the company, many will pay it not realizing the ad was never authorized. What these companies do is simply copy legitimate advertisements and then bill the companies. They must get paid often enough to make it worthwhile because the scam persists.

What can the company do?

### (c) Solutions

The law says that anything that arrives in the mail unordered can be considered a gift. It is not the responsibility of the receiver to return anything. Keep this in mind and point it out loudly to those making threats regarding payment for goods not ordered. Some workable solutions to help get rid of these pests are:

- Make them prove the goods were ordered. They should have a purchase order or an order blank with a signature from someone at the company. If they can't produce that, don't pay them.
- Some companies, preferring not to be involved with such vendors, take a more conservative approach. As soon as goods are received and cannot be matched to a purchase order, they call the vendor and tell them the goods were not ordered. They then return the product.
- When an invoice is first received, check to see if there is a valid PO number on it. If missing, incomplete, or inaccurate, return the invoice unpaid to the vendor. Companies that follow this procedure report it is amazing how quickly all the legitimate vendors clean up their invoices.
- List all suspect vendor's names on the site. Flag these names in the company's system to prevent payments. However, be aware that some of these companies change names frequently.

Finally, if all else fails, threaten to report them to the attorney general or some kind of business watchdog group. The problem with paying these bothersome invoices is that these fraudulent vendors won't go away. Pay them once and they will ship the company more low-quality goods that were never ordered. So, it is not simply a matter of paying $25 and making the problem go away. Pay the $25, and a $50 or $100 dubious invoice will appear.

# 31

# Professionalism in the Field

This is a great time to be in accounts payable. The field is finally starting to get the recognition it deserves and with that the professionals who populate the departments are finally starting to be given credit for the hard work they do. At larger companies, the departments are sometimes headed by individuals with Masters degrees, principally MBAs, and it is not unusual to hear of someone being paid over $100,000 to run one of these departments. Some make accounts payable their lifelong career while others use it as a stepping stone to more responsible positions within the organization. Both of these options are attractive depending on the long-term goals of the employee.

No longer is accounts payable being viewed as a place to dump the unproductive employee that the company does not wish to let go. Companies are beginning to realize that it is important to put good, productive, innovative people in accounts payable in order to protect the company's bottom line.

Now that companies are starting to recognize the value of these professionals, it is imperative that the professionals who wish to advance and prosper do everything in their power to meet the opportunities they are being offered.

## 31.1 EVALUATING THE BIG PICTURE

It's quite easy to get wrapped up in the day-to-day responsibilities of one's job and lose track of bigger issues. This is true for both evaluating the accounts payable department and surveying your own career. Figure out what game you are playing and then act accordingly. This is critical for both professionals and businesses if one wishes to remain on the fast track.

It is imperative to adjust appropriately. The game will periodically change, and accounts payable executives who do not step back and evaluate will find themselves playing the old game when the focus has switched.

Coordinate and work with peer organizations within the company. In the case of accounts payable professionals, this will probably mean working more closely with purchasing and receiving. This is particularly good advice, as a number of companies have begun to merge their accounts payable department with the purchasing function—a stance not all accounts payable professionals agree with. However, it is necessary to face reality and this is a trend (albeit not a huge one). By working with purchasing on a team basis long before anyone raises the issue of merging, the accounts payable professional will be situated well in case the accounts payable department ends up reporting to purchasing.

This is not the only reason that it is advisable to partner with other departments. Many of the productivity-improving procedures that accounts payable wishes to implement require the buy-in and cooperation of some of these other departments. Examples include purchasing cards and ERS. It would be next to impossible to run a successful purchasing-card program if purchasing refused to cooperate.

## 31.2 LEADERSHIP AND PREPARATION

Leadership, as always, will be the single most important skill acquired by the accounts payable manager and it can be learned. Always be open to new ideas. Look upon technology as a tool, not a replacement, and, most important of all, maintain an inquisitive mind.

The accounts payable manager of the twenty-first century will be the one who grasps the importance of dealing fairly and honestly with people and who knows how to handle day-to-day problems with confidence and knowledge by looking for solutions, not pointing fingers.

## 31.3 TECHNOLOGY

Identifying the right technologies for accounts payable is a necessary skill. Internet and intranet technology will be ideal tools that can even become weapons, helping an accounts payable department spend less time researching problems offline. It will also help get belligerent vendors off their backs. The successful professional will identify the emerging technologies and learn all there is to know about them—regardless of whether the company is currently using them.

## 31.4 COMMUNICATION

Good communication skills are important to the person who wants to succeed in any field, including accounts payable. The accounts payable professional must be able to communicate with vendors, company employees, and the accounts payable staff. While some accounts payable professionals are quite good in this area, others could use a little help—and then some. On top of this, accounts payable managers must be able to resolve vendor problems. Good communication skills will smooth this often rocky road, as well. The following skills will be required:

Logic and reasoning.

Computer and technology—some of which indirectly affects accounts payable through other departments.

Information processing.

The ability to conduct research and interpret and apply data.

Self-discipline and responsibility.

Adaptability and flexibility.

Conflict resolution and negotiation.

Teamwork.

The ability to function in a diverse and multi-cultural environment.

### (a) Keeping Skills Up-to-Date

Accounts payable professionals who don't upgrade their skills are like dinosaurs trying to compete in a modern world. In order to remain attractive, both to a present employer and possible new ones, it is imperative that the professional continue to learn new strategies and techniques. Standing still and doing the job the way it always was can be the kiss of death in the job market today.

### (b) Why Is It Necessary?

Professionals who are holding on to the belief that they are entitled to lifetime careers are not in for an easy time. They should examine the risks associated with change and then compare them with those of not transforming themselves. It doesn't take much introspection to identify the real danger.

Clearly, it pays to reinvent yourself both personally and professionally. The business community is changing on many fronts. Companies institute cultural changes as they merge with, or acquire or are acquired by, other companies. The result of all this turmoil is a tremendous amount of uncertainty and pressure—both for businesses and for individuals.

### (c) How Businesses Are Responding

Companies respond to this turbulence in ways never anticipated by most accounts payable professionals. Specifically, they are:

Mergers, acquisitions and spin-offs at levels previously unimagined.

Evaluating and reevaluating bottom line, or value-added contributions of whole departments.

Replacing people with technology.

Downsizing via benchmarking.

Becoming more customer focused.

By identifying the specific pressures their business is experiencing, accounts payable managers begin to see why and how they must change.

## 31.5 RELEVANT TRENDS FOR PAYABLES PROFESSIONALS

The constraints experienced by businesses have a way of filtering down to its operations. In this case, payables departments have begun to feel the brunt as companies react to competitive pressures. The pertinent trends for accounts payable professionals are:

Merging of customer service and payables functions, or purchasing and payables.

Reduction of staff through automation.

Retention and training of personnel who will be customer-oriented.

Creation of internal partnerships, breaking down existing barriers.

By recognizing these innovations in the workplace, accounts payables professional can begin to adapt.

## 31.6 GRABBING MANAGEMENT'S ATTENTION

It is rare for management to fully appreciate the contribution their accounts payable professionals make to the company's bottom line. Too often, this contribution is overlooked or taken for granted. Fortunately, this can be changed. Here is an approach used by one professional to get management to sit up and pay attention to the fine work their departments are doing. Note that communication and the sharing of valuable information is at the root of all their strategies.

### (a) Communication

"In the past," explains the manager of cost and budgets at a large southern insurance company, "senior management expected accounts payable to 'do everything' without regard to the additional time required to complete the process." This could include manual checks, special handling, and checking for a dozen different things before processing. This tale is all too familiar in a large percentage of accounts payable departments.

By communicating to management the time needed to complete each of these "special" requests, this shrewd professional was able to make them appreciate what was involved. Although the number has been decreased, a reduced number of special requests are still received.

### (b) Information

Accounts payable professionals have a tool that can greatly improve their standing within their companies. Unfortunately, few fully exploit this valuable resource. The wide array of information at the fingertips of those who run accounts payable departments puts them in a unique position. See Chapter 24, Benchmarking, for more information on this topic. Making sure this information is current is also important. Otherwise, the statistics are meaningless.

## 31.7 TAKING CONTROL OF YOUR OWN DESTINY

Sometimes accounts payable managers feel like they are operating in a vacuum. Many don't realize that there are a number of professional resources to help them keep up-to-date on the latest developments in the field. In addition to this publication, there are a number of professional organizations that address the needs of the accounts payable professional. They all have slightly differing focuses and, depending on your organization and your interests, a number may be of interest to you. Additionally, there are a number of organizations which give conferences addressing the needs of accounts payable each year. The professional who wants to keep abreast of the latest changes affecting their careers has options. The question is which should you choose?

## 31.8 PROFESSIONAL ORGANIZATIONS

The following list provides professional organizations as well as contact information and a brief description:

**The American Payroll Association** *(APA) (212) 224-6406, www.americanpayroll.org*. This group was established over 15 years ago and runs both an annual conference and many local seminars. At the current time there are also 99 local chapters. Those who also handle the payroll function might find this organization quite helpful.

**Institute of Management Accountants** *(IMA) (800) 638-4427, www.rutgers.edu/accounting/raw/ima*. This organization is for those with an accounting bent. It is the largest of all with 80,000 members and many local chapters.

**International Association of Accounts Payable Professionals** *(IAPP) (407) 240-8830, www.accountspayable.org*. This relatively new group has a number of regional chapters and holds an annual conference. It's main focus is the accounts payable professional.

**The National Association of Credit Managers** *(NACM) (800) 955-8815, www.nacm.org*. This is the oldest of all the organizations discussed, looking forward to celebrating its 102nd birthday this year. This organization focuses on credit and collection issues. It has an annual conference along with many local chapters, many of which have their own annual conferences. Those subscribers with responsibility for accounts receivable might look into this fine organization.

**The Treasury Management Association** *(TMA) (301) 907-2862, www.tma-net.org*. The group can also be reached by e-mail at communications@tmanet.org. This group was formed in 1978 and has many local chapters. It holds an annual conference in the fall and another in January devoted to electronic topics. Many of the local chapters have their own conferences, as well.

## 31.9 CONFERENCES

In addition to the conferences run by the professional organizations listed above, a number of other organizations run specialized conferences directed solely at the accounts payable professional. These include:

***The IMI/IOMA Managing Accounts Payable Conferences***. The issues covered at these multi-speaker, day-and-a-half events include intermediary and advanced topics along with leading edge subjects. Several are planned each year. For more information, call IMI at (212) 370-1518.

***RECAP holds its Enhancing Accounts Payable*** *conference each year in March*. At this day-and-three-quarter event, a variety of speakers address issues of import to the accounts payable community. For information, call (201) 697-6430 or visit the Web site at www.recapinc.com

***Basic Accounts Payable***. The following three organizations offer one- and two-day seminars that address introductory through intermediate accounts payable issues. They are generally taught by one instructor and are offered at many locations around the country. The organizations are:

**Dun & Bradstreet**, (212) 692-6600.

**Padgett Thompson/AMA**, (800) 433-3635.

**Pathmasters**, (800) 611-0088.

The accounts payable professional with a staff might want to consider one or more of these courses for staffers who also wish to enhance their careers.

# 32

# Success Stories

This chapter contains real life success stories that demonstrate what innovative accounts payable professionals have done in their organizations.

## 32.1 CASE 1: REDUCING A SERIOUS BACKLOG AND GETTING THE COMPANY BACK ON THE DISCOUNT TRACK

Taking discounts on invoices is something near and dear to the hearts of most accounts payable professionals. But this is difficult, if not impossible, to do when there is a serious backlog of work in the accounts payable department. However, one intrepid accounts payable professional has demonstrated that it can be done. Teamwork, a hardworking staff, an intelligent manager, and a little management support were all that was needed in this success story.

### (a) The Case History

When Waters Corp. was divested from its parent company in 1994, Joe Henry was given the opportunity to run the newly created accounts payable department. Henry, who has since gone on to become the corporate accounts payable manager for Boston Scientific Corp., faced many challenges in his new position at Waters. Specifically:

Inheriting a serious backlog of invoices.

Invoices carrying a variety of discount terms.

Many suppliers not offering discounts to the company.

Inadequate staff to handle the workload.

Existing staff members handling either vendor payments or T&E reimbursements, but not both.

Resolution of discrepancies was the responsibility of purchasing, which did not give it a high priority.

No cross-training within the department, and little teamwork.

The net result of these issues was that the company had trouble paying in 30 days and was in no position to aggressively chase discounts. Additionally, Henry says that quite a few vendors were on the aging list. Asking such vendors for discounts for early payments would make the company look ridiculous.

### (b) Solutions

"We overcame these issues by getting properly staffed and trained," says Henry. "Once fully staffed, I took the backlog total at that time and added the average incoming new mail and basically assigned a number that each coordinator had to process on a weekly basis to get us at an acceptable level of backlog."

He gave the staff three weeks to get all old invoices in the system. He set a standard of getting them all in the system within five days based on invoice receipt date into the accounts payable department. He date-stamps every piece of mail sent to the department. His group was up to the challenge and one additional one as well. Henry urged them to beat that deadline by three days . . . and they did.

"The group really pulled together as a team, as they did not want to be back in a backlog situation again," he says. The department also realized a huge decline in vendor phone calls and problems—an added bonus.

By the same token, the people who previously only processed

vendor payments now had to also process expense reports as well. Henry also had his own accounts to manage. He did this for several reasons. "For one, it was clear that I was not getting any additional help. I could see from my weekly key activity reports that the staff was working to full capacity, and yet I still was not comfortable with the level of backlog and making sure that discounts were taken and vendors were being paid. So, I know it helped to boost morale within the department when they saw me entering my share of invoices each week," he explains.

Once the backlog was under control, he set a goal of five days in which all new invoices had to be entered in the system. In most cases, the staff was now operating with practically no backlog, although the norm is zero to three days. With weekly check runs, getting the discounts is not a problem. With the ability to make timely payments, Henry was in a position to take advantage of discounts for early payments—if they were offered.

### (c) The Discount Problem

Waters did not really have that many vendors offering discounts at this point. But once Henry felt comfortable that Waters could remain current with its workload, he recommended that Waters change its payment terms from net 30 to net 45. He got support from upper management, including purchasing, and changed every vendor not currently offering a discount to net 45.

"Knowing Waters was now a stand-alone company ($350,000,000 in sales), I was well aware that float was more important now to Waters than it had been before. Management agreed that extending virtually all of our vendor base to 45 days and using that as leverage to get more discounted terms for quicker payments was a great opportunity. We told our larger vendors of this change, but the majority were not notified. As a matter of fact, even vendors who were offering a discount—say, 2%10 n/30—were also impacted if the discount was not met. They were now 2%10 n/45," he explains.

The company worked with its vendors if they complained. "If one of our large vendors or any of the others approached me or purchasing noting they wanted their old terms back, we honored their old terms if there was indeed a signed agreement in place," he says.

Once the company had moved the majority of its vendors to net 45, it was in a good position to ask for discounts for early payments. "All vendors were told we would pay them sooner but they would have to offer a discount or continue to be paid in 45 days. In most cases, if the vendor wanted to keep us as a customer it would offer us a 1% to 2% discount—and some offered more than that. If they chose not to offer a discount, we benefited with the net 45 terms," Henry recalls.

By changing its terms, Waters generated many more discount opportunities through negotiating. With a more manageable workload, Waters could take advantage of these discounts. In approximately 10 months in 1995, the first year the new program was in effect, the company took discounts totaling $360,000.

This was not the only benefit. Based on when the invoice was received, it was paid. Waters followed a practice used by a number of leading edge accounts payable departments of using the receipt date of the invoice rather than the actual invoice date. The vendors accepted this practice. "Periodically, a vendor would claim a discount was unearned and we would pay the discount back, but again, this request was not made often," says Henry.

### (d) Ongoing Efforts

As with most effective efficiency programs, the one at Waters is continually monitored. "On a monthly basis I ran and analyzed a discount taken and lost report. Each A/P coordinator was given a copy of this report for his or her vendors," says Henry. This accomplished several things. For starters, the coordinators were more aware of who the discount vendors were. The coordinators would become familiar with them and prioritize their mail so these vendor invoices were processed first. This guaranteed they would be in the system for our weekly check run.

Second, the coordinators were expected to get back to Henry with the explanations of why they missed any discounts. "I can tell you that if a discount was lost, it usually was as a result of a dispute over the shipment or satisfaction of the product, which we obviously want to resolve before any payment is made. I was able to convince the purchasing managers that their buyers need to resolve issues quickly, especially as it relates to a discounted vendor. By making them aware of the dollars lost as a result of not making the time to resolve purchasing and receiving issues and getting an invoice off of hold was critical," he explains.

His reports gave him some leverage with the purchasing department, where he had none in the past. "One of the new metrics for the buyers as far as their performance goes is directly related to how quickly they respond and resolve problems pertaining to these invoices for which they are responsible," he says.

"We also put an automated alert message in place. We use Oracle, and if accounts payable entered an invoice and it went on hold for a PO, pricing, or receiving issue, the buyer automatically received an e-mail message regarding their PO every day until the issue was resolved and the invoice came off of hold," says Henry. This technique is quite effective in bringing visibility to the buyers and their managers, if necessary. Explaining his squeaky-wheel approach, Henry says, "We all know what it's like to get too many e-mails, and the last thing you want is to see the same one coming to you every day for a month or longer."

### (e) Further Use of Reports

Many accounts payable managers implement cost savings programs and then get no credit for them. This is often their own fault because they do not let management know what they have done. This was not the case with Henry. "I made upper management aware of the savings on a monthly basis. I would provide them with an analysis of the discounts taken and lost each month," he explains.

He also would try to set a goal for the department to reach collectively. For instance, if the total amount of discounts offered for one month was $30,000 and the department hit 90% of that, or $27,000, Henry would ask the staff to work at increasing that percentage the following month. Now, 90% is excellent, especially considering where the department started. Henry says the accounts payable staff really enjoyed seeing the results they were now achieving. Henry says that the key to a successful program such as this has three components: managing your backlog, negotiating better terms, and knowing who your discounted vendors are.

What Henry did is quite impressive. Other accounts payable managers facing similar situations can take a page from his book and emulate some of the programs he instituted.

## 32.2 CASE 2: HELL ON EARTH—HOW ONE COMPANY SURVIVED THE IMPLEMENTATION OF AN IMAGING SYSTEM

A growing number of companies are investigating imaging for their accounts payable operations. These firms hope it will provide a panacea for problems plaguing their day-to-day operations. Imaging can and often does help, but (and this is a big caveat) implementing it rarely goes smoothly. Many of the lessons cited in this tale are applicable to the installation of any new system or process. For obvious reasons, the identity of the company has been changed.

### (a) Chronology

As background, the accounts payable professional involved in this story revealed that although the company had installed its current accounts payable system in 1989, it had what he referred to as "1959 technology." In July 1994, this company, like every other big company in the 1990s, commissioned a reengineering study. In November of the same year, an imaging project was approved and implementation was scheduled for August 1995.

August 6, 1995, is a day that the accounts payable professional says will live in infamy. It was the day the new imaging system was supposed to go live. He describes the August through October period of that year as "hell on earth." He says he's been told that such a description is not professional, but he stands by his characterization of the situation. On September 29, 1995, the system finally went live.

He calls October through December 1995 the "early recovery"

period, though he says it was not until January 1996 that the company had fully recovered. By April 1996 the company began to see significant improvements—the ones the firm had expected on August 6, 1995! What went wrong, and, more important, how readers can avoid similar catastrophes follows. Read on—the professional has lots of advice.

To make imaging work for its accounts payable department, the company broke the process down into four distinct personnel units: imaging, indexing, purchase order review, and non–purchase-order review. Each presented unique challenges. Accounts payable professionals considering using imaging will benefit from the recommendations in each component.

### (b) Imaging Unit

"Do not underestimate the amount of time it takes to make a batch scanable," he warns. He is not alone in this advice. It also comes from a number of other professionals who have introduced imaging into their operations. The advertised speeds are rarely, if ever, met. He advises that "the skills of the imaging unit must be carefully reviewed." He says the company was badly burned by not fully recognizing this fact.

Much of the "intelligence" is moved to the beginning of the process. At this company, personnel in the mail center became responsible for opening the mail. This certainly seems reasonable. They also became responsible, however, for deciding what was PO related and what was not. This, unfortunately, is not a skill that most mailroom personnel have been trained in.

The company had decided to throw the hard copy away after it is first imaged. Not all companies take this route. However, the company, fully anticipating the possible problems this could lead to down the road, got IRS approval *before* the system went live.

### (c) Indexing Unit

"It is important to have good reporting of what is in the queue—what is waiting to be imaged," says the accounts payable professional. The queue can be perceived as a "black hole." When he arrived at the company during the "hell on earth" phase, the backlog of invoices waiting to be imaged was 35 days. This, of course, was unacceptable and he now has it down to an admirable one day, except at the end of the month. It is imperative that identification of items in the queue be readily available.

He also cautions that the indexing and imaging units must work well together. Otherwise, additional inefficiencies can be introduced into the process. He relates that when the project started, the managers of the indexing and imaging units did not get along. Any opportunity to send work back to the other unit was taken advantage of.

How did he resolve this problem? He had the two report to the same boss. He also says cross-training between these two units is particularly useful, since it allows each group to understand the other's problems.

### (d) Purchase Order and Non–Purchase-Order Review Units

The company uses the three-way match. Items that do not match are pended for further research by the purchasing department. "A real joy," he quips. Like many other accounts payable professionals, he found that getting purchasing to do the necessary research and respond in a timely fashion was not easy. In order to get the issue under control, the company had to set strict limits on the response time.

The non–PO-review unit handles invoice transmittals, check requests, and employee reimbursements. These are all sent in by the end user with a cover sheet that includes the request, the authorization, and the G/L distribution.

### (e) Benefits

The company has seen some real productivity boosts since the imaging system made its debut less than two years ago. There is a nearly 60% increase in the number of invoices processed, while head count has dropped by slightly more than 10%.

Not only did the work flow improve, the company experienced some increased productivity in its Check Audit and Release units. When checking for duplicate payments, the imaging system allows the staff to bring up both copies of the invoice simultaneously. The ability to view the two documents at the same time makes it much easier to detect invoices that have already been paid. And very little effort is involved—just a few clicks of the mouse.

The process of reviewing and setting up new vendors has also been simplified, as has the check printing operation.

The biggest savings of all, however, has been realized in the customer service unit. He breaks down the savings into three areas: faster response time, better information, and a smaller "black hole." As with duplicate payment review, the ability to find information with simply a few clicks turns a process that could take hours or even days into a few minutes. And, satisfied customers generally translate into more business.

The company has incorporated the online image query capabilities for end users throughout the company. This helps reduce the number of phone calls coming into the accounts payable department.

### (f) Caveats

This professional is still a big fan of imaging but he warns that the implementation of a system does not come without some aggravation. He strongly advises that accounts payable professionals undertaking such a project adhere to the following guidelines:

Obtain early senior management support. You'll need it when things go wrong.

Be sure to communicate the upcoming change to end users and vendors. "Believe me," he warns, "they'll notice. The transition won't be seamless—no matter what the imaging vendor has promised."

Don't do a "Big Bang." Phase in both the implementation of invoices in the pipeline and new work. When the company started, the accounts payable staffers were instructed to bring all outstanding invoices to the mailroom. The company had estimated that a day's work was about 1,200 invoices (he says that in reality it is about 2,500), so the project was overwhelmed when 22,000 invoices arrived in the mailroom. It seems that every clerk who was hiding problem invoices in his or her desk took advantage of this opportunity to unload difficult invoices.

Be sure to have a good reporting mechanism in place. You will need to watch the backlog carefully in order to avoid a "black hole."

Do not underestimate the labor needed to prepare batches for scanning.

"There is a learning curve," he says. "Make sure you can measure productivity at the beginning to better align your staff." Other companies that have implemented imaging systems warn that you should expect a decrease in productivity for the first few weeks.

Reorganize the department to better fit the new flow of the work.

Do not ignore exception processing. "Worry about it," he warns. When faced with the naysayer who asks: "How often does that really happen?" be ready with the answer: "Too often!"

### (g) Future Enhancements

While the company is thrilled with the improvements it has garnered from its new imaging system, the company is not ready to rest on its laurels. He says the company already has its eye on the future and is planning additional enhancements. For starters, the next generation of activities will include better information on EDI and other uploaded invoices.

The company also plans to take advantage of other technologies to improve its new imaging system. While some of the firm's plans may seem quite high tech—and beyond the scope of the average midsize company—it is only a matter of time before some of the company's ambitious plans become commonplace. Remember when direct deposit of payroll seemed like an application only for the Fortune 500? Today, companies of all sizes are using it.

Other expansion plans include:

An extension of remote scanning via the use of fax-server technologies.

The use of the existing phone system to include Integrated Voice Response (INV) and associated fax copy requests.

The use of COLD technology to include EDI and diskette upload information as an image.

The use of OCR technology for certain items, including bar coding for online T&Es.

## 32.3 CASE 3: AN ACCOUNTS PAYABLE DEPARTMENT OVERHAUL

Boosting morale and fashioning a payable system everybody can work with are two of the biggest accounts payable issues to consider when restructuring your accounts payable department, one manager says. They are by no means the last, he adds, and in fact are part of a list of many important issues an accounts payable office needs to address during an overall evaluation of the department.

Paul Soltrenz joined Criet, Inc., as their accounting manager in 1992. His duties required him to work on the company's financial reports and deal with few people. His office was next to the accounts payable supervisor's office, and the things he saw drove him crazy. "If I am ever in charge of that area things are going to change," he thought.

"Most of us are accounts payable people, and other people are never nice to us," Soltrenz says. "Who would agree that the biggest group in a corporate environment is the second-guesser and the smallest group are the people being second-guessed?" he asked, drawing a laugh from the audience.

In August 1995, the unexpected happened, and suddenly, he says, "I was the most second-guessed person in the company."

### (a) Background

A department overhaul was requested and Soltrenz began his mission. He started by talking to the eight accounts payable staffers.

He'd already come to know them personally through his three years there. Despite this, he interviewed each of them, and put aside their old paper performance reviews. Everyone began with a clean slate. He sought to discover their individuality and work ability, and what would mesh with what.

"I also wanted to just sit back and observe," says Soltrenz. "I've always been the type of person who can easily sit back, watch what's going on, form an opinion—I think we can all do that—and then think of ways a process can work better." He continues, "I discovered several problems existing in the process."

### (b) The Problems to Be Resolved

Low morale in the accounts payable department was the number-one problem. Anytime anything in the area went wrong, the accounts payable department was blamed. The accounts payable staff felt defenseless. Problems were rarely investigated. The staff wasn't getting along. In addition, there was little opportunity for advancement.

There was just too much paper attached to an invoice—receiving documents, purchase orders, a copy of the check, and a voucher preparation sheet. By September, the files were full.

Excessive overtime was an issue. Clerks would stay at night, unsupervised, without a manager's approval.

There was no cross-training. If someone was absent, especially a supervisor, work didn't get done because no one else knew how to do it. People were getting blamed for not doing the work in someone's absence. This only increased already low morale.

Staff was not familiar with the chart of accounts. If account coding was accepted by the system, it was entered. Supervisors needed to have more confidence in workers at the clerical level, and give them the required training so they could recognize when the numbers didn't make sense and do more troubleshooting.

There was an excessive amount of manual checks, many of which were being returned to employees to process them. In addition, numerous vendors were picking up their own checks.

Checks were being processed prior to their due dates. Employees concerned with keeping vendors happy were pressuring the accounts payable staff to process checks prematurely.

Checks did not have proper approval authority. Secretaries and administrative assistants were requesting checks that were approved by managers for whom the goods and services were intended. Also, payments were being made from statements instead of invoices.

Discounts were not being fully utilized. The process was inefficient, and discounts were being lost because of missing information.

The vendor file was excessive, and vendors were being added without proper approval. In some cases key information was missing. Often, there were multiple files for the same vendor.

Direct employee expenses were being paid by accounts payable, including seminars; association and professional dues; and subscriptions. These items should have been included on the employees' T&Es.

Expense reports were missing required information. Receipts would be missing or meetings would not be documented. They also would not be properly approved.

Credit was not taken on returned goods unless it was issued by the vendor. Stale checks were numerous.

### (c) The Revamp's Solutions

The road was rough, but Soltrenz says hard work and a set of goals have turned around the department. Soltrenz's efforts have also injected new life into accounts payable. Some of the things he did to solve the accounts payable department's problems include:

Open communication is key. The biggest thing they did was break up cliques and treat everyone fairly, taking into account individual personalities. A fresh start was welcome and, although past reviews were looked at, personal judgement was reserved. Staffers were praised and defended in public. Private issues were kept private. "Getting people to work together and get along is important," says Soltrenz.

An accounting stamp has been created. It eliminates voucher sheets and reduces paper as well as processing time.

A departmental overtime policy has been established. Basically, it says, when a manager leaves, clerks leave.

The staff has been cross-trained on other's responsibilities, including the manager's job. Clerks now know how to do a manager's work if the responsibility should fall on their shoulders.

The staff and accountants have been reeducated and trained on chart of accounts.

Check-processing policies are set in writing and distributed to department managers. Invoices are paid by terms. Checks are mailed directly, and unless there's an extreme hardship, a vendor can no longer pick up checks at the office. An enforced approval authority has been implemented on invoices. Employees are required to pay for their own dues, subscriptions, and seminars under $350, and are reimbursed on expense reports.

The vendor file has been cleaned up and policies have been set for adding new vendors.

### (d) Keys to Success

Revamping accounts payable is a cumbersome task that, however tedious, can make work for a whole bunch of people a lot more efficient and enjoyable. Soltrenz's observations are a lesson and a case study that can serve as an invaluable benchmark. The following five keys to success are guides learned from this accounts payable department's long, hard trip toward improvement.

The most valuable resource is people.

Communication is key, both from the top down and from the lower levels up.

A team concept is the best way to accomplish goals. If people feel they are participating in a process, rather than adhering to it, they will be more involved in its success.

Support the staff, especially to outsiders.

Promote from within.

Accounts payable managers who follow Soltrenz's plan will find that their department runs smoother and that staff gets along better. And that will ease the load the accounts payable manager carries.

# Index